DATE DUE

10-1-10	

GAYLORD

PRINTED IN U.S.A.

The Craft of Community Study

University of Florida Monographs

Social Sciences Number 65

The Craft of Community Study

Fieldwork Dialogues

Solon T. Kimball
and
William L. Partridge

A University of Florida Book

University Presses of Florida
FAMU/FAU/FIU/FSU/UCF/UF/UNF/USF/UWF
Gainesville / 1979

University Presses of Florida is the central agency for scholarly publishing of the State of Florida's university system. Its offices are located at 15 NW 15th Street, Gainesville, FL 32603. Works published by University Presses of Florida are evaluated and selected for publication by a faculty editorial committee of any one of Florida's nine public universities: Florida A&M University (Tallahassee), Florida Atlantic University (Boca Raton), Florida International University (Miami), Florida State University (Tallahassee), University of Central Florida (Orlando), University of Florida (Gainesville), University of North Florida (Jacksonville), University of South Florida (Tampa), University of West Florida (Pensacola).

Library of Congress Cataloging in Publication Data

Kimball, Solon Toothaker.
  The craft of community study.

  (University of Florida monographs: Social sciences;
no. 65)
  "A University of Florida book."
  Bibliography: p.
  Includes index.
  1. Ethnology—Field work. 2. Ethnology—Colombia.
3. Colombia—Social life and customs. 4. Marihuana.
5. Partridge, William L. I. Partridge, William L.,
joint author. II. Title. III. Series: Florida.
University, Gainesville. University of Florida mono-
graphs: Social sciences; no. 65.
GN346.K55   301.2'07'2   79–10172
ISBN 0–8130–0631–7 pbk.
ISBN 0–8130–0647–3

Acknowledgments

MANY INDIVIDUALS contributed to the development of the research activities that are reported in the next several chapters. Even a categorical inventory of those who were involved reveals the extensive diversity of participation, directly or indirectly, with one or both of the coauthors. These include university and government officials in the United States and Colombia, colleagues, community residents, friends, students, conceptual and technical helpers, and editors. Only a few of those who inhabit the categories listed above have been directly involved in the preparation of this volume. None of those from Colombia has been so involved, although they provided advice and encouragement in the beginning and during its progress and they appear as actors in the events which are extracted from the field notes.

We regret that it is unwise to list by name those Colombian colleagues who made important contributions during the two-year research and subsequently. The reason they remain anonymous is discussed more fully in the epilogue. Basic scientific research is not protected in Colombia by the principle of academic freedom, and scientists are vulnerable to government censure if their work is thought to be controversial by those in power. Indeed, foreign research in Colombia since 1974 has been severely restricted in a government effort to decrease international knowledge of internal social and political realities. Our colleagues are, therefore, vulnerable to criticism for assisting us. Under such conditions we can not identify those to whom recognition should properly be extended. We can only express our gratitude to them privately, accept the burden of obligations still outstanding, and appreciate the much greater burdens borne by our Colombian colleagues.

The people of Majagua who assisted in many ways must also go unnamed here. No great harm would come at present from mentioning their names or identifying their community, but we cannot be sure this will continue to be the the case. It must suffice to say that the people in Majagua made Partridge's work possible. They were gracious in their reception, they were courageous in their cooperation, they were generous and honorable in their dealings, and they bestowed their trust as they incorporated him as a friend. Although only Partridge benefited directly from the expression of such manners, we are both deeply grateful for this display of traditional hospitality and intelligent cooperation in the objectives of the research.

There are others who should be mentioned since they were directly involved with the development of the original research, the interpretation of findings, or the work of bringing the manuscript to a publishable condition. Dr. William E. Carter helped initiate the research through discussion with Colombian anthropologists. Dr. Charles Wagley offered wise advice on the community system of Majagua based upon his wide acquaintance with Latin America. Valuable suggestions were received from Dr. Antoinette B. Brown, Dr. Reginal Byron, and Ms. Patricia C. Griffin, who read all or portions of the manuscript, and from the discussions with Dr. Barbara G. Myerhoff on fieldwork.

We are also appreciative of those whose managerial and technical skills are so essential in the emergence of a completed manuscript. They convert scribbled copy to smooth typescript, verify biographical and bibliographical detail, and do endless other chores. We express our respect and gratitude to Lydia Deakin, Joan James, Luz Graciela Joly, and Sandra Westmoreland, who contributed so much to this enterprise in the ways designated above.

Thanks must go also to the Graduate School of the University of Florida for making possible the publication of this monograph.

Contents

Preface

THE ANCIENT Celt invested his sacred grove with qualities not unlike those which the anthropologist attributes to the "field." Initiations, celebrations, and sacrifices are associated with both. And there are other parallels; but we must not push our metaphor beyond its capacity to dramatize the deep significance of the field experience for the anthropologist. In our discipline the field has often been a crucial factor in shaping the future professional and personal life patterns of the individual.

During the field experience the fieldworker is frequently engaged in one of several dialogues. Awareness of empirical setting and behavior comes to the investigator through these dialogues, as does the intellectual ferment which adds knowledge and shapes theory. It is surprising that a process of such significance has attracted so little attention. Rarely does the traditional ethnographic monograph, for example, specify the analytical methods by which data are gathered and ordered. Sometimes in the relaxed recollections of memoirs are the processes of ordering and discovery mentioned. One of the purposes of this book is to draw attention to the importance of the subject and to add understanding of the dynamics of the dialogues.

An enumeration here of the principal types of dialogues in the field may alert the reader to recognize them as they appear in the text. The most common dialogue engages the fieldworker and his informants. In observations and interviews the fieldworker records happenings, seeks descriptions, asks for explanations, and challenges conclusions. From such a procedure there emerges an adequate, accurate, and comprehensive data base.

On another level is the dialogue between the fieldworker and his advisor or colleagues. Where the relationship is that of graduate student to faculty advisor the contextual content of their communications can range from delayed funds to social theory, but the significant aspects focus on creating models, conceptual formulations, and research directions. This level of dialogue in the field is exemplified in the exchange of letters between Partridge and Kimball and the accompanying commentary.

Most of the dialogues of the third type occur only cerebrally and remain unrecorded. These are the orderly processes of thought in which the congruency of conceptualizations and data are tested by the fieldworker. Two synthesizing processes are at work. First there is the need to order the data of field observation and learning through categorization and to find interconnections between categories. Second there is the need to test the resulting model against prevailing conceptualizations and to confirm, modify, or seek additional data to correct for deficiencies. Out of these processes comes an enhanced comprehension, a knowledge of those interconnected regularities we identify as community.

Introduction

ANTHROPOLOGISTS carry not only cameras, tape recorders, notebooks, and supplies with them into the field, they also carry conceptual and methodological tool kits. In this book, we have joined as coauthors to describe the use of the conceptual and methodological approach of community study in social anthropology in an actual field setting. We achieve this by presenting the field notes and correspondence exchanged between us, in our roles as faculty advisor and graduate student, in 1972 and 1973. It is our central thesis that from the ongoing dialogue between us there emerges an element essential to the successful development of skill in the uses of the community-study approach.

Anthropologists do not merely observe. The tool kits we carry determine in large part the data we collect and what these tell us about the subject of our study. Anthropologists collect information systematically, data that represent only a fraction of the total available information; these data are then further selected as they are studied for patterning, representativeness, and complementarity with other data. The relevance of this point can be better understood if we now turn to a brief theoretical orientation to community study in order to show why anthropologists select and study the data they do. Our purpose here is not to analyze the history of thought out of which the community-study approach evolved, but rather to acquaint the reader with the nature of the theoretical propositions that underlie this scholarly tradition.

The theoretical orientation from which the present study was undertaken is that of community studies in the natural history tradition of American social anthropology (Arensberg and Kimball 1965, 1969). A *community* is defined by the systems of interactional regularities and cultural behaviors that exist within an environmental context (Arensberg and Kimball 1965:4). This is a minimum definition, which generalizes several points of technical significance that will be developed here.

The emphasis upon interactional regularity calls attention to the biological basis of human social organization. Incest prohibition, which requires

1

exogamous groups to interact in some predictable manner, is a primal survival technique of the species. The implications of prolonged infancy and late puberty compel us to view society not as based upon the nuclear family unit but as consisting of organizational structures that relate several family units into larger groups. Three generations, two sexes, and the structures by which these are articulated are the fundamental elements of community.

The emphasis upon cultural behavior stems directly from these requirements for social organization. Organizational structures that link families vary from culture to culture, and they stem from learning experiences of preceding generations. Patterns of mate choice, settlement, subsistence, belief, and the like express the regularities in responses of individuals to comparable situations. We do not think of them as "rules" to which individual actors conform but as constraints that delimit the field of possible responses through the designation of value priorities.

The emphasis upon environmental context adds to the definition the importance of territory and the functional interdependencies that exist among individuals and social groups by virtue of their spatial relationship within a natural world. Community is a storehouse of adaptive responses that have temporal and spatial aspects; the responses reflect the heterogeneous and complex configurations of elemental behavior patterns, the intensity and frequency of which change in relation to incentives stemming from the environment. Community, therefore, should be viewed as the organizational system that ensures the succession of lives and culture through time and over space.

Community provides patterned social relationships that constitute "conditioning influences from the organization of one's fellows about the individual" and channel choice for succeeding generations (Arensberg and Kimball 1965:45). The role of specific individual behavioral items chosen for study is understood, therefore, only in relation to these structures of social relationships that channel choice for members of a community.

The central concern of the method of community study is with the observation *in vivo* of the varieties of social systems and cultural patterns in the context of ongoing human activity. The central problem facing the observer is the reduction of the multiplicity of social facts into a system of priorities of relevance. These priorities are established by examining patterned relationships existing between individuals who are temporally and spatially related. The concern of the method, most simply put, is with the regular and recurring behavior of individuals in groups, for the community is the minimal unit of cultural transmission, whose organizational structures ensure the transmission of the culture from one generation to the next. Inevitably, beliefs, customs, and objects derive meaning from their communal context.

Cultural traditions, particularly in complex societies, are derived from the diversity of their constituent communities and the patterned interconnections among distinctive communal organizations. In general terms, the broad geographical territory encompassed by a unique or distinct cultural tradition and manifest in its constituent configuration of human communities is called a culture area. Latin America is one such broad culture area. In order to place in proper context the community study conducted by Partridge and shaped by the processes that are the subject of this book, we shall summarize the major community traditions that make up Latin American culture.

The varieties of human communities in Latin America have held a particular fascination for American anthropologists. The conquest of indigenous societies—some of them empires of a scale equaled only infrequently in world history—and the subsequent Spanish and Portuguese colonization have produced kinds of human communities that are quite different from those of Europe and Asia. The fundamental legacy of the origins of Latin American culture and society in conquest can be found from the lowland tropics to the altiplano. It is this heritage of civilization, conquest, and colonization that has attracted a great deal of scientific investigation, for the cultural traditions of both conqueror and conquered have synthesized to produce the culture of the majority of people living in the area today. Anthropologists have conducted two kinds of cultural research in Latin America, each of which reflects a distinct intellectual and professional tradition.

The first kind of community research grows out of the tradition of museum collections and the classification of traits observed at the community level according to museum taxonomic schemes. The classification framework used is largely intuitive and is generated from the study of similarities and differences in collections of artifacts, word lists, house forms, food taboos, patterns of dress, and other traits. For example, Parsons (1945) described the community of Peguche, Ecuador, from this perspective. She concentrated upon the categorization of observed traits as either Indian or *mestizo* (mixed Spanish and Indian origins). Using this method, many anthropologists believed it possible to classify whole communities according to the extent of change or degree of acculturation from the time of conquest to the present. For example, people of Indian descent who continued to cook over firewood with a clay griddle supported by three stones were classified as less acculturated than those who cooked on charcoal fires built on a platform elevated on four legs to about waist height. A long list of such simple polar contrasts was compiled in order to provide a taxonomy of contemporary people from the perspective of proximity to and conformity with ancient practices. Similarly, Gillin (1947) studied the community of Moche, Peru, and devoted the bulk of his analysis to the relative proportions of surviving Mochica, Tiahuanacoid, and Chimu culture traits (each an archeological phase in Peruvian prehistory). Little attention was devoted to the analysis of ongoing behavior, the relationship between this community and others, or the distinctive social structure and processes that distinguished this community from others. In neither Parsons's nor Gillin's accounts can we find information on the processes by which traits survive or disappear, for there is no discussion of the interconnections and interrelationships among traits.

Although the museum research approach may be employed at the community level, it is not founded in any theory of community. With its characteristic concern with the mapping of the distribution of traits, it culminates in such reference works as the *Handbook of South American Indians* (Steward 1946) or the *Handbook of Middle American Indians* (Wauchope 1969). The typologies used to order such vast quantities of data are generally not explicit and have little reference or relevance to contemporary communities; for the purpose of the museum research tradition is not to discover the processes by which communities evolve but to catalog the products of that evolution. It is the second method of community research that resembles our own and provides greater insight into the origins, persistence, and modification of human communities in Latin America.

Redfield (1930, 1934, 1941) undertook the first of the studies attempting to analyze social structure, world view, and organizational systems through the observation of ongoing behavior in a cultural context. Like Parsons and Gillin, he was concerned primarily with the continuity of Latin America Indian culture. In his study of Tepoztlán, Mexico, Redfield developed the concept of folk society in which he was able to include not only the traits that typified the community but also the social processes in which they were embedded. Redfield's later work in several communities in Yucatán, Mexico, expanded this approach to include the analysis of interrelations among communities, resulting in his concept of the folk-urban continuum. His findings have been expanded and added to by subsequent community studies, such as Wagley's analyses (1941, 1949, 1952, 1953) of economic exchange relationships in Guatemala and Brazil, Foster's work (1942, 1948) on acculturation and social change in Mexico, Steward's work (1956) on the interrelationships among Puerto Rican communities, Fals Borda's analysis (1955) of peasant social organization in Colombia, and Stein's study (1961) of *hacienda* laborers in Peru. Although this list of "classic" community studies is not exhaustive, it includes those that have contributed most to our understanding of Latin American culture and community. From these studies and those by Wagley and Harris (1955), Wolf (1955), Arensberg (1955, 1959), and Aguirre Beltrán (1967) have emerged typologies based on empirical evidence from contemporary communities. These represent a distinct departure from earlier classificatory efforts of museum science.

We can best illustrate this by summarizing the major community forms that have emerged from earlier studies and, without attempting to exhaust the major and minor variations of these forms, we can understand them as the loci of processes that shape Latin American culture today. They are seen as discrete elements of an essentially multilineal, multifocal, and complex process that is partly a product of the interaction among diverse community traditions, partly a product of geographical factors, and partly a product of the role played by Latin America in the international arena of global economics and nation-state politics.

We have identified four community forms that have come to be representative of Latin American culture: the *Indian peasant hamlet,* the *monoculture plantation,* the *cattle estate,* and the *mestizo peasant hamlet.* Each transmits to succeeding generations a distinct organizational structure and system of interpersonal relationships, manifests a typical settlement pattern and distribution of inhabitants in space, exists within a bounded territory, exhibits functional adaptation to a set of ecological conditions, and perpetuates a characteristic world view. These patterns also reflect the linkages that connect community and urban centers and the functional relationships through which diverse parts are integrated into the whole. When we encounter several community traditions articulated to the same nodal center (for example, in the case of cattle estate traditions and Indian peasant hamlet traditions, which compete in the same valley and are articulated to the same market town), it is necessary to determine empirically not only the vertical articulation of hinterland traditions to node but also the kinds and levels of horizontal interconnections between these traditions. In some cases what historically had been distinct communities may now be fused into one, each becoming in the context of community life a subcultural tradition. In other cases they may be physically contiguous yet remain culturally distinct, semiautonomous communities.

The *Indian peasant hamlet* is typified by satellite Indian villages dispersed about a *mestizo*-dominated market town. The extensive territory is interlaced with footpaths and trails for mule trains. Because of the distances that separate hamlets and town, the observer may assume initially that the settlements are distinct communities; however, examination of interpersonal relationships reveals the systemic connections. An obvious biological interconnection is found in the centuries-old interbreeding between the two populations. The shared system of markets to which Indian farmers bring crops and other products for barter or sale to townspeople is also evidence of interconnection. Less obvious is the small corps of bilingual Indians who function as intermediaries between town and country and whose offspring are integrated into the town subculture.

The territory is usually remote, yet land is in scarce supply. The combination of population pressure, advance-purchase credit at usurious interest rates (which prevents capital accumulation), and the successful expansion of the townspeople's landholdings results in a steady out-migration of indigenous offspring in search of work. The *mestizo* townspeople cultivate the land of the fertile valleys, while indigenous farmers are pushed into more remote mountain regions.

In the hamlets the indigenous elders dominate positions of political, religious, and social authority through the "cargo" system, which bestows prestige and power on wealthy families that serve the community. Authorities in the towns are politically powerful mestizos, both elected and appointed. Despite close biological and economic ties, the world views of townsmen and Indians repudiate any close interdependence. The Indian world view is founded on respect for elders, for the obligations of community service, for land transmitted to them from ancient times. Indians view townsmen as lazy individuals with skills inadequate for extracting a living from the land; thus, their survival depends on the exploitation of Indian labor. In the world view of townsmen, Indians are backward people condemned to poverty because of their traditional values, a caste whose only role in society is labor for low wages.

The *monoculture plantation* community displays a settlement pattern composed of slave (worker) quarters, immigrant (mixed-blood) administrator family units, a plant for processing and loading crops in vehicles, and a grand house (which frequently contains a chapel for use by resident family and worker alike), in which the plantation owners (corporate managers) live. The monoculture plantation produces a single crop for export to international markets. This feature links all personnel of the plantation in an enclave economy vulnerable to transnational conditions, such as volatile price changes, production quotas, and commodity accords. The boom and bust cycles of major plantation crops produce a sense of dependency reflected in the strong personal relationships that workers, administrators, and even part-time laborers seek to establish with the plantation owners or managers.

The territory of the community includes the expanse of fertile flat land where cultivation takes place and the equally important territory of the nodal center: the offices of the corporation, the homes and townhouses of urban owners, the shanties occupied by migrant workers. Political, social, and economic power are vested entirely in the plantation owners or managers, for the plantation monopolizes good land so that few if any peasant hamlets and towns exist in the same area. While labor unions may exist, their capacity to affect transnational conditions is slight; leaders are therefore rarely recruited from their ranks. Real and effective leadership stems from the production process and the role relationships that structure production, and workers who rise to prominence do so through the status and skill hierarchy of the plantation.

The world view of the owners or managers is that of an urban elite concerned with the replication of political power, the control of human and nonhuman resources, and the realization of profits sufficient to meet social obligations toward dependent families—a responsibility that elite status carries with it in Latin America. The world view of workers is structured by the necessity to achieve some security in a situation of seasonal labor, fluctuating market conditions, and high unemployment. Consequently, the laborer attempts to maintain extensive kin ties wherever migration takes him, always seeking to secure permanent employment in the production process.

The *cattle estate* displays a settlement pattern made up of clusters of residences for cowboys and administrators, a physical plant for processing and transporting live cattle and/or beef products, and an estate store. Today the cattle ranch characteristically occupies the less fertile and rougher country, although at one time it enclosed the richer lands as well. The expanse of land is generally huge, particularly in remote areas. Production and animals per hectare are low, dairying is limited to household needs, natural pasture grasses predominate, and calf mortality rates are often high. Under these conditions, few workers and administrators are required. The owners reside in urban centers, delegating the daily operation of the estate to administrators and workers. The patron-client relationship unites owner, administrator, and worker into a tightly knit pattern of reciprocal obligations. In addition to their cash wages, administrators and workers are given estate housing; a small plot of land for farming; rations of milk, salt, and beef; and credit at the estate store or stores in nearby towns. Employees reciprocate with intense loyalty, protection of estate land from invasion, and a willingness to work extraordinary hours during infrequent periods of intensive production. The structure of relationships on cattle estates is highly personalistic and, while political and economic power are monopolized by the owner, a degree of social mobility is possible for energetic employees through the sponsorship of the patron. The world views of all personnel, save the owner, are remarkably similar, in that all are concerned with the maintenance of patron-client ties and with the lineal transmission of these; because migration in search of work is not typical of estate personnel, there is less concern with extensive kin ties. The owners utilize extensive kin ties in meeting social obligations toward dependent families, in retaining access to political power, and in maintaining control of human and nonhuman resources.

The *mestizo peasant hamlet* is understood not as the counterpart of the Indian peasant hamlet but as the culmination of processes that begin in the Indian peasant hamlet, the monoculture plantation, and the cattle estate communities. Offspring from Indian peasant hamlets who seek wages find work on the great plantations within the flow of migratory labor upon which plantation production depends. It is here (and on the cattle estate, if the migrant is lucky enough to find employment) that cultural synthesis occurs, a process that is partly biological, resulting in ''mixed bloods,'' and partly cultural, resulting in acculturation to the norms of a plantation community. Generations later the offspring of these *mestizos*—either by establishing a relationship with a powerful patron, obtaining credit, saving their wages, or finding a region where colonization is possible—acquire a farm. Like the Indian peasant, *mestizo* peasants plant subsistence crops, a portion of which they market to storekeepers who advance credit and with whom strong bonds of interdependence are formed. Unlike the Indian peasant hamlet, the *mestizo* peasant hamlet is not divided ethnically, and the caste-like attitudes of *mestizo* townsmen are absent here. Nor does there exist the dual pattern of political, religious, and social authority in a *mestizo* peasant hamlet. Consequently, the patron-client bonds of interdependence and interconnection among townspeople and farmers are openly acknowledged, publicly cultivated, and ritually confirmed in drinking and feasting, in the marriage of offspring, and in the apprenticeship of peasant offspring to shopkeepers, artisans, and other townspeople. The world views of *mestizo* peasants and the townspeople are similar. Both are concerned with the lineal transmission of rights and obligations through the generations; there is little concern with maintenance of wide kin networks, although extensive fictive kin ties are important; and both believe in the possibility of socioeconomic mobility given the right combination of luck, hard work, and personal sponsor.

Any one of these four major community forms may exist in pure form quite separate from the others, or they may be found in combination with each other. In the community studied by William Partridge, the distinct traditions of the cattle estate, the monoculture plantation, and the mestizo hamlet were articulated to the same nodal center. Just as personnel, patterns of interaction, organizational structures, and world views vary in each of these traditions, so too do the townspeople connected to them vary in the nature of their participation in these traditions. And just as the people of the hinterlands are culturally heterogeneous, so too are the townspeople variously linked to identifiable community traditions.

These four community traditions that encompass countrymen and townsmen alike continue to influence the direction of change and development in Latin America. Yet as surely as they persist into the present, they must continually adjust to new conditions. For example, public health advances have altered morbidity and fertility rates and sparked tremendous population growth rates, leading directly to urban migration into the regional and national capitals. In response to population growth and slowly growing economies, most Latin American governments have become committed to ''the green revolution," the energy-intensive alternative to traditional systems of agriculture. Agrarian reform has been married to this process of industrialization of agricultural production. Similarly, large-scale central government development schemes, often affecting entire regions and sometimes involving resettlement of entire communities, are eating up great portions of the total national development budget. Government programs are moving into the hinterlands with the express purpose of transforming community traditions. Examples of such efforts include the spread of rural technical schools devoted to changing agricultural, livestock, and manufacturing production and distribution systems, and an increased emphasis upon health care, transportation, and taxation in the hinterlands.

It is understandable that such plans to modify Latin American communities may engender conflict, personal insecurity, and uncertainty. Oftentimes, the response of Latin American leaders to resistance is to order compliance. Community traditions have mediated the specific response of Latin Americans to these new conditions. The adaptations have become the object of problem-oriented community studies carried out in the last few decades. Examples include Cancian's studies (1965, 1972) of changes in the Maya culture stemming from new opportunities for cash cropping introduced by the Mexican government; Carter's work (1965) on the impact of agrarian reform on land tenure among the Aymara of the Bolivian altiplano; Doughty's and Mangin's studies (1970) of urban migrants and culture change in Peru; Hammel's studies (1969) of changes in economic conditions and social stratification in Peru; Peattie's analysis (1968) of the multiple dilemmas facing Venezuelans caught up in the creation of a planned city; Whitten's study (1965) of changes in kinship patterns and social mobility as a response to new economic opportunities in Ecuador; Moore's work (1973) on the impact of the development of public education systems on Indians and Ladinos in Guatemala; and Modiano's study (1973) of the bilingual education of indigenous people in Mexico. There are many others, but these examples are representative of problem-oriented studies in community context.

The purposes of problem-oriented community study are to describe and analyze the nature of systems of interpersonal relations, organizational structures, world views, and ecological adaptations that shape community responses to changing conditions. Such a study also traces the impact on community traditions of new constraints and incentives that arise from new conditions. From such an approach, the processes by which the four community traditions sketched above persist into the present, and with them the nature of Latin American culture, can be better understood.

Partridge's work in Majagua, Colombia, is a problem-oriented community study. The research design was focused upon cannabis and human social groupings. But it was not concerned with cannabis *qua* cannabis. Rather, the study concentrated upon the variety of human groupings found in the community, the social relationships that characterized each of these, their distinctive activities and world views, and the system of relationships by which these groups were articulated into a community. Cannabis was expected to be associated with some groups, but not with others. Data of interest to the anthropologist would necessarily come from all groups. The proposal originally called for the study of cannabis use, but this was quickly expanded to include cultivation and marketing when these were found to be present in the community studied.

Social group structures and social relationships that permeated systems of production, distribution, and consumption of cannabis in a community on the north coast of Colombia were studied between July 1972 and October 1973. The origins of the community were traced and certain subcultural traditions were found to be adaptations to the ecological, historical, and geographical conditions of the north coast region. These subcultures were linked through certain exchange relationships, yet they were also clearly identifiable in their differing social, economic, and domestic arrangements.

Once these components of the community were outlined, social group structures and social relationships characteristic of each subculture were examined with special reference to systems of cultivation, distribution, and consumption of cannabis. Two systems of cultivation and two systems of distribution were found, corresponding to two distinctive subcultural traditions present in the community. Cannabis consumption was found to be characteristic of only one of these subcultures. As a result of controlled comparison between these subcultures, cannabis consumption was found to be instrumentally and expressively related to certain kinds of social groupings and social relationships present in one subcultural tradition but absent from the other. Cannabis cultivation and distribution were associated with still other groups. In this manner the locus of cannabis in the natural human grouping was described (see Partridge 1975, 1977, for detailed discussion of the results).

The results of the study summarized here were the product of many months of painstaking data collection and continuous dialogue concerning the evaluation and interpretation of the data. The findings were presented as a dissertation (Partridge 1974). However, the processes by which the data were collected, evaluated, and interpreted are not apparent in that volume. It is to these processes that this volume is addressed.

There has been minor editing of the field notes and letters for purposes of adding clarity, eliminating duplication, and deleting some personal items that are not relevant.

1. Prologue

THIS BOOK is about anthropological field research as an operational system. Our first objective is to delineate for the reader the processual structure of the craft of community study, a procedure for discovering, describing, and analyzing the interconnected systems of human relationships that constitute a community. To accomplish this we have drawn from the original field notes written by William Partridge during a 15-month period in 1972 and 1973, in which he employed the methods of community study to investigate a specific problem: the social place and cultural meaning of marijuana (or cannabis) in a community in Colombia.

The method of community study is part of a larger process of transmission to another generation of the purposes and skills of professional anthropology. Our second objective, then, is to portray the intellectual dialogue between professor and student engaged in a search for new knowledge and to demonstrate the role of this dialogue in shaping field operations. Thus, interspersed chronologically among the field notes are samples of the correspondence between Solon Kimball and Bill Partridge, professor and student, during the period of fieldwork. This documentation and accompanying analysis provide an intimate view of the process through which community study research emerges, for we see the processual structure of the fieldwork and the dialogue as the twin elements of the craft of community study.

Our focus is not limited to the sequential response of a fieldworker to his environment. We are also concerned with the transformation in role behavior of the fieldworker during the various developmental phases of the research project. These phases, as they are developed in the chapters to follow, we have called: visitor, guest, explorer, participant-observer, participant-operator, and research-evaluator, leading in the end to withdrawal from the field and reentry to the university. These stages are the product, we contend, not only of the continual adjustment of the individual fieldworker to a distant or foreign society; they are also partly the product of the intellectual dialogue between professor and student as the latter seeks to order and report his findings (through the application of the theory and method in which he has been trained) and as the former seeks to react to these and contribute advice that will facilitate achievement of the research goals. Each is engaged with the data, and through the data with each other, as they attempt to order the data from different perspectives. As the student fieldworker moves with greater ease and skill into the various domains of the life of the community being studied, so too the dialogue among partners in this research endeavor intensifies and deepens.

To our knowledge, field research as an operational system has not been viewed in this way. We are aware that the prevailing mode speaks of advisor and advisee, master and apprentice, or mentor and novice. While recognizing that some aspects of our relationship, particularly in the early stages, might legitimately be so characterized, we find that the distinguishing feature of an anthropological research relationship is the joint quest for new knowledge. The findings flow from mutual effort and, we believe, are not possible through the efforts of either professor or fieldworker acting independently. The developmental phases, as we will show, are marked not only by changes in the nature of Bill Partridge's activities in Colombia but also by changes in the depth and tone of his dialogue with Solon Kimball. These changes are reflected in the field notes and correspondence, which we accept as written evidence that the model of community that emerges is the product of a mutual effort.

We characterize our working relationship as a research partnership, the success of which depends upon mutual but differing contributions. Some colleagues may protest that their own experiences do not correspond to ours, and this would not be surprising. The mythology that surrounds anthropological field research includes the quest of the erstwhile student who ventures forth alone into the world of cultural contrast, while the aloof professor, with the indifference of a sidelines field judge, observes whether the neophyte will endure the difficulties and attain his quest for knowledge. In most cases the mythology of a people encompasses only the highlights of ordinary experience, and dramatizes these in order to communicate to the uninitiated that which is unique and the object of particular pride. If this is the case with others, so too it is probably the case with anthropologists. What lies behind the myth?

As far as it goes, our anthropological mythology is accurate. Following a period of academic preparation that requires the student to prove his intellectual competence through course work and examinations, there follows a trial by ordeal in the field. The field offers the crucial situation of our profession for testing individuals and validating their competencies, a stage of development charged with an emotional essence exceeding any other. For those who live the culture and speak the language of another people for extended periods of time, the metaphor of the field as crucible is valid, and ample evidence of this will be found in the pages to follow.

But the field research experience is much more than the culmination of academic preparation. Following his initial exposure to the new environment, or culture shock, which in extreme cases involves disorientation and paranoid anxieties, the fieldworker enters a period of productive activity, which continues to intensify and deepen in both personal and professional significance until the time arrives for departure and reentry into academe. It is this period of productivity—a time of heightened engagement in the lives of informants, intense intellectual involvement in the interplay between data collection and theoretical model building, constant fine-tuning of research techniques and goals, and the confrontation of ethical dilemmas and corresponding commitment to their practical solution—that is of most interest to us here. It is this time of productive work, the bulk of the research endeavor, that receives the least emphasis in our mythology. Moreover, it is during this period that the dialogue between colleagues also becomes more productive. As will become apparent, the dialogue during the more productive stages of the field research is an essential part of the craft of community study. In it we find evidence of the powerful effect of the theoretical perspective on a course of scientific activity, and the interplay between research goals, techniques, and theoretical models. We will develop these points in the final chapter.

The reader may fairly ask a number of questions at this point: Is not the research partnership founded upon a deeper, personal relationship? Are the origins of the dialogue to be found in shared cultural origins, similarities of personality, or the chance convergence of other, more idiosyncratic factors in the participants' pasts? What are the origins of this mutual interest in cannabis in community context? We can best answer these by briefly tracing the beginnings of our collaboration and the genesis of the research project.

THE RESEARCH PARTNERSHIP

We first met in 1966 when Bill was an undergraduate student of anthropology at the University of Florida, where Sol (as he is known among his intimate friends) was graduate research professor of anthropology. Bill was born in Miami, Florida, and came to the university with an already developed interest in anthropology, having spent his free time in high school among American Indians. His mother is from a Scotch-Irish family of the hill-country farming tradition of the Carolinas, his father from an English watchmaker's family that immigrated first to Toronto, Canada, and then to the United States. Both families moved to Miami during the boom period of the 1920s. He was socialized, consequently, into the contrasting traditions of romanticism, independence, and respect for authority typical of the hill-country South, combined with the self-discipline and skeptical distrust of authority that marks the English working class.

As a beginning graduate student, Bill was intending to study culture change in contemporary communities of the South. Since Sol was recognized to be one of the pioneers of modern social anthropology of the South, it is natural that Bill sought him as his major advisor. Sol was born in Manhattan, in the Flint Hills of Kansas. He first developed an interest in anthropology through the study of geology and man's antiquity, later studying social anthropology under Lloyd Warner at Harvard. His parents represented the contrasting backgrounds of prudent New England and the ebullient Border South. He was socialized into the midwestern Main Street tradition characterized by cautious privatism, pragmatism, and public cooperation.

In the late 1960s Bill learned of the deaths in Vietnam of several of his high school friends; although he expected to be exempted from the draft, he was, nonetheless, frightened and outraged. He read avidly about the war and, in the summer of 1967, marched in protest in front of the Pentagon with thousands of others. By embracing the tactics of public confrontation, Bill achieved temporary release from the feelings of powerlessness that his dead high school companions had left as their legacy. Other students reacted differently. The hippie movement was then beginning, and to Bill this was cause for alarm. In place of the symbols of defiance he valued, these students substituted symbols of serenity. It was then that he decided, with Sol's approval, to make this phenomenon the subject of his master's thesis. Bill lived and conducted research in a neighborhood the hippies called the "ghetto," taught part-time at the university, and consulted from time to time with Sol. In the fall of 1969, he turned in a completed thesis.

Then and now, Bill and Sol hold different opinions on many of the controversial issues discussed in the thesis. For example, Sol dislikes public confrontation and display partly because of his cultural background and partly because he believes them to be politically ineffectual. In contrast, Bill's commitment to public defiance of the military, the munitions industries, and their dependent personnel stems from his cultural background and from his belief that it is politically appropriate. However, these and other differences of opinion were overridden during the writing, presentation, and defense of the thesis by a shared commitment to professional competency in its ethical, technical, and theoretical dimensions.

If Bill Partridge was an angry young man in the late 1960s, Solon Kimball was an angry professional anthropologist. Some professionals are too enamored of their own interests to have much time for students; in such instances the process of graduate research may be hampered, although the student may still draw upon other resources and generate worthwhile research. For example, Kalervo Oberg reported in 1931 at the University of Chicago that his conference with his advisor before he left for his study of the Tlingit Indians lasted no more than an hour. After that he was on his own. Laura Nader recalled Clyde Kluckhohn's response when, as a graduate student at Harvard in 1957, she approached him for advice prior to her departure for a Zapotec village in Mexico: "He told [me] the story of a graduate student who had asked Kroeber the same question. In response, Kroeber was said to have taken the largest, fattest ethnography book off his shelf, handed it to the student, and said, 'Go forth and do likewise' " (Nader 1970:98). But Nader also reported that Kluckhohn commented on the field notes that she sent him.

Senior anthropologists, as senior scholars in any field of science, have a professional obligation not only to contribute to new substantive knowledge themselves but also to ensure its continuing expansion through the younger generation of scholars. This includes the bureaucratically imposed chores of record-keeping, attending committee meetings, and preparing reports and progress summations. It also involves acting as guide, protector, prod, and developer. The significant goal, however, is achieved only at the intellectual level: in the formulation of research problems, in the operations of field research, and in the scholarly presentation of the findings. It seemed to Sol that many senior anthropologists, for a variety of reasons, neglected the more significant and time-consuming developmental goal and instead grew proficient at processing scores of students in assembly-line fashion. These young anthropologists were trained to replicate the work of their mentors, but most seemed intellectually unprepared to expand and extend the horizons of anthropology to encompass contemporary society and modern issues. The theoretical foundations for modern anthropology had been laid in the 1930s. Yet despite the affluent and prolific growth of higher education during the postwar years, little had been added to this base. For these reasons Sol Kimball was angry with his generation of anthropologists and was determined to pay special attention to the younger generation of scholars.

It has always seemed to Sol that anthropologists should extrapolate from their knowledge of cultural behavior parallels that are applicable to the academic situation so that they might better know their own behavior. The sequential phases of induction, testing, and claiming, which occur in rites of passage, resemble in broad outline the graduate training process. Too often, however, this process is conceptualized entirely in terms of the neophytes' progress from one phase to the next. It should not be forgotten that the elders of the Australian Murngin (and their counterparts in other places of the world) carry the burden of bringing the novices successfully through their struggle for passage to the new status by transmitting the heritage of their group. Only thus does the group endure.

From our short biographies it should be apparent that the research partnership was forged by two distinct individuals. We are from different generations in a society in which divergent interests and commitments based on age frequently erupt into generational conflict. We are the products of distinct cultural backgrounds, manifest in contrasting personal styles of behavior and thought: the emotionally closed and cautious interactional and intellectual style of the Midwest contrasted against the emotionally open and risk-oriented interactional and intellectual style of the South. Finally, we are very different in our political actions and beliefs.

Yet it should also be apparent that overriding these contrasts were points of tangency upon which the partnership was built. The first of these is a shared professional commitment to high standards of ethical, theoretical, and technical competence. We first discovered this mutuality when Bill was working on his master's thesis and, later, when he was revising it for publication following Sol's encouragement to write a book on the topic (see Partridge 1973). Such mutual interests are rarely discovered outside the context of joint involvement in scientific research and writing. Second, we share a view of anthropology as an offshoot of natural science and consequently distrust *ad hoc* theory-building and the hypotheses generated from such theories in the social sciences. In the natural science tradition, value-critical research (in which we attempt to scrutinize the observable implications of values and inductively construct theories to explain the evidence we find) and value-committed research (in which we state our values and seek empirical evidence that demonstrates their behavioral implications) are based on scientific induction. Much social science, on the other hand, is increasingly bound by deductive logic and is increasingly concerned with hypothesis testing using secondary data. Our third point of congruency derived from our very distinct cultural traditions, which endowed a degree of flexibility that has permitted us to withstand individually the stresses of conflict, ambiguity, and tension when these occur. Probably not all combinations of cultural backgrounds would result in mutual flexibility, but it is probably the case that this capacity made possible the emergence of the points of tangency in the development of our separate yet shared commitments.

It would be naive—and perhaps arrogant as well—to represent our research partnership as a model for others, nor is this our intention. The conditions, after all, have changed. Today's student either has never heard of Ho Chi Minh or imagines him to have been an adolescent guru. Much of the tension of the immediate past that infused the academic environment and other parts of the world with a sense of involvement and commitment has today been supplanted by an overarching feeling of uncertainty. New concerns for personal security and individual gain have superseded the concerns of the past. However, we do think that the lessons we have learned from our relationship can serve as stimuli for others; for, whatever the issues, problems, and concerns of the moment, the anthropological research experience as an operational system will remain the hearth at which personal and professional talents are forged.

THE RESEARCH PROBLEM

The processual structure of anthropological field research and its series of developmental phases begins with formulation of a research problem. Before we join Bill Partridge as he enters the culture of the north coast of Colombia, we should briefly sketch the major steps that led to the field research.

In Partridge's study of the subculture called hippies, he discovered that cannabis smoking had been ritually organized and served a number of social and cultural purposes. But the literature on cannabis use seriously neglected the social and cultural aspects. Few investigators had studied the natural social and cultural setting in which marijuana use occurs, and cross-cultural studies were rare. At the time of Bill's research, the widespread use of cannabis among American youth was a national concern, as evidenced by the availability of public funds for support of basic research. It was hoped that the results of government-sponsored research would be useful in the development of national policy and programs on drug use. While the great bulk of the literature available at the time (*see* UNESCO 1965 for a bibliography including over 1800 entries) and most ongoing research was concerned with the botany, chemistry, pharmacology, and clinical effects of the plant, Partridge proposed to concentrate on social and cultural factors through the use of the community-studies method.

Solon Kimball was uncertain about the desirability of such a sharply focused study, a doubt that arose from his knowledge of other restricted efforts. These concentrated on a single facet and failed to examine the setting in which activity occurs. Their lack of contextual substance resembled the ephemeral smile of Lewis Carroll's Cheshire cat. Meaning cannot be extracted from the thing itself; only when behavior is placed in context can understanding emerge. Kimball agreed to the proposal with the stipulation that the community context would be the essential component of the problem. In retrospect, no other approach could have made sense out of the complicated behavioral variations that Bill encountered in the Colombian community. In addition, the value of specific problem orientation was also demonstrated. In following the elusive and sometimes dangerous trail on which the search for cannabis led him, Bill was able to analyze community structure in a way that contributed not only to our understanding of drug use but also to our knowledge of contemporary Latin American communities.

The proposal called for 15 months of study in a community located on the north coast of Colombia. During June and July of 1971, Bill visited Colombia in order to perfect his Spanish. At the conclusion of his intensive course he visited the major cities and interviewed physicians, psychiatrists, pharmacologists, and government officials regarding the incidence and location of cannabis use. The north coast emerged as a prime area for the study of traditional cannabis consumption and cultivation. During August 1971, Dr. William E. Carter, then director of the Center for Latin American Studies at the University of Florida, conducted a feasibility study of the prospects for cannabis research in Colombia for the Center for Studies of Narcotic and Drug Abuse of the National Institute of Mental Health. His report also confirmed that the north coast would be an excellent research setting.

Numerous studies existed that purported to provide data on social or cultural dimensions of cannabis use in Colombia, but these were uniformly undertaken in prisons, asylums, or clinics (Wolff 1949, Perez 1952, Ardila Rodríguez 1965). Although no scientists had sought sample populations outside of the selected groups present in Colombian prisons, schools, or hospitals, enough was known at that point to postulate that the observed effects and social and cultural characteristics of the populations studied were more the product of the special conditions associated with confinement and institutionalization than of cannabis use itself. The proposal described a research project designed to provide data concerning that area which had received the least attention: the social and cultural meaning of cannabis in the natural setting in which it is used.

In November 1971 the research proposal was submitted to several funding agencies. The Fulbright-Hays Dissertation Research Committee and the Cultural Anthropology Committee of the National Institute of Mental Health (NIMH) responded favorably. The NIMH grant provided not only for 15 months of research in Colombia, but for 9 months of write-up as well. That grant was activated in June 1972 and preparations were begun for starting fieldwork the following month.

2. Entry into the Field

ALONG the northern rim of South America a fertile coastal plain sweeps inland until it meets the edge of the Andean highlands, which stretch northward into Colombia out of Ecuador, Peru, Bolivia, and Chile. Separated from this massive chain of mountains is the Sierra Nevada de Santa Marta, perched on the coast and transecting the broad expanse of humid flatlands that lies between the ocean and the Andean highlands (figure 2.1). Occupying a portion of the plain and the Sierra Nevada highlands is the *municipio,* or county, of Majagua. A town of the same name serves as the seat of local government and a center of commercial activity.

The varied activities through which residents of the town and country pursue the business of living reflect the diversity among them. In the fields and pastures one encounters farmers, ranchers, and laborers. In the towns there are multiple divisions within the professional, commercial, and industrial spheres. Such occupational contrasts are only the more obvious manifestations of the diverse secular and symbolic functions of corporate life. For example, Majagua not only serves as the point of convergence for innumerable activities originating in the surrounding countryside, but it also acts as a connector with comparable nearby towns and the regional cities of even more impressive complexity.

The flavor of the locality, however, is garnered from the myriad distinctive sights, sounds, and movements. The stranger traveling the local highways notes the large number who travel on foot, an occasional horseman or commercial van, and the infrequent jam-packed local bus. Country women busily laundering the family wash squat alongside irrigation canals and streams flowing down from the sierra. Tin-roofed huts and palm-thatched *bareques,* sometimes clustered in hamlets, are sprinkled along the roadside. Gangs of workers laboring in fields or along roadsides contrast with the infrequent tractor and its solitary operator. The sights and sounds of the town are no less distinctive. Children laugh and chatter on their way to school,

19

elderly women gossip as they go to church, beggars extend an empty hand to passersby, and male voices echo from the doorway of the *cantina*.

These surface behaviors acquire contextual meaning as one explores the history of these people. The cultural successions have been few but dramatic.

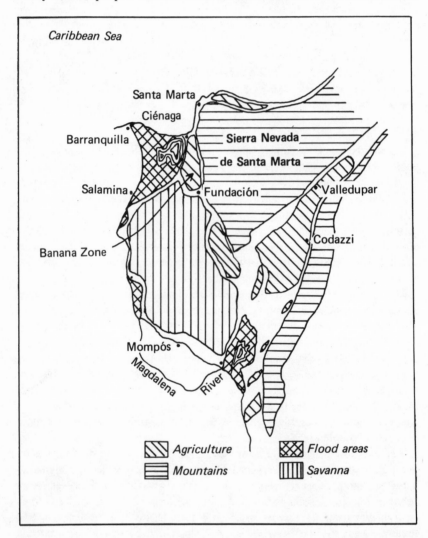

Figure 2.1.   Map of Magdalena region. Source: Comisión de Planificación, 1964.

The original village cultivators of pre-Columbian days were first over-
whelmed and then incorporated into the great cattle baronies established by
the Spanish conquerors. Centuries later an equally severe transformation
occurred when the United Fruit Company introduced banana plantations. The
company's abandonment of the effort a few decades later opened the way for
the appearance of the contrasting commercial and subsistence economies of
today.

These word pictures offer an initial glimpse of the setting in which Bill
Partridge conducted his community study. In July 1972, he arrived in
Majagua seeking a suitable site for his work on the use of cannabis in a
community context. In October 1973, 14 months later, he departed.

The events described in this chapter occurred during the period from 30
June 1972 to 15 August 1972. The initial date marks the activation of the
research grant that financed the field research. The period ends with the
submission of Partridge's first field report to Kimball. This six-week period, called the period of entry, is marked by its distinctive configuration
of activities, all designed to facilitate a successful entry into a new social
field.

Entry into a new social field always implies exiting from an older, more
familiar one. In the following account the process of exiting is described in
relation to the subsequent process of entry. Its flow is recorded in letters and
notes. Partridge's initial impressions of the new setting are reported in his first
letter from the field. In it he describes the preliminary work carried out in the
cities of Colombia that led to his selection of the research site, including the
events that led to the selection of a specific community on the north coast.
This accomplishment, the selection of a community, signaled entrance into a
new social field. In the pages that follow, the reader will gain an appreciation
for the complex and varied adjustment that accompanies entrance into a
society and culture different from one's own. We trace out the progress in its
detail. Entrance into another society or culture may be viewed as a sequence
of steps, each one bringing the investigator closer to his subjects and more
deeply into the role of researcher. But entrance does not automatically confer
upon the anthropologist the role of ''participant observer'' (a much misunder-
stood and misapplied phrase that has come to mean anything from conducting
a few interviews to spending several weeks in prison to learn ''what it is like''
to be an inmate). Participant observation is a valuable and respected technique
of anthropological field study, but it must be developed with time. During the
period of entry, the anthropologist assumes the role of guest. As a guest, he is
neither fully a participant nor fully an observer.

Guests are intruders into the private space of a household, a neighborhood, or a community. Their presence automatically elicits the ordinary rituals all peoples have evolved to deal with such invasions of privacy. Characteristically, such rituals are cordial. The people of Colombia are no different from others in this regard. They offer the visitor a chair and a cup of hot coffee, a glass of water with raw sugar and lemon juice, or a beer, and converse pleasantly with him on general topics. But just as the ritual is cordial, so too is it cautious, preserving the boundaries between members of the host group and the visitor. By such ritualized interaction, the intrusion into private space is controlled, standardized, and dealt with effectively.

Entrance into a new social field, therefore, means that the anthropologist has gained only an initial access to persons and situations that constitute his data. He is not yet interacting as participant observer any more than any other stranger who momentarily enters the space of a people. The behavior that the stranger's presence elicits limits access to the private space through ritualized actions and words. Thus does any social group neutralize the disturbing effect of an intrusion.

In this chapter, then, we trace the events through which Partridge gained entry into a community on the north coast of Colombia. The full story encompasses succeeding stages of fieldwork, but it is this one that constitutes the important first step.

DEPARTURE AND ARRIVAL

During the weeks preceding his departure for the field, Partridge's activities had centered on assembling materials and equipment; packing and storing personal belongings, books, and files; and withdrawing from a social network of friends, professors, and students, some of whom were likewise preparing to enter the field. Removing oneself from a social setting can be pleasurable as well as traumatic, especially when uncertainty remains about the new locale that one expects to enter.

Several friends from graduate school hosted a going-away party in Partridge's honor. Thus, aided by food and drink, the separation that was about to occur was ritualized and commemorated. One unusual aspect of the affair was the bestowing by Partridge of an amulet, a trinket of small monetary but great ceremonial value. The amulet had been passed through a successive line of graduate students as each one successfully completed his doctoral qualifying examination. In such manner it had come to Partridge, and now the time had come to transmit it to another. This ritual on the eve of his departure could also be viewed as symbolizing separation from the ranks of one's fellow graduate students. Although Partridge did not leave for Colombia the following day as he had intended, his embarcation had been celebrated by friends that evening.

The departure of the plane from Miami International Airport on July 11 and its arrival a few hours later at the Aereopuerto Internacional de Barranquilla was another in the sequence of endings and beginnings. Only two weeks earlier Partridge had been sorting and packing the accumulated possessions of years of graduate study. He had been feeling euphoric, his anticipation mixed with uncertainty, since receiving notification that his grant proposal had been approved. Now, on new soil, the prospect of finally beginning fieldwork in a society and culture different from his own only heightened such feelings.

But there were the sobering problems associated with the purely technical and mechanical aspects of preparation. There was concern about establishing cooperative liaison with institutions in the host country, becoming adjusted to a new culture and a different language, and being separated for a lengthy period from family and old friends. The two weeks before departure had been a time of excitement, but it was also a time of reflection on the nature of the task that lay ahead. Upon his arrival in Barranquilla, Partridge was greeted by a mixture of sights, sounds, and smells of a different world.

Barranquilla is a large Caribbean port on the north coast of Colombia, situated at the mouth of the Magdalena River, which flows from the mountains of the interior to the humid tropical lowlands bordering the Caribbean Sea. Farther up the coast lies colonial Cartagena, and in the opposite direction is found the first permanent Spanish settlement in South America, the sleepy little city of Santa Marta. In stark contrast to these two ancient ports, Barranquilla is industrial, densely populated, and huge. Yet the scale of the peculiarly Latin American modernization—the factories, the warehouses, the port—does not obscure the Spanish Caribbean flavor of the city. The smells of mangoes, salt, and flowering trees and shrubs mingle together throughout the year. Barranquilla is surrounded by lowland swamps on one side, savannas dotted with peasant hamlets and cattle estates on another, and the Caribbean on the third. The city streets are alive with activity: peasants bringing produce to market on their burros; fishermen hawking their catches in the streets; and market women selling twisted roots, crushed leaves, and other herbal remedies gleaned from the countryside for sale to urbanites.

The residential areas of the wealthy on the surrounding hills overlook the fascinating fusion of modern industrial society and traditional coastal subcultures. Here are the homes of cattle barons, banking executives, professionals, and others who attempt to direct the growth of the metropolis. El Prado is one such neighborhood, a combination of the boom-period architecture of the 1920s, with its flare for the Spanish-Moorish iron grills, tile floors and roofs,

heavy carved wooden doors, and breezy patios; and the more modern structures designed by sons of the elite educated in Europe or the United States.
These homes, which bring to mind Wright and Le Corbusier, display sweep-
ing and massive concrete facades punctuated with expansive plate glass
windows and sculptured steel.

Partridge's first evening in Barranquilla was not spent in appreciative
observation of these charming features of the city in which he found himself.
Having checked into a hotel in the downtown area, close to government and
customs offices where his trunks and luggage would have to be cleared, he
spent his first evening walking the streets of this area, where bars, stores,
poolrooms, movie theaters, hotels, restaurants, and business offices crowd in
upon one another. Here, in the old center of the city, an air of decay pervades
all but the most recently built structures. The streets are littered with rotting
vegetables and the storefronts are barred with heavy metal sliding doors or
wire mesh screens. Political posters, advertisements, and funeral notices are
printed on paper and pasted on the old buildings; the paste dries and cracks
under the hot Caribbean sun, and soon the streets are lined with peeling
posters and announcements. Policemen carry automatic carbines over their
shoulders. The din of automobile horns, so characteristic of Caribbean and
Latin American cities, unnerves the unprepared visitor. Barranquilla seemed
at first a strangely familiar yet, at the same time, an inhospitable city.
Although it shared features with many industrial cities of North America, the
distinctive Latin American flavor was a constant reminder to Partridge to be
suspicious of his first impression.

The following few days he was engaged in recovering his supplies, clothing, and professional equipment from the customs officers at the Aduana
Nacional. For the first time he was to plunge into the culture of this region as a
participant. His activities soon convinced him that, despite the similarities he
initially perceived, this culture was indeed quite different from his own: the
factories, the banks, and the offices of the government were externally similar
to those in the United States, but when he came into contact with those who
inhabited these familiar places, the differences leaped to the foreground. The
differences were real; initial sensory impressions had been valid.

Partridge's letter to Kimball dated 19 July reflects the transition outlined
here, a transition from disoriented spectator to guest in a new society and
culture.

Within a few days Partridge had made contact with Colombian anthropologists working in Barranquilla and, through letters of introduction, had
been granted working space at the Museo de Antropología of the Universidad
del Atlántico in that city. His letter to Dr. William E. Carter of 19 July reflects
his progress in selecting a research setting, a community in which to work on

the north coast. In that letter Partridge refers to a trip he made to Bogotá, the national capital, in order to consult with anthropologists in that city who had previously indicated they would be willing to assist him. The conferences in Bogotá and his research in Barranquilla eventually narrowed his search to a smaller region of the north coast. In addition, through his consultation with other anthropologists who were willing to assist in the project, Partridge was able to secure the joint sponsorship of the Instituto Colombiano de Antropología of Bogotá and the Universidad del Atlántico in Barranquilla. Such assistance and sponsorship were crucial factors in the eventual success of the project.

19 July 1972

Dear Dr. Kimball:

On the thirteenth I began a letter to you re Initial Impressions of the Lone Anthropologist amongst the Natives. I never finished it, but will enclose it here, together with more recent impressions and a brief progress report.

13 July 1972

After 60 hours in Barranquilla I can testify that I am having no picnic. Hour by hour, though, I feel more and more at ease with the people, almost like a gradual warmth seeping through a window. The first evening was difficult, even though I was able to remember more Spanish than I had expected.

The city of Barranquilla is unlike Bogotá in some ways and like it in others. First, it is big and very dirty. Hunks of rock, brick, trash, and rotting vegetable matter line the streets, along with dirty adults and children. In fact my strongest first impression is dirt. Second comes heat and humidity.

Today, after arguing (badly) with the customs people about my trunks of books, typewriter, cameras, etc., I felt much more at home. The argument took an entire day, and was concluded only when I had paid for the paper upon which were required the names, titles, and signatures, as well as the seals, of some 15 minor officials. Everyone here who occupies an office has a seal that must be stamped over his or her signature. Likewise, an official is not important unless there is a line in front of his or her office, and in this weather it is a hot and sweaty line. To complicate matters further (for the uninitiated), the business of any given office is cut off whenever a friend arrives, or when someone goes for coffee; it also ceases at noon until 2:00 each day, but continues until 6:00 in the evening. The experience was an intriguing one, for although I hated every minute, I felt much better after it was over. I had a couple of beers with the cab driver who waited throughout the afternoon with me, cracking jokes about "El Rey." El Rey is the head administrator (everyone in the building is *"jefe"*—head—of something) whom people called *"Doctor."* I like El Rey better.

As I was saying, Barranquilla is dirtier and more run-down than Bogotá, but its people are just as talkative and enjoy the cafes and clubs. Groups of men gather to talk throughout the day. It seems they are more open and friendly than Bogotanos, but in both places the people like to get together and chat.

It is truly amazing the change that came over me after the day in the customs office. Walking the streets the first night I felt very ill-prepared for all that I saw (this was the center of the city, in worse condition than other parts). But tonight after dinner I felt more at ease doing the same thing, although I did not talk to anyone about anything in particular. I just felt better being around these people. . . .

Well, that was where my letter of 13 July ended. Today is a different story. I have just returned from Bogotá and the coolness of the highlands. There I met a Colombian anthropologist who showed me around and made me feel very comfortable. He helped me to secure the sponsorship of the Instituto Colombiano de Antropología for my work here. The director and subdirector signed a letter (complete with two seals of office!) introducing me to the authorities here on the north coast and authorizing me to undertake a study of the social and cultural aspects of marijuana. They were very kind and offered their help should I run into any difficulties in the course of my studies. I'm sure this will be helpful since sponsorship of the Institute is a national level function and will open more doors than association with the museum here in Barranquilla.

I have not yet visited a site for the proposed research, but have concentrated upon contacting various anthropologists and officials here and in Bogotá. This groundwork will cease at the end of this week when I undertake a site survey in the Santa Marta region to look for a place to settle down. Then of course it will resume as I begin contacting the local *alcalde* (mayor), the curate, and the police. I am looking forward to the site survey as it will give me a chance to see the country. I have seen little besides the cities so far.

The survey will be undertaken with the help of the director of the Museo de Antropología. He has kindly offered me space in the museum to work, which I occupy at this moment. Several of his students have worked in the Santa Marta region and will accompany me on the survey. I'm of course grateful for their companionship, in that I will probably learn more this way.

Aside from formal contacts and conversations I had some time in Bogotá to read what the Instituto had on marijuana. It was of general interest, very little of it original. There was nothing in the area I'm pursuing, but I did find some leads to other documents regarding the ethnohistory of the plant, etc. Also, I may get some help from the librarian there in the future.

I will write again when I'm settled someplace near Santa Marta and have an address to give you. If the need arises to get hold of me before then (say two weeks or so from now), I can be reached through the Museo de Antropología in Barranquilla.

Your student and friend,
William L. Partridge

19 July 1972

Dear Dr. Carter:

A week has passed since my arrival in Barranquilla and I thought I should keep you informed of my progress to date.

I have not yet visited a research site, but have spent my time making contacts with the anthropologists. First I talked with the director of the Museo de Antropología who kindly gave me space in the museum to work. We are making plans to visit some sites he knows of near Santa Marta, especially Ciénaga and some others near the base of the sierra. Arrangements are being made for this. I hope it does not eat too great a portion of my budget.

Secondly, I went to Bogotá and met your friend. He was very helpful, gracious, and tolerant of my Spanish. He was quite eager to have me affiliated with the Instituto de Antropología in Bogotá.

As your student, I was treated royally and shown around the Instituto as an honored visitor and doctor of anthropology. I didn't mind that at all and was reluctant to correct my hosts!

Through this visit I have obtained the sponsorship of the Instituto. The director has written me a very good letter of introduction, stating that I have the support and authority of the Instituto Colombiano de Antropología for the study of marijuana. He further instructed me that, should trouble arise in the course of my work, I should contact him. With his support I feel a little more secure here.

Your friend at the Instituto strongly recommended that I contact the mayor, curate, and local police as soon as I have chosen a site in which to settle. (I am ready to settle now, as I dislike hotels with a passion.) I will follow his advice, hoping it will not prejudice my reputation with informants. . . .

Sincerely,
William Partridge

THE FIRST FIELD REPORT

Having completed some preliminary library research at the Museo de Antropología of the Universidad del Atlántico and in the national capital at Bogotá, Partridge was now ready to explore several locations as the site for study. The region at the base of the Sierra Nevada de Santa Marta was selected as the area in which a community would be sought.

Through the assistance of a Colombian anthropologist, who will remain anonymous due to the politically sensitive nature of the research topic, Partridge was introduced to a Colombian journalist who had studied anthropology and had been born in the Santa Marta region. (All names which appear are either fictitious or permission has been granted to use actual names.) He was then working in Barranquilla. This man, José Ramon Martinez, consented to assist Partridge in his site survey.

The field report written between 13 and 15 August summarizes that exploratory trip and traces out the decision to set up the base of operations in the town that will be called here Majagua. Although José Ramon started out as Partridge's guide, he soon became his close friend as well. During the weeks between 27 July when the exploratory trip was initiated and 15 August when it was concluded, the two spent many hours together, discussing the region, its people, and the various settlements. After Majagua was chosen, Partridge spent many more hours with José, learning about the widely diverse inhabitants of the area: the old and respected families who live in the town, the cowboys and rice estate workers, the highland and lowland peasants, the professionals and teachers, the town drunks, the beggars, the contraband runners. José recounted the stories and legends that had grown up during the period when the United Fruit Company was located in the town. Out of his initial dialogues with the Colombian journalist, Partridge came to understand some of the complexity that was the community called Majagua. It was only later, however, after many months of study, interviewing, and observation, that Partridge was able to construct a model of community organization.

In order to clarify for the reader the characters introduced in the following report, a list of persons mentioned in the notes is provided in table 2.1. Such a listing is useful as more than a guide for the reader, however. The list is also integral to an analysis of the social networks through which

Partridge moved during the period from 11 July to 15 August 1972. When compared with later lists of characters, the progressive changes that developed as Partridge continually refined and altered his research focus will become apparent. It will then be possible to construct several generalizations about the stages through which the field research progressed. These stages will be seen to be, in turn, related to the development of preliminary models—conceptualizations—of community organization that emerged from the addition of new data and the dialogue between Partridge and Kimball.

13 August 1972

Dr. Solon T. Kimball and Dr. William E. Carter:

The past month has come and gone like a whirlwind, leaving this student rather confused. I have seen so many things and talked to so many people that I am not sure what I know and what I don't. There will be time to sort it all out, but for now my report will be rather hazy and disorganized. I have had some successes, although I am not happy with the situation at present.

In the company of the Señor José Ramon Martinez, a former student of anthropology at the Universidad del Atlántico, I set out to survey the region known to my guide, following his suggestions most of the time and following my nose the rest of the time. I took José entirely within my confidence regarding the topic [the use of marijuana]. We spent some time discussing the study and what exactly I was seeking, and José understood perfectly. And as far as I can tell, he has told no one of the exact objective of my mission.

The survey began the morning of 27 July which was my first meeting with José. I asked when he would be ready to leave for the Sierra Nevada region. He said "immediately," and we were off. We got to know each other on the bus to Santa Marta. Although I had agreed to pay expenses, these turned out to be greater than I had expected: for José it was a paid vacation. But his assistance was invaluable. He grew up in Santa Marta and his contacts there are excellent. When we arrived, we rented a car from a friend of his in Santa Marta. (Renting a car is next to impossible here on the coast and is usually done on a person to person basis; there are no agencies in Santa Marta.) According to José, the area around Fundación is famous in Magdalena for the cultivation of cannabis, and so we set out for Fundación.

Along the way I found out that José's family is quite large and all hail from the town of Majagua during the heyday of the United Fruit Company. He suggested we stop there before going to Fundación and he would show

TABLE 2.1   Key Informants in Majagua 11 July–15 August 1972

José Ramon Martinez	Initial contact in the town; born in Majagua but now living in Barranquilla; cousin of the mayor of Majagua
Luis Bernal García	Mayor of the town, professional politician, and descendant of one of town founders
"Melo" Angel and "Melo" Luis Hernandez	Twin offspring of notary public and one of the original founders of the town; sells insurance and works for the municipal government, respectively
Pedro Pertuz	Local politician, descendant of a founding family of a nearby town, and resident of community for last 23 years
Manuel Sánchez	Wealthy owner of several estates, including one in Majagua; descendant of founding family in Majagua and cousin of the mayor; lives in city of Valledupar
Pedro Goméz	Manages Valledupar estate for Manuel Sánchez; cousin of the mayor and Manuel Sánchez
Francisco Goméz	Brother of Pedro Goméz and cousin of Manuel Sánchez; administers Majagua estate for Manuel Sánchez
José Manuel Ardila	Born in Antioquia, migrated to town during the banana industry days; now retired and living in Majagua; rented a room to Partridge, assisted in surveys of the region and in collecting census data
Pedro Martinez	Father of José Ramon Martinez, retired and living in Barranquilla; important Conservative party politician who held office in Santa Marta and Majagua
Cristina Hernandez	Sister of "Melo" Angel and "Melo" Luis, teacher in primary school; center of a large network of single professional women, all of whom are descendants of old families from Majagua and nearby towns
Jorge Laurientino Durán	Mayor of Majagua during the military government of Rojas Pinilla; migrated into banana zone from interior in early 1950s and married into old family of the town; today peasant farmer in the highlands
Guillermo Castrillon	Highland peasant who migrated to municipality in 1956, successfully colonized a farm in the mountains, and is today a respected peasant household head

me around. I was interested in the United Fruit Company so we stopped.
After a brief and depressing tour of the town, José suggested we talk with
the *alcalde* (mayor). We located him in his home about 12:30 P.M. and we
had an interesting conversation about medicinal plants. He produced several volumes on the flora of the region and graciously loaned them to me,
offering his complete cooperation and support.

[Initially, all informants were told that Partridge's research focused upon
medicinal plants of the lowlands and foothills around the base of the Sierra
Nevada. The specific medicinal plant that was the focus of the study was
not revealed until more was known about the situation.]

A street in a wealthy neighborhood in Majagua, next to the plaza.

After a few beers I was introduced to Melo Luis. He and his twin brother
Angel are from one of the important families of the town; their father, I am
told, is sort of the elder statesman of the community. The *alcalde*'s house
seems to be a clearinghouse for various types of business, ranging from
socializing to municipal affairs. People drop in at all hours, and many of
these are relatives. Melo Luis was enthusiastic about my study and immediately set about the task of finding out something about me and my
needs. Discovering that I would need to rent a house and secure a maid for
cooking, laundry, etc., he offered to assist me. Other persons, notably
Señor Pedro Pertuz, dropped by during the afternoon. Pertuz was very
interesting and seemed to know a lot about plants used for treating illness,
including cannabis and coca. But José informed me that Pertuz simply
"liked to talk" and was not to be trusted for research purposes.

Later José and I, accompanied by the twins, took a brief tour of the town on foot. It is a dusty and run-down place, giving the impression of having once been more prosperous. José and Melo Luis pointed out buildings, bridges, irrigation ditches, etc., built by the United Fruit Company. All of these were in bad need of repair, except for the irrigation ditches, which are apparently carefully maintained. The buildings are old. All of them appear to be fortifications, with barred windows, huge doors with sliding bolts and several locks, and brick and plaster walls about a foot thick. The buildings in which the townspeople live appear much the same, except that many do

One of the poor neighborhoods in Majagua, bypassed by major roads and electric power lines.

not have windows at all and the building material is wattle and daub with a plaster coating. The town plaza contains the church, the building in best repair in the whole town, the mayor's house, and the homes of a few formerly important families. The rest of the town is composed of relatively poor workers, artisans, and farmers.

There are no large landowners in the town—they live in Barranquilla or Bogotá. The problem of Magdalena, I was told, is the *latifundia* and not the *minifundia*. This is readily apparent when one scans the countryside, sparsely populated with large tracts of rice and cattle. On the outskirts of the town are extremely impoverished *morenos* or mulattos, who live in wattle and daub houses without plaster coating or in simple cane structures without windows but with ample gaps in the cane for the breeze to pass through. In all, there are probably about 3,000 people in the town proper.

Well, as you might be able to tell, I was fascinated by the story of the
rise and fall of the town in connection with the history of the United Fruit
Company. I could envision the title of my thesis already: "Heirs of Pueblo
Bananera," or something like that. Slightly intoxicated with all that I had
learned in two days, I returned to Santa Marta with José. We had spent the
night in the mayor's house and had gone to Fundación the next day. I found
Fundación to be rather large and inhospitable. It is the commercial center
of the region, providing a market for the various products of the sierra
region as well as the stores and services necessary for the lowland towns

A highland peasant house of wattle and daub with a thatched palm roof, typical of housing in the
foothills of the Sierra Nevada.

and countryside. Majagua is about eight kilometers from Fundación and is
completely eclipsed by the larger town.

We spent the night in Santa Marta where I was robbed of some 1,500
pesos and José of his trousers. Around 10:00, when we retired after an
evening of beer and fine food, I found the room a little warm and suggested
we leave the balcony doors open. José didn't think it was a good idea, and
it wasn't. The next morning my wallet was lying on the bed, empty except
for my papers and documents (fortunately), and José's trousers were
nowhere to be seen. We cashed another traveler's check, bought José
another pair of trousers, and set out for Barranquilla.

I had decided, and José enthusiastically agreed, that Majagua would be a
good place for setting up a base of operations for the present. We stopped

in Ciénaga, just the same, for a brief survey. Ciénaga is terrible and, if there are cannabis users living there (which there are—we purchased a small packet after only three hours in the town), I will not be the one to study them. Incredible heat and dust obscure the quite interesting fishing industry. Ciénaga, the fishing capital of the region, is located on the road between Santa Marta and Barranquilla. It is, therefore, a major trading center. During centuries past it was a minor trading center for this region of the coast, due to its location at the mouth of the freshwater lagoon.

But my reception in Majagua and the impressive history of the town left me unimpressed with Ciénaga. No doubt it is an important center of marijuana trade and consumption, and no doubt I will be forced to spend some time there in the future. But to live there would be unbearable, I think. This is not a very good way to choose a research site, perhaps, but I feel that my own mental health and my warm reception in Majagua are the deciding factors at this time.

Returning to Barranquilla, I transferred my gear from the Museo de Antropología to José's parents' home. His family was most hospitable and quite eager to tell me all about Majagua. Together we set about the task of selecting which of my various trappings should be carried to Majagua on the next visit. I decided to store most of my books and winter clothing at their home, taking only my radio, typewriter, books concerning Colombia, and summer clothing. On 31 July José and I flew to Santa Marta, rented a taxi at the airport, and set out immediately for Majagua, arriving about 10:30 A.M..

We left our luggage at the mayor's house, then went to his office to inform him that I was indeed going to spend the next year in his municipality studying medicinal plants of the region. In his office we found Melo Luis and two other of the mayor's right-hand men. All were delighted with my decision.

In the company of Melo Luis and José I set out to rent a house. The first spot I was shown was an abandoned warehouse and office building of the United Fruit Company. I could not abide living in such a structure. I visualized my solitary bed, desk, and typewriter swallowed by the dark corners and empty rooms and a chill ran through me. I politely declined. Second, we went to visit another man named Luis, who escorted us to the house in which his grandson lived. The boy's parents—Luis's son-in-law and daughter—now lived in Fundación. They wanted about 700 pesos a month without water or electricity. On top of this I would still have to pay a maid and cook. (It seemed like a lot at the time, although it is actually only about $31 a month.) In addition they wanted full payment for a year in advance. Again I declined. Returning to the mayor's house for a midday beer and some lunch, we met Manuel and Pedro, cousins of José's who live in Valledupar.

Manuel is the son of a relatively well-to-do landowner living in Valledupar, and now has his own *finca* (estate) here in Majagua. He divides his time between his father's farm and his own. He has had the *finca* only three years and is just now getting the place fixed up. His cousin Francisco lives there and is treated as an employee, or so it seemed to me. Manuel is a husky lad of about 28 or 29 years of age. He has the bearing of a child raised to take over his father's role someday, a kind of self-assured arrogance tempered with a keen sense of humor and wit. He is a confident young man, but is worried, as are most middle-range farmers, about his land being invaded by *campesinos*. [A campesino is any person who works in agriculture; he is not necessarily a subsistence farmer, which the literal translation ''peasant'' implies.] The problem of invasions, according to Manuel, is common in Colombia, but especially here in Magdalena. Since there are some squatters on his land in Majagua and on his father's in Valledupar, he is primarily concerned with the rural manifestation of it, but he was also interested in my familiarity with the urban end of the process. Our discussion ended with an invitation to visit his farm and his father's. This I will do.

Pedro (whose exact relationship to Manuel is unknown) administers a cotton plantation owned by Manuel's father in Valledupar. He also seems to be involved in selling contraband. During my conversation with Manuel about the problem of invaders of the estates, Pedro had simply suggested shooting them. Manuel is a bit more farsighted, however, and I learned that he was about to make a visit to Santa Marta to see the lawyers representing the squatters. When I expressed surprise he explained that INCORA (the Colombian Institute of Agrarian Reform) offers legal services to *campesinos* who wish to colonize land. This was his main problem, and he had retained a lawyer to deal with it. I asked Manuel whether the problem of squatters affected the large landowners, the *latifundistas*, as well. He said it did, that all landowners were being affected. I expressed an interest in learning more about this problem and he said he would be glad to inform me.

The discussion was broken up by Melo Luis, who came to announce he had found a good deal for me. A family on the other side of the plaza had a room for rent. I could have the room and take my meals with the family for 1,000 pesos a month. The idea of living with a family nearby appealed to me since I would be making various trips into the surrounding countryside and would have to leave my possessions, notes, tapes, etc., for long stretches of time. Melo Luis emphasized this aspect of the

situation as well, warning me that thieves abound in Majagua and that my
things would be secure in the home of a family. We went immediately to
the house across the plaza and investigated the room. It was large, barren,
and quite warm. Like the other houses in the center of the town, its
windows are barred and the doors huge and heavy. I sit now in the room.
Señor Ardila, the owner, has just brought me a tall glass of limeade—most
welcome, as the sweat is running off my back as I type these recollections.
I decided, obviously, to take the room.

After concluding the deal and paying Señor Ardila half of the August
rent and board, Pedro and José suggested we drive to Fundación and search
for a table fan, since the room was so hot. I agreed and off we went. We
stopped at several bars and stores asking people where we could get a small
fan. We were directed to a store that sold only ready-made clothing and
some fabrics. After the initial inquiry the proprietor produced a table fan,
brand new and still in its plastic wrapper, for which he wanted 800 pesos.
But Pedro informed me that he could pick one up for only 500 pesos on his
way back from Valledupar. I agreed that this was a price I could afford and
asked him to bring me one next time he came to town. I am expecting a hot
but short wait, since Manuel and Pedro apparently visit Majagua frequently.

That evening around 5:00 P.M. José suggested a bath in one of the
irrigation ditches referred to as the *chorro*. This is a site where a sluice gate
creates a small waterfall in the brown running water. Off we went. I was a
bit nonplused to think that cows, burros, horses, humans, and God knows
what else up the river use the waterways as a latrine, but despite my
reservations, the water was cold and refreshing. Back at the house during
dinner we discussed my plans for the coming weeks and outlined my
further needs. The sister of the mayor's maid was contracted as my
laundrywoman and instructed to check every few days at Señor Ardila's
house for my dirty clothes. I mentioned that I also needed to find a guide
for a trip up into the farmlands of the Sierra Nevada and would need a desk
and chair for my room. We decided to take care of these things the
following day.

I spent the evening drinking rum and coconut water at the mayor's house
with Pedro, Manuel, and José. The mayor joined us for several drinks at
one point, but in general did not participate. The old man named Luis,
from whom I had almost rented a house, stopped by for a few drinks to find
out more about me and to visit the mayor. He told several jokes and stories
for the younger men, but I could not fully understand. A guitar was
produced and Manuel was invited to sing several songs. He composes
ballads known as *Vallenatos,* or songs from the region of Valledupar. He

sang several original, quite beautiful songs, pausing before each one to explain them to me or talk through them once so that I would understand the words when they were sung. One in particular stood out—a protest ballad, as Manuel called it, about the United Fruit Company. It decried the well-known facts that the company had paid wages in script, developed no local industry, and eventually left the region to its own fate. Manuel made reference in the song to the killings in Ciénaga in 1928, when a workers' strike was put down by the government. [Although this event occurred on 6 December 1928, it is important enough in the minds of the local people to be remembered in ballads such as this one and in conversations in stores and bars. The United Fruit Company brought prosperity to the town of Majagua and the region in which it was located, but it also brought tragedy such as the strike of 1928 and the subsequent massacre in Ciénaga. Townspeople continue to debate the ultimate impact of the United Fruit Company: those who grew wealthy laud the American corporation, while those who experienced no dramatic increases in their social or economic status generally condemn it.] We whiled away the evening in this fashion, most agreeable and quite educational.

Wednesday was spent visiting Manuel's farm. This trip familiarized me with the miles of irrigation canals, the dusty dirt road turned to mud by the winter rains, and the cattle, rice, and other kinds of estates in the countryside. Upon my return I visited the bank and talked with the president about opening an account. After lunch José and I visited Cristina, the twins' sister, and listened to records and drank Cokes. Little was accomplished during the day. Late in the afternoon the mayor's wife, Carmen, returned from Barranquilla where they have a second house, and so José moved out of the mayor's house and in with me. That evening Pedro, José, and I took in the local house of prostitution and spent a pleasant evening, even though everyone got quite intoxicated. This event proved to be of no minor significance when the following morning I received compliments from Manuel, Señor Ardila, and the others. Apparently, such an evening is one of their great pleasures, and they were happy to see that the foreigner enjoyed himself also.

Thursday morning José proposed another swim in the irrigation ditch to rid us of our hangovers. On the way to the swimming area I noticed a man on horseback watching us, but thought little of it. While we were bathing this man rode up and José introduced him as Jorge Laurientino Durán. José explained that Señor Durán had a farm up in the foothills of the Sierra Nevada and would be able to show me around that part of the municipality. I expressed eager acceptance of the offer and we made arrangements to meet later that morning to discuss the details. After Jorge left, José

informed me that he had been mayor of Majagua during the years of
General Rojas Pinilla's presidency, a period during which almost all
government officials in Colombia were military personnel. Jorge was
familiar with the entire municipality and, having a farm in the hills, he also
knew the people of the highlands. This all seemed fine with me, as I was
most eager to make contact with this region of the municipality. It seemed
that the clandestine nature of cannabis cultivation would make the sierra a
natural place to look. But José continued by warning me quite strongly
about Jorge. He explained that, though this man knew the mountains as
well as anyone in Majagua (and better than most), he was not to be trusted.
He characterized Jorge as a fox on the make for a dollar. The warning was
so strong that I took notice.

   This was not the first such warning I had heard, however. After a few
hours, almost everyone I had met so far offered me his undying friendship
and sealed the pact with a handshake, gravely warning me against all others
who would only be after the foreigner's money. But this warning was
specific, against someone named and identified. Later that morning, in
conversation with others, it became known that I had met Jorge and
planned to go to the mountains with him. Cristina and Señor Ardila added
their warnings to José's, advising me strongly against trusting Jorge. I
began to feel that I might have made a mistake.

   At this point, however, Jorge was my only contact with the highlands
and I felt as though I couldn't afford to sever it without some more
information. Later, at our designated meeting place (a humid little bar with
cold beer), I discussed the trip with José and Jorge. It was apparent that I
would need a horse, and Jorge quoted a price of 80 pesos a day to rent one.
Then he pointed to his fine horse and asked if I would be interested in
buying it. I looked the beast over and said I couldn't tell sitting down at a
table, whereupon Jorge left the bar and motioned me after him. I rode the
horse around the clearing in front of the market building. It was a highly
spirited animal, six years old, and a little difficult to control, but this suited
my tastes perfectly; so I purchased the horse. Jorge was delighted, as the
price was a good one. He explained the custom of having a drink to finalize
a business deal and then bought a round of beer. As we drank we discussed
the journey into the mountains. It was decided that we would go on
Wednesday or Thursday of the following week. Jorge would make all the
arrangements. This was convenient for me since I needed to go into
Barranquilla or Santa Marta in order to cash some checks and make some
purchases. We all parted with handshakes, Jorge promising to care for the
horse and have it ready for the trip.

   [The highlands are divided into *veredas* or neighborhoods of rural peasant farmers, all of which lie at the end of a single rutted road that winds up the side of the mountains. Each day at 7:00 A.M. a broken-down truck journeys up this road into the highlands and returns each afternoon. Peasants pay for passage on the truck and for the transport of produce and animals down to the town and for the transport of supplies and equipment up to their farms. The truck's final stop is at a store run by a highlands family. Beyond that store all travel is by foot or by mule and horse. It was at the store that Jorge agreed to have the horse waiting.]

I spent the afternoon at Cristina's with José drinking coffee, eating sweet cakes, and exchanging pleasantries. But all I could think of was how I was going to get at cannabis. Up until that point I had described my study as of "medicinal plants of the lowlands and foothills." I foresaw great problems if I took off with Jorge and confessed the more precise nature of my interests. If he was a grower I could expect real problems, and the warnings I had received made me suspect as much. Brooding on this, I was in no mood for the small talk of the afternoon and soon suggested to José that we get a beer. We left immediately and I told him the problem bothering me. He advised that I tell no one, taking notice of what I saw in the highlands, but asking no questions. After I returned, he continued, I could—if I thought it necessary—inform the mayor, Cristina, and others of his family and friends of my precise objective. He thought they would understand and pave the way for me. I felt his suggestion a good one and took the advice. This journey would be for learning the ropes.

Early the next morning José and I caught the bus for Santa Marta and from there the bus for Barranquilla. Before returning to Majagua I had purchased a blanket, a desk lamp, and some snakebite serum and syringes to carry in my saddlebags; everything else I needed could be purchased in Majagua.

I spent a pleasant weekend with José's family in Barranquilla and did not leave for Majagua until Tuesday morning. When I arrived, about 9:00 A.M., Señor Ardila informed me that Jorge had already been looking for me; so I sent a message with a boy to look for him. Soon Jorge showed up and we took off to get letters of permission and introduction from the mayor to the police commissioner of the highlands. [The police commissioner of the highlands is himself a peasant who is appointed by the mayor.] The letter was obtained easily. The mayor, Luis Bernal García, asked after José. It should be noted that José had wanted to return with me to Majagua for the duration of the study and act as my field assistant. Of course, he expected to receive a salary, which I explained I could not afford to pay, though I would need someone from time to time to help with house-to-house census work. He was disappointed and still wanted to come, telling me that I

didn't understand Spanish well enough to elicit information on such a
sensitive topic as cannabis. I concurred, but reminded him I would never
learn if he did the talking for me. At any rate, I reported to the mayor that
José was tired after so much drinking and eating over the weekend (it was
his mother's birthday), and a hearty laugh was had by each of us.

Having obtained the letter of introduction, Jorge and I set out to buy the
remaining gear: a flashlight, food for the trip, a machete, an axe, and
several bottles of rum and *aguardiente*. We each paid half for the food. I
purchased the tools and paid Jorge a commission for his guide service, out
of which he then paid for his share of the rations. At the local pool hall,
where we stopped for a beer, I was invited to play with the owner of the
establishment and a few regulars, five pesos a game. Having once been
hustled by an apparently drunk Ponca Indian in a place called Red Rock,
Oklahoma, I was aware of being set up. But I got lucky, even after
shooting poorly, and managed to come out a few pesos ahead.

Jorge invited me to dinner at his house about 6:00 P.M. At about that time
he came for me in the company of a tall, thin, and quite intense man whom
he introduced as the inspector of schools in Magdalena. This man, named
Fernandez, joined us for dinner, and it was the best meal I have yet had in
Majagua. We talked of politics in Colombia and the United States most of
the evening. When asked about my research I explained to Jorge and
Fernandez that I was generally interested in medicinal plants of the lowlands and the foothills of the sierra. Fernandez pressed me and confessed
that he thought that my true interest was the study of such drug plants as
marijuana and coca. I agreed that this was part of my purpose, but not my
entire objective. I stressed that my study encompassed the entire community and all customs surrounding plants that they consumed or grew. I was
sure, however, that Fernandez did not buy this argument.

Morning came at 6:00 and the truck for the highlands left at 7:00. Jorge
and I were on it, along with three young men, the driver, and a young boy
who assisted the driver with passenger fares, gates along the road, and tin
cans of water for the leaking radiator. We made several stops in Majagua
for more passengers and one stop on the outskirts of town where a peasant
loaded some recently purchased supplies on the truck. Jorge ran into a
nearby store to purchase two beers and a bottle of rum. In spite of our
hangovers—or, perhaps, because of them—we emptied them during the
first hour of our journey.

The road climbs through the foothills, meandering around various farms
as the altitude rises, and eventually into the rugged terrain of the sierra. It
crosses several streams, none of which have bridges. (When flash floods
come up, all traffic out of the highlands stops.) The passengers in the truck

sit on the floor or on sacks of salt or produce and are jostled around as the truck dodges holes and bumps in the road. I did not exactly fear for my life, but I was uncomfortable. [A similar vehicle links the people of Aritama with the outside world. See Reichel-Domatoff 1966.]

We arrived at the station in the late morning, and there waiting were the horses and a burro. Several of the passengers, all of whom have farms in the highlands, assisted us in packing the bags on the burro (and, I discovered later, lifted two bottles of rum from the supplies—perhaps in partial payment). Almost all of the travelers got out at the station. We had stopped only twice to discharge people along the road.

We began on our journey and started climbing the steep trail on horseback, accompanied by our fellow passengers. Most stayed with us for several hours, and then began dropping out of the caravan as we passed paths leading away from the main trail to houses. The journey was made light—for the males in the caravan, that is—by consuming several bottles of *aguardiente*. When traveling, people seem to drink a lot, or maybe it is just when the *gringos* are buying. At each house we paused for a swig from the bottle and a cup of *agua con panela* or *agua con limón* (water with raw sugar or lemon juice) offered by the owner of the houses. This pattern continued throughout the journey, but we ran out of *aguardiente* the first day and none could be purchased in the sierra, thank God.

Late that day we arrived at the home of one Alberto, where we were to spend the night. Jorge had wanted to stop earlier at another house we had passed, but I wanted to push on and see more. That turned out to be a mistake. I was using muscles I had never used before, and was so stiff I could hardly get off my horse—a lesson to remember. Alberto was not at the house when we arrived, but his wife was there to accept the money Jorge presented for dinner that day and lunch the next. I thought this meant we would stay at Alberto's house the next day, but as it turned out either the money or a message was passed along to a house in the next valley.

Around dusk that evening another resident of the sierra joined us, one Guillermo Castrillon, *comisario de la policia* for the highlanders. Without my noticing Jorge had apparently passed the letter from the mayor to someone who had delivered it to Guillermo. The police commissioner is the owner of a large and beautiful farm where we were to spend the following night. I explained the nature of my study to him shortly after he arrived as we washed down the animals in one of the numerous mountain streams nearby. Later, over the *aguardiente* he had brought, he pledged his cooperation as an *hombre de confianza* or a trustworthy individual. I was pleased with the results of the first day.

I slept little that night, being sore and unaccustomed to the hammock I had recently purchased. Jorge joked about this the following morning, as I stayed in the hammock a little longer than the others. They were off getting the animals when I climbed out and drank some coffee. When they returned we had breakfast, consisting of manioc with an egg on top and a side dish of rice. Guillermo explained that there were Indians living within a few hours' ride from the house, so we could leave the burro and bags at Alberto's house. I had stressed that I was interested in plants used by both *mestizos* and *indios* of the region, and that part of the reason for this trip was to meet the highlanders and the Indians. [In this manner the limits of the highland area claimed by the Colombian farmers could be determined.] The place to which Guillermo was referring is called by the highlanders *compartimiento* or dividing line. It is a cluster of wattle and daub houses that functions as a way station for the Indians as they journey down into the area of *civilizados* or civilized Colombians. [To be an *indio* or *indígena* in this part of Colombia is to be savage; to be peasant or townsmen, even if of mixed blood, is to be civilized.]

When we arrived at the *compartimiento,* I was told by my hosts that we were standing at the outermost limit of civilization: the cluster of huts marks the dividing line between the *Ijka* or Arawak Indians and the peasant farmers of the highlands. The mountains beyond the huts belong to the Indians; those we had just been through, to the Colombian peasants. Curiously, the houses at the way station appeared to be better constructed and more finely finished (being freshly plastered with white clay) than any we had passed in which the *civilizados* lived. I did not mention this. No one was home at the way station, and my guides nosed around the houses like a pack of dogs inspecting an area for the scent of other dogs.

The return journey was much easier for the *gringo,* since it was downhill. As we approached Guillermo's farm a storm blew up and we got good and wet, but I didn't mind because the view coming down into the valley was splendid. The vistas here in the mountains are inspiring in general, especially since the roads often run parallel to the river Majagua and you can sometimes see the river. But Guillermo's valley was particularly spectacular, with streams running through it, cattle and horses grazing, and the house sitting on top of a small rise in the center. Gardens of corn, manioc, plantain, and sugarcane climb the steep hillsides. We approached the house and sàw four children, an old man, and Guillermo's wife. The house is much larger than many of the others I have seen, consisting of three rooms, a porch, a kitchen, and a tack room. We slept in the room where grain, beans, and rice are stored in burlap sacks; in that room alone was there room for four hammocks. Before dinner Guillermo showed me his cattle and his prize bull. He asked me to take a picture of him with his newly born grandson sitting on top of the bull, which was a most docile animal and obviously the object of some affection. I agreed, but suggested that we wait until I could bring up my Polaroid so he could have the print immediately, rather than waiting to get the 35-mm film developed. He was happy with this arrangement.

The other houses we had passed during the preceding two days were much smaller than Guillermo's. They generally had two rooms, a kitchen, and a garden. Most were of wattle and daub, though a few were of adobe with plastered clay surfaces. All were in poor repair. People in the highlands generally dress in rags, which is to say old and patched work clothes. Women wear pants under their dresses to protect their legs. I saw only one woman with a dress and uncovered legs. Back in the other valleys such as this one, there are probably other large farms and relatively well-off peasants, like Guillermo. The ones along the road are probably the poorest.

The next morning we saddled our horses and set out for the truck stop at the store, a trip of about three hours from Guillermo's. Saying goodbye to Guillermo and thanking him for his hospitality about 10:00 A.M., Jorge and I boarded the old truck and left for town. The return trip was interesting. We stopped about ten times for farmers waiting on the road with loads of corn, manioc, and other produce. By the time we reached Majagua the truck was brimming with produce and human beings sitting on top of it all. As we entered the town the truck stopped in response to calls from passengers, who took their load off into this store or that home. The majority, however, unloaded at the warehouse of a general store near the center of town, where the owner could be seen at the door weighing the sacks and handing out dog-eared pesos. I found out from Jorge that one *arroba* [25 pounds] of rice is valued at 50 pesos, one *arroba* of manioc at 80, corn at 20, beans at 75, and cheese at 250. I will of course have to get other information.

Jorge and I parted to clean up but met later at the poolroom for a beer. All of those I had met there previously came over to inquire about the journey. We told them stories about the *gringo*'s walk up to see the Indian woman, about Jorge's horse almost falling off the road, about the missing bottles of rum. Pedro Pertuz was present and, like everyone else, enjoyed the stories greatly. But he immediately began extolling the virtues of his home town, Ciénaga. He invited me to go there with him this coming Friday. I agreed, since I might learn something from him; but I was less than enthusiastic.

This brings me to an important point. During the entire journey I never saw any cannabis being grown or smoked. But from comments made by others and pointed questions asked of me I know it is there. Both Manuel and Cristina had told me that the highlands were full of cannabis plantations.

The problem of access is perplexing. This trip was for the purpose of getting acquainted, but I am thinking now of roles I might play. I don't want to play the role of buyer, but I may have to buy some cannabis in the beginning. I don't want to play the role of consumer, but I may have to, initially. I would prefer to play the role of observer, but I am not sure this is wise. Finally, playing any role at all may be a bit dangerous if the cultivation and use of cannabis is as clandestine as it seems to be at this point.

Guillermo came to town today, 14 August, as expected. I decided sometime last night that the best time to divulge the precise object of the study would be when Guillermo, the mayor, Jorge, and Cristina were all in town at the same time. I hope to hit them all in the same day, thereby preventing the story from becoming twisted with retelling, at least among my current informants. I hope, also, to swear them all to secrecy (knowing this will be fully impossible).

I met Guillermo and Jorge around noon at the pool hall. Guillermo was as cordial and friendly as before. His mission in coming to town was to buy horseshoes for his horse, and so I asked him to put new ones on mine, too, and bought shoes for both horses. We talked some more about the study, and planned a trip to Serancua. I said that 28 August would be a good time, but Guillermo explained that the roads this time of year, the rainy season, would cause real problems. I then suggested that we wait a few months. In the meantime, the study of the highlander in his *vereda*, and perhaps the surrounding *veredas,* can be carried out during the rainy season. Come summer, January or a little earlier, we will make the trip to Serancua. Upon this Jorge and Guillermo agreed. The *gringo* seems to be making sense finally. We again discussed the need for a census and map of the region. Guillermo said all this could be accomplished with his help.

It was then that I decided the time was right to produce the letter written for me by the Instituto Colombiana de Antropología in Bogotá and let Guillermo, the mayor, and Jorge read it. But I soon learned that the mayor was out of town (today and tomorrow are national fiestas—in actuality, only Tuesday is, but everyone takes off today to visit relatives over the four-day weekend). I decided I would show the letter to the mayor as soon as he returned, and that I would talk with Guillermo and Jorge about it immediately so they would not get the story secondhand. I am fairly sure of the mayor's support.

15 August 1972

I am nursing another hangover. At about 9:00 P.M. I sent a message to
Guillermo that I wanted to see him. A few minutes later he showed up
and I took him into the house. I produced the letter, which he read rapidly
and handed back to me. It was apparent he did not comprehend it, which I
can understand since it is mostly useless honorifics. I pointed out the
sentence regarding marijuana research and he became more interested. He
reacted by rereading the letter carefully, pronouncing each word carefully
on his lips. When he finished he looked up and I quickly assured him that I
wanted his help, but I did not wish to cause any trouble for him or his
family or for the people I studied. He looked perplexed and said he didn't
see how I could cause any trouble. I explained the need for secrecy, telling
him who else knew or would be told about the study, and saying again that
this was to protect the people studied. He put the letter down and tried hard
to put my mind at ease, saying he would be glad to cooperate fully. At this
I was delighted and invited him for a drink and suggested we might discuss
my plans in greater detail. He accepted, saying he knew a perfectly safe
place to discuss them.

Guillermo took me to a bar about a block from the pool hall. We went
into the back and ordered a bottle of *aguardiente*. We were the only patrons
in what proved to be a hotel, used primarily by the highland peasants when
they come to town for business. Guillermo at first placed a table for us near
a closed door, but after a few minutes of talk about marijuana he moved the
table to a spot near an open door, saying he wanted to be sure no one was
listening. Our conversation centered on the kinds of information in which I
was interested. I stressed I wanted to learn about the customs surrounding
cultivation, sale, and consumption of cannabis, just like one would learn
how corn or manioc was produced, sold, and eaten. He understood but
warned me it would be difficult. I asked if there were cultivators in the area
under his jurisdiction. He said there were many; it was a booming business
in the municipality. I asked if the rumors I had heard of huge plantations
were true. He said no, the plots were small, hidden away so as not to attract
attention. When I asked if he knew who grew it, he answered that he knew
some and could find out about others. He said he knew who smoked it as
well, and described them as a class of thieves, low-class bums, and vulgar
people. But, he said, the growers were not the ones who smoked it; they
did not use it. Rather, they grew it for trade with the people in the lowland
town. I asked if he could introduce me to people who smoked it and he
replied that he could, but that it would be dangerous to poke around where
it was grown. I said I understood, but repeated that I needed both kinds of

information. He thought about this and then told me that if I really wanted to learn how it was cultivated he would show me on his own farm. My answer was an emphatic *yes*. His eyes lit up and he said that would be safe, but he was obviously thinking in terms of requesting a fee. I asked if he knew how to grow and prepare the plant. He assured me he did. Then I decided to push no further. We shook hands on the deal and I purchased another bottle.

Then our conversation turned to general things, such as his job, the agricultural cycle, the way the municipality was organized politically, political parties, and the like. At one point I asked Guillermo if there were many arrests for cannabis growing or smoking, and he said no. He explained that there was no judge in Majagua, and that those arrested were usually fined (though sometimes not disciplined at all) and then set free. The police would only be causing trouble for themselves if they were to arrest people by making enemies of the families of the violators. He noted that the reason a person arrested could get off free was money. Since cannabis is expensive, the vendor has enough money to pay off the officials of the government. In such a situation the police would only be making enemies by bucking the system. I agreed it was an intelligent decision. Besides, he said, the police in the town of Majagua were users of cannabis and would accept a bit of it as a bribe.

I explained that I had a full year to work and that I would work very slowly. He said that this would be the only way to do it. He cautioned me strongly. Bringing up the topic of cannabis smokers, I asked again if he could introduce me to any. He said there were plenty of them in every town, not just in Majagua, but that he did not have personal friends among them. He did not like them. I said that I would still want to learn about their customs and why they smoked the plant. He agreed this would be interesting, and suggested that I pay them for information. My response to his suggestion was enthusiastic, even though I could probably only afford to pay them once. He said that I could pay them at first and later visit them and simply talk about the subject. That sounded fine, I told him. We downed several more drinks and the bottle was empty.

(My reaction at this time is one of caution. Everyone is eager to assist the foreigner with whatever it is he might be doing, thinking he is probably just crazy. But the *gringo* does have some money and he just might pay for such help. I feel Guillermo probably wants to help and will expect something in return. For this reason I am not sure I can rely too much on his instructions regarding the cultivation of the plant. He may just fake it. But then I know a little about it too. On the other hand, he is more sincere than many of the people I have met to date, a hard worker and responsible

family man; he has my respect for this. Moreover, I am a stranger whom he
has known only a week, and so he must have some doubts, too.)

I felt good, having confided in someone that knew a little about the local
situation. I hadn't learned much, but I felt that I was on the right track. If
I'm careful and move slowly, I think I can learn a great deal.

At this point I reminded Guillermo how important it was that I get the
census and the farming data that we had discussed earlier. I emphasized
that I did not want names of cultivators or of consumers. He thought this a
silly precaution, since there was little I could do to harm them. I explained
that I wanted the data about the region because I was writing a book about
Majagua. The data about cannabis was for the University of Florida; the
information about the people and the municipality was for me and my
students. I tried to make this distinction clear, but I am not sure he
understood—or cared. Still, he agreed to assist me in any way possible. . . .

Jorge showed up about 10:00 this morning and invited me to lunch at
his house. I went over about 1:00 P.M. Guillermo had caught the morning truck for his farm. I had decided to take Jorge into my confidence
as well and this seemed like a good time. I explained the study in much
the same way, leaving out this time the emphasis upon studying customs
of smoking. Jorge's eyes lit up as he explained that cannabis was expensive, costing 500 pesos a pound. (This is more expensive than it
really is, of course.) He said there were many cultivators and many
people of the town who smoked it, pointing off in the direction of a
neighborhood behind his house. (This neighborhood is inhabited by
coastal subculture people, as are most neighborhoods of the town.) Although I had told Guillermo that I did not want to purchase any cannabis, I did not tell Jorge this. I wanted to find out if he could procure
the plant. He acted as though he could, but did not say so outright. He
also mentioned that the police smoked it. After lunch he explained that
the problem would be getting a contact in Barranquilla who would want to
buy the stuff. I agreed, but said that it shouldn't be too hard for a
businessman to do. He suggested that the safest thing to do would be to
contract with someone in the highlands to grow the crop, paying in advance
for part of it, and have it grown specially. I agreed that this was simple and
safe. Then Jorge suggested that I speak to Guillermo about this. He
suggested that Guillermo could grow it on his farm for me.

At this point I realized what was going on: I am perceived as a buyer
from the States and it is going to be hard to get around this. Obviously,
Guillermo and Jorge spoke about this matter this morning before the truck
pulled out for the highlands. Where I go from here I don't know. I think the

best thing to do is to play along in the role in which I have been cast until I find out more about the situation.

At this time you have a good idea of my situation. If you have any suggestions please make them. For my part, I have been following my nose and will continue to do so until I discover something. As you can tell, I have not taken any systematic notes. This letter is the first chance I have had to get anything down on paper, and I really don't know much yet. The way things are working out I think the best way to proceed is to take week-long trips to the highlands every month. During those trips I can collect data regarding the highlanders and their farms. The other three weeks of the month I can work here in Majagua, trying to contact smokers and making a survey of the town. I feel sure I can lay my hands on census materials for the towns in the municipality. I will be checking this out on Friday in Santa Marta. I also plan to purchase an aerial photo map of the municipality there. I intend to plot residences and farms and the lines of communication for a start and see where this leads. My feeling is that a study concentrating only on the town of Majagua would miss a great deal. Given my experience in the highlands it is apparent that the traffic in and out of them is great. I would not be surprised to discover that the people of the highlands are in town as often as three times a month or more. The problem will be to define the limits of the community, as it may take in Sevilla, Fundación, El Retén, and other settlements as well. We will see how much I can accomplish. One thing is certain: the distances in the highlands are great and these peasants live on dispersed individual family farms, so plotting more than one or two *veredas* is going to be a big job. We will see.

Well, that's it for now. I will be sending along better organized notes in the future. Hope all is well with you both and your families. I have not yet obtained an *Apartado Aereo* number yet, as all are occupied in Fundación and they don't exist in Majagua. Without one, mail will take a month to get here. So contact me through the *museo* in Barranquilla for now.

Best wishes,
Bill Partridge

The letters from Kimball and from Carter that Partridge received in response to his first field report are introduced as part of the dialogue. Both Kimball and Carter perceived Partridge's situation in Colombia as potentially dangerous. Cannabis cultivation, distribution, and consumption are illegal activities under Decree 1699, Articles 23 and 24, of the Colombian Penal Code. Consequently both men advised caution in seeking information about cannabis. Partridge's response to Kimball of 27 September 1972 indicates that he had agreed to make haste slowly in pursuit of information regarding cannabis.

From this correspondence the reader is given another context for judging the selections from Partridge's second field report. While there is some overlap between the time Partridge recorded some of these notes (those from late August, for example) and the time that he received Kimball's and Carter's letters, the letters stimulated Partridge to embark upon the second stage of the fieldwork, the stage we shall call "exploration."

31 August 1972

Dear Bill:

Your lengthy letter and report arrived Friday a week ago, to give you an idea of the time elapse.

This reply will be somewhat brief because there isn't a great deal that I feel needs to be said. It seems to me that you have moved with extraordinary rapidity in getting into the field and making contacts, especially when compared with some other situations I'm familiar with that required weeks just to begin to get started.

Your reports are well written and entertaining, and without too much effort you'll be able to extract sections to make an account of "my" experience as an anthropologist. But that isn't the first objective. I recognize that at this time you are simply reporting the situations you move through and the people with whom you come into contact. Over time these will build a picture of the system, if you move through enough of them, but I do feel that you are not getting in enough of the detail of specific situations, which would permit another and deeper kind of analysis. This doesn't mean that you report in detail every situation, because this is impossible, but you have to do enough of it to sharpen your own powers of observation and to provide important specifics for later analysis when you cannot trust your memory as to what happened.

Bill Carter is on vacation and so he has not seen your material. I do have one further comment. Do not let the pursuit of the research objective cause you to move too fast in that you may get yourself into some kind of dangerous situation. It is always possible to withdraw for a while and pursue other interests, like looking at markets, while those through whom you work have a chance to digest and muse over your plans. *Cuidado, cuidado!*

Hasta luego.
Solon Kimball

12 September 1972

Dear Bill:

Just after I sent my last letter, I received from Dr. Kimball the field notes you had dispatched on 13 August. I found them fascinating—so much so that I think you have the makings of a good travel book already. I do sympathize with your dilemmas, however, and wish I were there to help you to cope with them. Barring that, I shall try to give you a bit of advice.

You need to be careful, as you well know. From reading your notes, it strikes me that one of your problems may be that you have been in too much of a hurry, and have allowed yourself to get committed to people, places, and approaches before you were ready for such commitment. I can see how your perception of the situation has changed from day to day. Just be careful that you do not get locked into situations from which you cannot retreat.

Your basic problem is, of course, establishing an acceptable and fruitful role. This is particularly difficult with the subject that you are studying. It is complicated by the fact that you have one set of objectives, your grant foundation has another set, Dr. Kimball and I have another, and each of the persons you deal with in Colombia has yet his own set. As a result, a single action by you may be interpreted in many ways. Dr. Kimball wrote a little note to me saying that he has warned you of the need for *cuidado*. I can only reiterate that warning. Dealing with a topic as sensitive as yours has all sorts of special problems; it, however, also has its rewards.

You have plenty of time. Don't feel that you have to rush. It is better to really pave the way and have three or four months of extremely fruitful research than to close doors the first month of fieldwork and encounter frustration for the rest of the time there.

Sincerely yours,
William E. Carter

3. Involvement and Exploration

ONE CANNOT remain the guest in the house of another for too long. As reported in the previous chapter, Partridge found the role of guest to be confining, frustrating to his desire to learn more of his hosts and their social world than could be perceived from the vantage of a guest. He soon branched out and began to explore new dimensions of life in Majagua.

It will be remembered that Partridge's initial and excellent informant, Señor José Ramon Martinez, sought to join the research by becoming a full-time field assistant, guide, interpreter. Had Partridge accepted this offer, he would have been ensured immediate access, but at the expense of limiting the direction and depth of his research. It seems likely that Partridge would have remained tied to the social network and situations in which José habitually engaged. The field research under those conditions would have followed the inclinations and objectives of José more than those of Partridge and Kimball. While there are advantages to such long-term associations with one informant, family, or household (for example, detailed recording of systems of symbolic logics or other beliefs that can be elicited only through long-standing personal confidences), such reliance upon a few informants would seriously limit the investigator and distort his data.

Exploration, then, is the process of expanding the social field in which one is a guest by seeking alternative sources of information, new situations, and unknown areas to investigate. In this search the anthropologist does not necessarily deepen his relationship with anyone; rather, he becomes acquainted with many different people. In this way he increases his understanding and conceptualization and establishes contacts with a large number of informants, situations, and areas for more intensive exploration at a later time. Through the process of establishing this broad base, the anthropologist encounters the many facets of the lives of individuals and the varieties and interconnections of the social systems in which they interact. From these data he formulates the tentative hypotheses that explain the social dynamics of the groups, situations, and areas in which he originally participated as a guest.

In retrospect, Partridge's activities during the period from 15 August to 27 September were largely exploratory. With each invasion into unknown social territory he established new referential outposts, while at the same time his familiarity with known situations increased his ability to comprehend, not just witness. The field notes of this period reveal both the outward excursions and the perceptual changes that occurred in Partridge as he gradually abandoned the role of guest and assumed his new role of researcher. Furthermore, a hazy outline of the order of life in Majagua began to emerge from the gathered information.

In this chapter we have grouped the field notes under five major headings based on topical content and selected a representative sample for each category. To further contribute to their usefulness we have introduced each section with an explanation of significance and, where needed, we have provided comments to add contextual meaning. It should be noted that these categories represent Partridge's major areas of activity during the exploratory stage. These sections have been labeled: Doing Fieldwork; Expanding Social Networks; Patterns of Social Life; Visit to La Piedra; and Groups and Their Activities.

The arrangement and presentation of activities by categories may mistakenly convey a sense of order. It should be remembered that the activities in which Partridge engaged did not result from any precise plan of operations but occurred randomly, primarily in response to the situation or at the initiation of informants.

27 September 1972

Dear Dr. Kimball:

Under separate cover I am sending the latest of my field reports, covering the time since the last batch to the present date.

I appreciate very much your advice about my last report. After criticizing the work of other anthropologists and social scientists, the student can use all the advice he can get when he tries to do better himself.

I too think I am making good progress. I was fortunate to have excellent introductions here. Your advice on taking more specific notes refers, I think, to keeping records of interaction regularities. I have not done so for want of a comfortable situation. I have only recently begun carrying my black notebook in town. During my trips to Cerro Azul it was only after a good length of time that I felt comfortable taking notes in front of my informants. I think in the future I will be able to do so here in town as well, particularly now that my horse is here and I can get around to the various farms to talk to people.

I have taken your advice regarding cannabis. I have made sufficient contacts, I believe, and am now waiting. In the coming weeks I will concentrate on defining the community here by looking at markets, kinship, and land tenure patterns. I will be attempting to cast myself in the role of student of life in the *municipio*—but a student who enjoys a good time, thus leaving the door open.

I am having just a little difficulty with José Ramon Martinez. He is a fine informant and a good friend. But I get fed up with his revolutionary diatribes. It would not be so irritating if he knew what he was talking about—revolutionaries can be interesting. But he knows nothing. He knows Russia and China from the newspaper and movies. Likewise he has only blurry impressions of the United States. Therefore, his lectures on world politics and revolution are most revolting. At this time I am having difficulty containing myself. Upon one or two occasions I have told him off by arguing him down on a specific point. But still he persists in badgering me about revolution! For a man who likes his meals prepared for him, clean shirts, polished shoes, and long stretches in bed, he makes a most curious revolutionary. He reminds me of people I knew in the ghetto in Gainesville: romantic dreamers who could talk for hours about ''the revolution,'' but couldn't lift their hand to do anything to bring it (or anything else) about even if their lives depended upon it.

Forgive me this brief digression, but I guess I am experiencing a frustration familiar to many anthropologists: wanting to be themselves, but at the same time not wanting to upset or muddy the waters by expressing their views. This I find most disturbing as I am accustomed to saying what I think. I suppose I will be more open in the future, but right now it seems unwise to let José or the others know what I know and what I think.

Other frustrations beset me, not quite of the same importance. One of these is music—I didn't realize how much I enjoyed or was used to the music of the United States. The lack of music bothers me more than the lack of the food I am used to. I don't know why. When I go to Barranquilla I find myself magnetically attracted to bars that have American music and theaters with American films. And I think of poor Malinowski, deprived of all contact.

The field report which follows is no better, I am afraid, than the previous one. I will be trying to make the improvements you suggested in the future. In the meantime, if you wish to make specific comments such as ''what about___?'' or ''why didn't you ask___?'' I will be quite willing to receive them. I am retaining copies of the notes so I might understand such comments.

Best wishes to your family and to the people at the department for the coming term.

Sincerely yours,
William L. Partridge

DOING FIELDWORK

Anthropological fieldwork contrasts strikingly with research conducted in an office or library. From the point of view of the fieldworker the most marked difference is the lack of control over the course of events. The events that Partridge described in his early field notes were largely controlled by his informants. As a guest, Partridge was stimulated by and reacted to these events, people, and situations. Informants appeared at unexpected times at his door or stopped him on the street where they initiated conversations, issued invitations, warnings, and threats, and gave advice. In the initial stage of fieldwork, the anthropologist possesses neither the command of language and custom by which to gracefully extricate himself from such situations nor the understanding of the social system and life of the people that would enable him to make a judgment about the desirable degree of involvement.

Orderliness is a condition of graduate study—schedules, deadlines, class and office hours, tables, charts, and summary statements—but not of the field. To the anthropologist in his beginning stage of research, ambiguity and randomness seem to prevail. He does not know for certain what is happening. From day to day he tries to figure it out, each day revising what it was he believed the day before, eventually giving order to his perception of the setting.

In addition, he is as prone to illness, fatigue, and accident in the field as elsewhere. Furthermore, the initial stages of fieldwork generate unique tensions arising from problems of communication. For example, the anthropologist needs periods of rest and planning from time to time. Data must be recorded, figures compiled, books read, and plans for investigation laid out. But time is never sufficient to do all these things: informants call at one's home in seemingly endless succession, disturbing sleep or meals, interrupting time set aside for rest, work, and planning. As a guest the anthropologist possesses none of the means whereby he can gracefully handle such situations as he is accustomed to doing in his own society.

Such situations are illustrated in the selections from Partridge's field notes between 11 July and 21 September 1972. They provide evidence of the kinds of problems he encountered and the actions he took. Another situation, not recorded in these selections, is summarized here to illustrate one such problem and its eventual solution.

When Colombian peasants or estate workers conduct business it is frequently in a bar, poolroom, or store. Consumption of alcoholic beverages invariably accompanies marketing of produce, hiring laborers, negotiating the sale of a cow or pig, and horse trading. Partridge became aware of this immediately and sought to join such clusters of individuals engaged in business negotiations in order to learn about economic relationships among his informants. Hence, when invited for a beer by several men in a bar he often accepted. But Colombians also spend considerable amounts of time drinking for the pleasures of companionship, conviviality, and intoxication. Such occasions generally yield useful data. Moreover, certain groups of men are habitually seeking the pleasures of the bar, and one soon learns to identify such clusters as distinct from those involved in business negotiation.

The problem arises when the anthropologist sets out on an errand in the early morning, perhaps about 7:00 A.M., and is invited by a group of informants to join them for a beer. If the situation and the participants are interesting, the invitation might be accepted. But if the group is one of those that has not quit drinking since the previous evening, the anthropologist will want to decline the invitation. Yet to drink with one group and not with another is to ally oneself with that group and risk offending the other. Clearly, an acceptable excuse is needed to avoid spending all of one's waking hours in bars, stores, and poolrooms, becoming intoxicated. Partridge tried various excuses, but none seemed to satisfy persons who were turned down. It was not until several months had passed that Partridge observed an acceptable excuse: "*Estoy tomando una pastilla,*" or "I am taking a pill." The pill referred to was a medication commonly prescribed for the treatment of venereal disease. Since drinking alcohol is prohibited while using this medication, this excuse permits one not to offend, to affirm interest in the group and their invitation, and at the same time to communicate virility and manliness. Once he learned it, Partridge used that excuse often among the workers and peasants when pushed to accept a drink, and his informants did not take offense.

16 August 1972

Today was spent writing letters to family and friends. I feel like I accomplished very little. I spoke with Pedro Pertuz late in the afternoon about historical material on the municipality of Majagua. He most enthusiastically offered to help me trace these down, saying that obtaining them would be no problem. He pointed out that the plaza was only constructed about 20 years ago as was the mayor's office ("Palacio Alcaldía," reads the sign); the Telecom office, about 25; and the market, 30. I inquired about the effects of the United Fruit Company, and he said the town had been prosperous in those days. This was the *Zona Bananera*. When I mentioned that Fundación had also been a major port, he emphatically said no. Majagua had been the center, not Fundación. He called Majagua the father of Fundación, saying that Fundación used to be the *corregimiento*, Majagua the capital. Things are apparently different now. I'll have to sit down with Pertuz and perhaps Melo Luis and draw an organizational chart so I will understand how this municipality is organized.

[Fundación is actually the older town, dating from 1788 and the days of a colonial road connecting the ancient Magdalena River port of Salamina and the cattle-rich valley of Valledupar. Its original name was San Carlos (Reichel-Dolmatoff 1951:44). But the townspeople of Majagua are correct in stating that Fundación was designated merely a *corregimiento* or satellite of Majagua during the banana boom. The older marketing center only regained its former prominence when the United Fruit Company left the region during World War II. Majagua was clearly the most important banana producing municipality of the banana zone. Today it remains the seat of a municipality or *cabecera*, and ancient Fundación has long since been designated the seat of a separate municipality.]

17 August 1972

Random notes for a day of rain and diarrhea.

I had to cancel my trip to Santa Marta for the maps for today. I will go instead tomorrow, and from there to Barranquilla for money. My trip to Ciénaga has also been canceled. I've arranged to obtain maps from the Edificio Caja Agraria.

The grandchildren of Señor Ardila and his wife are here with their mother. Arrgh. They were here Sunday and Monday and I thought they would leave with their father on Tuesday. Alas! With the screaming and crying I am hard put to sit in this hot room and work. Likewise, the music from Cristina's house (her two sisters and their numerous girl friends keep the stereo or radio going all day) contributed to a day of general ill feeling and ill will against my fellow man.

I accomplished nothing today: laid in the hammock and reread *100 Years of Solitude*.

[*100 Years of Solitude* is a novel written by the internationally famous Colombian author Gabriel García Márquez. García Márquez was born in one of the small towns of the banana zone during the 1920s when the banana boom was at its height. For the reader who is aware of the social perspective that the author brings to his task by virtue of his origins, his social status, and his experiences, this novel provides an excellent intro-

duction to the culture of the north coast of Colombia. The usefulness of
such a novel to an understanding of the culture of a people has been
stressed by Wagley (1971). Partridge (1974:16*n*1) considers some of the
limitations of the use of novels for understanding a culture. The major
limitation is that the novelist eschews historical fact in the interest of his
plot. Extensive cross-checking is needed if the novel is to be any more than
suggestive.]

23 August 1972

Friday, 18 August, I went to Santa Marta to investigate purchasing maps
of the *municipio*. I went to the offices of the Instituto Geográfico Augustin
Codazzi and was able to obtain an excellent set. If I need more exact maps I
can get them at the main offices in Bogotá, I was told.

From Santa Marta I went to Barranquilla to José's house. I had to check
on the transfer of money down here. I am not yet running low on funds, but
I wanted to be sure the process was working. Since none had arrived yet I
wired an inquiry. I am now waiting.

I spent Saturday conversing with José. He wanted me to buy a hand gun
for self-defense. I objected that an armed stranger would only raise suspi-
cions; people would wonder why the *gringo* was carrying a gun around,
thinking I was either a troublemaker or a CIA agent. (I have been con-
fronted with that question before—José expressed doubts about my stated
objective earlier on, saying he suspected I worked for the CIA; likewise,
Julio, José's friend who knows the sierra, expressed the same belief. In
time I convinced José, but not Julio.) Saturday afternoon we went to the
cockfights in Barranquilla, at a place called the Pico de Oro. We had a
grand time. I plan to return with my camera to take some photos.

24 August 1972

Today was spent lazily, bathing in the irrigation ditch and talking about
very little at all. I plan to go to Barranquilla tomorrow to take care of my
bank business.

Only two things were accomplished with regard to the study: first, I
wrote down José's genealogy; second, I saw my first marijuana plant in
this town.

3 September 1972

When I returned to Majagua Friday I was met by José. He had brought
mail for me from Barranquilla. I was happy to get some, although most of
it was bills.

I spent most of Saturday writing. Jorge showed up Saturday afternoon
after lunch. He was rather drunk. I invited him in and we talked about the
trip to the highlands. José added little and seemed a bit sullen. At one point
he went out and I began asking Jorge questions about the municipality. He
explained the *consejo* (council) to me and gave me a list of its current
members. He also asked me to buy him a horse, since he had sold me his
last one and needed one for his *finca* to work. I told him I didn't have that
kind of money and he dropped the question.

Pretty soon José returned and we all talked about local politics. Jorge is
of the conservative party, as is the mayor. Therefore, I had difficulty
understanding many of his complaints about the political situation. He
proceeded to berate the mayor, explaining that he needed money. The
mayor's daughter lives in Spain and has no money, and so he has to support
her. Also, the mayor wants to be a senator from Magdalena to Bogotá. For
this he works hard doing favors for important friends. Jorge expressed the
conviction that he could never make it to senator. He asked José if he was
right or wrong: "Sí or no, Martinez?" José said nothing. A few minutes
later Cristina from next door poked her head in the door, asking if I could
come over for a minute and translate the instruction booklet for her Singer
sewing machine. I agreed and all rose to depart. On the porch I accepted
Jorge's invitation to meet later for a beer at Manuel's store. Cristina, it
turns out, had been asked by José to call me to her house in order to get rid
of Jorge—Cristina told me this. Later, José explained that Jorge knows
nothing. If I want information about the pueblo and the *municipio,* he said,
I should go to the mayor or to Cristina's father. García has been mayor five
times and knows everything about the *municipio.* Cristina's father was
mayor and knows the history not only of this pueblo but also of Ciénaga,
where he served as secretary to the army during the strike when the banana
workers were killed.

In short, I have discovered Jorge is an enemy of "my family." In the
future I must be careful with him. The warnings about his character betray
generalized hostilities.

[An ongoing conflict involving much distrust on the part of certain
informants placed the fieldworker in the position of choosing among the
rival groups. In seeking information about the history of the municipality,
Partridge had made contacts among informants supportive of the current
mayor as well as among informants who disliked him. As the confrontation
recorded in the field notes demonstrates, Partridge sought information from
both of them, yet each wanted to make sure that it was his version that
would be recorded. In such a situation the anthropologist finds himself
being treated as an agent by which antagonists can bring greater glory to

their friends and supporters and themselves. This occurs when the anthropologist treats any one informant as an authority on a subject to the
exclusion of other informants. There are two sides to every dispute, and the
anthropologist must not permit himself to become committed to one or the
other. If this were to happen, the data would be distorted by one group,
quite naturally, as it attempts to present itself to the anthropologist as most
correct, most important, and most cooperative.

The conflict involving Jorge and José, and ultimately involving the
social groupings from which they come, is not an isolated incident. Rather,
it is a surface manifestation of a deep division in the life of the community.
Jorge was denounced as untrustworthy by members of José's group, yet by
maintaining good relations with Jorge the anthropologist learned that it was
not Jorge's personal traits that were at issue. It was, instead, Jorge's social
and cultural identity—his membership in another social grouping—that
was the cause of denunciations.]

12 September 1972

I have just recovered, or almost recovered, from a good case of flu—*la
gripe,* they call it. I ran a fever Saturday, Sunday, Monday; it finally broke
last night. Señor Ardila and Cristina were most attentive and I was made
quite comfortable for the duration. One thing about being sick in a strange
place—everything is stranger than usual. I have spent today relaxing, but I
am still weak. I am hoping not to have a fever again tonight.

Given such a mental state, I was happy to receive Dr. Kimball's good
letter of 31 August (received in Barranquilla on the fourth, but delivered
here today). It contained some welcome advice about not pursuing my
research objective too quickly. I am now beginning to feel that the time has
arrived to let the contacts I have made work themselves out, as Dr. Kimball
suggests.

13 September 1972

The day was spent socializing and writing up notes. It should be noted
that Melo Luis and Melo Angel are so called because they are twins. They
are the older sons of the notary public and the brothers of Cristina. The
elder Luis mentioned in the notes of the first week is named Luis Ramirez.

Gregorio (who runs the *tienda* across from the *alcaldía*) sells marijuana
in cigarette form. Jorge had warned me against talking to him about it:
"All he wants to do is sell some to you." Now José has made the same
observation about Gregorio.

27 September 1972

I returned to Majagua today and spent the afternoon resting. In the early evening Cristina and Carmen dropped in. Cristina reported that there had been a killing here Sunday. A man named Vargas was shot three times by a member of the Santana family. Cristina pointed out that the Santanas were a bad lot. She said he was killed for 20 pesos. Vargas was poor, she said, and is survived by his wife and seven children, the oldest being 14. He has some seven brothers in Santa Marta who are influential, so she expects justice will be done eventually. But the police have done nothing yet; the culprit is still free—*feliz,* as she put it. She added that last year another member of the Santana family had killed someone.

EXPANDING SOCIAL NETWORKS

The sensitive nature of the research problem investigated in Majagua placed certain limitations on the fieldworker. Due to the covert nature of cannabis use, as well as the illegality and danger of its cultivation and sale, Partridge did not deem it wise to inquire widely in the town or countryside about cannabis. Instead, the social networks of trusted informants were followed in hope that these would lead him to knowledge of the problem. Thus, Partridge expanded his social networks slowly, following the advice of trusted informants. Many informants could provide little valuable data, and initially there were few contacts with those who could supply any information at all, but this could not be known in advance.

Initially, his investigation of the topic proceeded along formal, even official lines, as he sought formal introductions and offered somewhat formal explanations of the nature of his research. Examples of this procedure are given in the selections of field notes that follow. Some contacts, such as those at the party at the agricultural research station near Majagua, proved to be a waste of time in that they led to no information about cannabis per se. But all such contacts were important to his objective of investigating cannabis in the life of the community; for, in following out the networks of social relationships, information was gained about the nature of the community and positions occupied by actors in the social organization of community life.

16 August 1972

About 5:00 I went to the *alcaldía* with the letter from the Instituto and showed it to Mayor García. He read it, expressing understanding when he came to the part about marijuana. When he finished he looked up, handed

me the letter, and said, ''¿Qué mas?'' ''Nothing else,'' I said. I told him
that Guillermo knew the object of the study, that the information was
confidential, and that I did not want to create any difficulty for the subjects.
He nodded his head, but said nothing. To him it was another task in the
day's work, so it seemed, in which he seemed to have no personal interest.
He talked of other things. I asked again what he thought and he said it
might be difficult to get at the cultivators—to see the plants, as he put it.
About this time we were interrupted. On the floor next to his desk were
about ten machetes. He explained that they belonged to some squatters who
had been detained by DAS. [DAS is the secret police, an office charged
with the enforcement of drug laws; in recent years it has been mainly
concerned with squatters rather than cannabis.] They had invaded some
land on the *finca* Zacapa and apparently all was not well with their
connections with INCORA. I could not understand well; the mayor speaks
fast, like a machine gun. I nodded my head as he explained. About that
time a peasant came in and started to tell his story. García interrupted him
to ask why he had given a false name to the police officer who arrested
him. His explanation was unintelligible to me. They talked on and I could
make out little of it, as three persons participated—Melo Luis, the mayor,
and the peasant. The mayor gave the peasant his machete and the fellow
left. Then he turned to me and embarked on a tirade against INCORA.

[Partridge was concerned that the mayor of the municipality learn the
precise objectives of his research, and on the occasion above presented
him with the letter of authorization from the Colombian Anthropological
Institute. The formal manner in which the topic of cannabis was presented
to the mayor did not produce any useful information about cannabis. The
mayor was concerned with another (and, in his eyes, more significant)
problem: the squatters who had invaded many of the large estates in the
municipality. It is a problem in all of Colombia, but is particularly acute
in Magdalena. INCORA is the Agrarian Reform Institute to which falls
the task of administering land purchased from or given by the United
Fruit Company when it exited from the banana zone. The fight between
local government officials, landowners, landless peasants, and the federal
government over the disposition of these lands is a constant problem for
the mayor. It is periodically exacerbated by the squatters, who seize
control of portions of large estates belonging to the government but leased
to some private party. The result is sometimes the formation of a peasant
cooperative agricultural unit, called a *parcela* among the squatters, and
the ousting of the former tenant. Such action, the mayor and others feel,
encourages the landless to make further invasions of the estates in the
municipality, including those for which private citizens have title.]

3 September 1972

This was a busy day. Later in the evening Jorge, José, and I met for beer at Manuel's as we had planned. After a few beers Jorge pulled José aside and spent a good while whispering to him. During the conversation José looked perplexed or even worried. Later at dinner José explained that Jorge put the question of marijuana to him, saying that he could produce four hectares if I could put up the funds for seeds and could market it in the States or Barranquilla. José became very interested when I answered his questions about the value of that much grass on the streets in the United States. He began talking airplanes and contacts, asked me if I had friends with that much capital, etc. (José thinks like a movie scriptwriter—just get a plane, fly down to South America, pick up the goods, fly to Florida, and collect one million dollars for passing ''Go''!)

I told José it was very possible, that although I did not have friends with airplanes, I did have some with that much capital. I would write and see what could be arranged. But this would take time as I would have to write to friends of my friends as I did not want to contact them directly for fear of being watched. This he understood. By stalling in this fashion I hope to have gained time—I can beg off later for want of a positive reply.

[Many situations such as this one illustrate a common ethical problem for the fieldworker: How does the researcher convey accurately his objectives when informants already have formed their own opinions? No amount of reassertion will convince them otherwise. In this situation José persisted in perceiving Partridge as a potential contact for drug trafficking, which Partridge did not then disavow. At a later point José did accept Partridge's explanation of his activity, but this evening Partridge felt that José would have been unwilling to accept it. A fuller treatment of the complex problem of situational ethics is presented in Bailey's *Stratagems and Spoils* (1969).

The fact that Partridge was American, young, and interested in cannabis was generally interpreted by informants to mean that he was (1) interested in smoking cannabis, (2) interested in buying cannabis, or (3) interested in transporting tons of it back to the United States. Of these, the third was the hardest to overcome and the most persistent explanation for Partridge's presence in the community. Upon leaving the field in October 1973, one of his most trusted friends and informants from Majagua confessed that Partridge was quite an intelligent businessman, since Partridge had managed to conceal even from him the contracts he had made with the cannabis growers to transport plants back to the United States.]

There was a party at IDEMA (a government purchasing station across the highway from Majagua) for one of Cristina's friends. Melo Luis showed up about 7:30 and we went to La Brasa (a bar) to warm up with a few beers. The band (three drums and an accordion) for the party showed up at La Brasa and likewise warmed up. They were good. We went to the party and drank a little *aguardiente*. Late in the evening I was approached by a burly fellow who I later found out lives in Santa Marta. He is the youthful heir to a large estate nearby. He wanted to fight about my opposition to the war in Vietnam and I obliged him for about half a hour. Cristina and Luis later informed me that he gets his kicks by getting drunk at parties and getting into fights. Luckily we had not come to blows, as he outweighed me a little bit. Cristina further described him as a *burro rico*—a rich donkey.

[This conflict between the fieldworker and an informant was personal and did not stem from any significant social group division among informants. The phrase ''rich donkey'' is not a particularly strong one, simply referring to a lack of manners, and it was later confirmed that the antagonist and those who so characterized him were in fact good friends.]

4 September 1972

Today José and I decided to go out to *finca* Virginia and ask Francisco about the table fan. We borrowed Dr. Santana's Land Rover (he is one of two doctors here in Majagua) and started out for the farm. We immediately got stuck in a mud hole about two miles from town. Some workers from a nearby *finca* helped us dig the car out, and we proceeded onward.

In talking with Francisco I discovered that José had apparently talked to him about my study, for Francisco volunteered his help in locating and talking with marijuana users in Majagua. He said he knew many people who used it. José explained that Francisco had lived here all his life. The people knew him and trusted him; they knew he was not a *sapo* (''a toad,'' meaning someone who sticks his nose into someone else's business or is a tattletale). I considered this most fortunate as I have yet to find a resident of the town who knows of my interest and also knows users.

I immediately decided that I should put my horse up at Francisco's farm, so as to make our arrangement a little more binding without making it directly so. He agreed and said there would be no problem. He would even bring it to town for me when I sent word that I wanted it. I declined this offer saying I could walk the 40 minutes or so it took to reach Virginia on foot. When we parted, I had the feeling that a good relationship had been established, and felt grateful to José once more.

[Seeking pasture for Partridge's horse enabled him to establish contact with farmers in the countryside surrounding Majagua, since care of the horse dictated almost daily visits to the farm. The horse was moved several times during the study to different pastures and several kinds of farms, in each case leading to excellent information about a host of activities such as cattle ranching, rice agriculture, banana plantations, and the like.]

8 September 1972

Today I went on a picnic with Cristina, Carmen, Guillermo (a student studying the African oil palm at the *finca* Andalusia), José, a fellow nicknamed "Chino," and a girl whose name I missed. I was a little miffed at José in that I wanted very much to go with Gregorio, the storekeeper, to the cockfights in Ciénaga. Gregorio raises cocks for fighting in back of his store as a sideline—I expect he has several and for this reason I wanted to go with him. He seems to be a hard person to get to know, clever but close-mouthed. I suspect that he could tell me much of marijuana. But José is a rather simple fellow who thinks sitting on a river bank with a bottle and playing grab ass with some girl he will never see again is a lot of fun. So we wasted the whole day.

[Such social events among the offspring of the elite families of the municipality were frequent occurrences. In this passage it is clear that Partridge was frustrated that the need to participate in the party at the river interfered with his wish to establish contact with an informant who he thought would be able to give excellent data on cannabis. Although both kinds of data were important to the purposes of the study, information of the kind obtained at the party was readily available, while that available at the cockfights was less easily obtained. Eventually, of course, both objectives were achieved. But frustration, it should be noted, is no small part of the fieldwork enterprise.]

PATTERNS OF SOCIAL LIFE

Ethnography is not merely description, but description illuminated by priorities of scientific relevance. At the exploratory stage the ethnographer is bound by the range of social networks that his informants have established. As illustrated in the previous section, such networks must be expanded and built upon. During this process the ethnographic data that fall into the orbit of movement are recorded, even though the full significance of a particular item may not be known at first or can only be guessed at. Careful recording during the exploratory stage makes possible the eventual construction of patterns of social life at a later date.

The excerpts from the field notes that follow contain a variety of ethnographic facts that became significant only at a later time. For example, the recurring debates in stores, bars, and homes about the actions of the Colombian army in 1928 fascinated Partridge. That such an event should remain a topic of current discussion so many years later proved to be a significant clue to the importance of the United Fruit Company in the lives of residents of

Majagua. Similarly, the description of the cockfight was recorded because it seemed a fascinating event in and of itself. Yet many months later when the social structure of the community was understood, it could be seen that the cockfight was a significant setting for social interaction among two important elements of community life. While cockfighting is an enjoyable activity for the spectators, the interaction among the participants had a greater significance than the overt drinking, betting, and shouting.

27 August 1972

The setting is an arena surrounded by bleachers. In the center are two upside-down baskets suspended from chains, numbered one and two. Outside the arena proper the atmosphere is that of a private club: a bar serves the patrons and owners and bettors, several groups of men sit playing dominoes, a cafe serves meals. All of this is contained within the walls of the cockfight arena. Around 4:30 P.M., while people drink, chat, and play dominoes, the owners of the cocks begin lining up fights for the evening. One can see them talking, striking bargains, naming prices. When they are about to make a match, one can tell. The owners go to the rear of the establishment where a bank of cages lines the wall, floor to ceiling. They return with their cocks and head for the scales. There a judge weighs the cocks and if the weights are relatively matched, the owners decide whether the match will take place.

When the match is set the owners move to nearby tables where they prepare their cock for the fight. First they pare down the cock's spurs to a point with a pocket knife. Then they fit an aluminum and plastic spur over it (the point is plastic and the base aluminum). To be sure that the spur fits snugly, they affix it with a few drops of lacquer melted over a candle or match. Then they wrap several short pieces of adhesive tape around both the leg and spur, finishing off the preparations with a long, thin strip wound several times around the leg and spur alternately. The owner usually holds the cock while an assistant, who carries all the supplies in his pockets, does the actual work of fitting and securing the spur. When this operation is finished, all of the spectators who have been watching get up from their tables and file into the arena, some stopping off to place a bet with the owner or one of his helpers or to buy a beer to take inside. Some of the men playing dominoes continue with their game, seeming not to be interested in the fight about to take place.

The fight begins slowly, as the owners finish their prepping at staggered times. The first one ready, with hands in pockets, stands near his cock, guarding it. The cock struts with great difficulty, as the spurs cross each other behind him and cause him to stumble at first. Soon he becomes used to them, taking large, elongated steps, lifting his feet exaggeratedly high, exploring the arena. He stops and picks at the spurs tied to his heels, trying to move the unyielding adhesive tape. The owner moves swiftly in his direction and he hops off to one side, resuming his struggle to remain alert and dignified in spite of his cumbersome weapons. His rival appears, held close to the breast of the owner, the eyes peering out from under a sweaty armpit. Both owners pick up their cocks and walk in a circle, holding their roosters in front of them, thrusting the contenders at each other. The cocks peck and grab hold of each other's beaks and are pulled apart. Then, as their owners let go of them, they jump to the floor for the attack.

The air is filled with the cries of the bettors, calling colors and names and amounts of pesos. Some of the men sit on the seats directly in front of the arena, ringside. These are well-dressed, professional bettors. Often they are called "*doctor*" by the others, who sit a row farther back, or stand, or walk briskly from one deal to another around the ring. A bet is sealed as one of a pair of negotiators shouts "*pago*." Amounts range from twenty to one hundred pesos at first, but as the fight mounts in intensity—as blood appears first above an eye and then on the neck, as a blow is struck deep beneath the protective feathered layer—the bargaining also increases in intensity. The cocks spin and turn and leap to avoid one another's beak and spurs. At times one can hardly tell them apart, especially when markings are the same, but still the din of shouts grows. Soon one cock staggers and begins to receive more abuse than he can deliver, but even now the betting continues since even a seriously injured cock may summon enough energy and luck to leap to his feet and strike the fatal blow to the lung. Finally, one of them lies quite still. His head continues to bob and weave in defense, but his body no longer responds as his opponent picks furiously, tearing at feathers and flesh. The owner of the winner rushes to pick up his prize; the owner of the dead contender grasps his cock by the wing and carries it off, twisting the neck if it still flutters about. The din breaks into shouts of victory, bills are produced and slapped into palms, and the bettors retire for a beer or drink at the bar to discuss the bloody event.

At first I was rather repulsed by the idea of watching bleeding animals battle for their lives, but found that there was not so much blood after all. Roosters bleed very little I guess. After watching about four fights I was approached by a bettor who asked why I didn't bet. I asked José what was the minimum acceptable to the gentleman and he suggested twenty pesos. I chose a reddish-brown contender, *chino* they call the color. My friend picked one almost the same color but slightly darker, called *negro* by the spectators. I watched intently and found myself a little excited to be involved. The fight was quick and my *chino* won handily. I was quite pleased. Then José whispered that I should give my friend the opportunity to recoup his twenty pesos. I called to him (*"doctor"*) and he came over. The next fight pitted a white cock against a black one. I liked the white one (I heard someone saying it was older and more experienced and would make quick work of the black one), but my friend liked it, too. So wanting to extricate myself from the obligation to bet I agreed to take the young *negro*. The fight was long and drawn out, *"el negro"* repeatedly being backed against the sloping orange boarder of the ring and having to kick and peck his way free. But he soon got lucky and hit the white one with a single fatal blow to the lung, and the *"el blanco"* fell. I was at this point shouting along with the rest. All the while the *negro* youth was being backed into the wall, the host of bettors had been shouting *"blanco, el blanco,"* and when my puny *negro* finally got lucky I was shouting *"negro"* at the top of my lungs. A most exhilarating feeling. We left after the next fight and I bet no more, and discovered it is not half as much fun to watch if you are not betting; even a measly twenty pesos heightens the fun.

14 August 1972

Jorge is a bit of an anomaly, making a fitting subject for a treatment like Robert Murphy's "What Makes Biboi Run?" The question for Jorge is "What makes Jorge unpopular?" He is an anomaly because he is obviously of high status in the town. I have seen him command the attention of everyone from the *alcalde* down—when he desired. Yet not everyone responds to him with deference. Most people in the *tienda* area will come over when he waves at them, except for Luis, Pancho, and the mayor (he goes to them and grabs their arm to talk). But he has the reputation of a Shylock. People warn me about him constantly. I find this very curious.

Cristina explained the other day that in the days when Jorge was *alcalde*, during Rojas Pinilla's regime, the police and military were recruited from the lower classes of society. They were a bad lot. But then Jorge rose in status, becoming the *alcalde* of the town and the *municipio*. If anyone happens to forget, there is a monument in the plaza to remind him. It is quite phallic in nature, with a pole for a flag I have never seen flying. The monument bears a plaque that notes that the plaza was constructed during Jorge's term as mayor. It is a rather permanent notice of his historic place in the life of the *municipio*. The plaque on the monument reads:

Administración
Jorge Laurientino Durán
Alcalde Militar
Junio 13, 1954

16 August 1972

I visited Mayor García this morning. He says there are four cases of *invasiones* in the works now. In total they involve some 100 families of squatters on four separate *fincas*. The squatters have *jefes* or leaders with whom the mayor talks. He says they are mainly interested in money and rum, not in work or cultivation. He takes a decidedly negative view of the subject. We arranged to talk the following week when I returned from Barranquilla.

Señor García is a perfect example of Colombian government in action. He is the strong leader who takes on all of the problems of the municipality himself. He of course has a staff, consisting of Melo Luis, Pancho, and a younger fellow whose name I have never heard. The last is like a shadow, showing up at intervals with papers to sign or problems to discuss. Melo and Pancho are more relaxed and more professional, perhaps because they have titles and secure positions. They take their time. The shadow runs from here to there almost like Senor García's personal errand boy.

16 August 1972

The town is rather deserted during the day. Most of the men are at work, I assume, in the *fincas* at the outskirts of town. Around 4:30 tractors, trucks, jeeps, and buses made from old trucks haul people back into town. Kids play on the plaza in the morning. I asked Ardila about this and he explained that there were two shifts at the schools, morning and afternoon. An excess of children and a shortage of teachers make this necessary. As a consequence, there is no time when there isn't a game of soccer in progress in the plaza. In the late afternoon the scrambling little boys are joined by teenagers returning from school who stop and chat and watch members of the opposite sex strut by. In the evening the scene changes little. A few adults join the crowd. And a burro might be seen grazing on the long grass. By 9:00 in the evening only a few men are left, talking politics and business and women; they cluster in one or two groups of two or three persons. The talk is relaxed, hushed, for it is late. Lights are going out in the houses around the plaza by 9:30, and by 10:00 I am one of the few souls watching the burro graze.

The physical types are interesting. Señor Ardila looks Spanish, definitely *blanco* or "white" by local standards—a *cachaco* from the interior, actually. Manuel, who runs the store in front of the *alcaldía,* is a Negro by both North and South American standards. Pedro Pertuz is a *mestizo,* and the treasurer of the *municipio* is a *blanco* who obviously had black parents or grandparents. Cristina is *mestizo* and black. Her father could have easily walked out of a dusty little town near Macon, Georgia; he is definitely black by North American standards. Cristina's mother is *blanca,* and I have no doubt hails from the interior. Jorge is a *cachaco,* and looks like an *Antioqueño.* Many of the girls seen on the plaza look Indian, as do the boys. And Negro features are not rare in the general population of the town.

Turcos or Arabs have the same folk reputation here as do Jews in the U.S. They are considered money-grubbing swindlers. And *Antioqueños* are more "Arab" than the Arabs, according to Cristina.

Jorge was *alcalde* for two years. When he came to office he was poor, says Cristina, a sergeant in the army. But when he left office he had a lot of money. Cristina explained that when public works were undertaken (and these seem to be substantial during this period) one bag of cement would be purchased for the work and one for Jorge: he simply reported two used for the project, keeping one for himself.

17 August 1972

On the return trip from Pedro's farm to town it started to rain cats and dogs. We ducked into a small *tienda* in the barrio across the road from Majagua. (They sell cigarettes, cigars, rum, a little rice, onions, soap, and not much else.) The owner and his wife, a hag smoking strong cigars, sat with us and talked to Ardila. They have known each other for some years. José asked about the strike in the years of the United Fruit Company. This started a series of stories. Ardila said he had personally seen 40 dead in Majagua, strikers killed by soldiers. José said Señor Hernandez, Cristina's father, claimed that there were in total seven dead in Ciénaga, one in El Retén, and one in Majagua. The owners and Ardila scoffed at this. The owner and his wife said that hundreds were killed during the strike: 188 in El Retén alone and 50 or more dead in Majagua. All agreed that Señor Hernandez was putting out bullshit. We departed when the bottle of rum was empty and the rain had stopped.

[The massacre in the banana zone on and following the morning of 6 December 1928 continues to be the subject of conversations in the stores, bars, and homes of the town. Acting on the request of the United Fruit Company and a loose association of independent Colombian banana growers who sold bananas to the United Fruit Company, the Colombian army moved into the banana zone in November 1928 to police the region. The resultant actions—the massacre of demonstrators in Ciénaga on 6 December and a mopping-up operation in the rest of the zone during the weeks that followed—are dramatically summarized by the famous Colombian lawyer and criminologist Jorge Eliécier Gaitán (1972). Despite United Fruit Company admissions that the total number of deaths were over 1,000 (Val-Spinosa 1969), the official Colombian army estimate was first set at 9 and now stands at 11 (Valdeblanquez 1964). Señor Hernandez is well known in Majagua for his defense of the official story of the massacre in support of the army, but townspeople still debate the issue 44 years after the event.]

VISIT TO LA PIEDRA

An important activity during the exploratory stage of fieldwork is making visits to all sections of the community under study. The journey into the foothills of the sierra, reported in the excerpted field notes that follow, brought Partridge into contact with a distinctly different way of life. Majagua, situated in the flatlands, had been the point of first contact; now it was necessary to extend research boundaries to include the highland peasant farmers.

Travel served to advance the research in several ways. First, Partridge gained a familiarity with the range of variation in settlement types, house construction, dress, farming activities, location, and use of space as these were associated with the various social elements of the community. Second, because travel was undertaken under fairly rugged conditions with one or more informants acting as guides, the fieldworker was able to establish important bonds of friendship and trust built on cooperative efforts. Third, travel exposed the fieldworker to residents with whom he was later to establish contact. He became known well in advance of his visits to interview the people in the outlying communities. Finally, through the hospitalities extended to him during the course of his travels, Partridge incurred numerous debts that demanded repayment. His attempts to reciprocate provided him an opportunity to reestablish contact with his former hosts. Requests for interviews and specific information flow quite naturally out of these early encounters.

These four functions of travel as an exploratory technique combined to produce significant data. During the journey itself, of course, little of lasting significance was discovered. But a few leads were picked up. In addition, Partridge discovered several clues as to the importance of travel for the highland peasants in maintaining contact with the lowland towns and their highland neighbors. This trip also resulted in an invitation to attend a future event in the highland neighborhood, one which proved to be of great importance to an understanding of the community as a whole and its highland subculture.

31 August 1972

I have just returned from an initial survey of the farmlands of La Piedra. On 28 August I joined Guillermo at the store at the end of the road that leads into the highland area. My horse was waiting and we went immediately to his *finca*, Villa Rica, about an hour and a half ride from the station. We spent the rest of the day, Monday, getting better aquainted and making plans to visit various *fincas* of the *vereda*. He was still not sure what I wanted besides information about marijuana. I tried to make it clear that I wanted information about the *campesinos* of the highlands as well.

We saddled up the horses after lunch and took off for a brief tour of the northern part of the *vereda*. We visited La Ye, El Estación, El Encanto, La Belleza, and *finca* Andrea. I am still unclear as to the names of the owners, but will sort them out in the future. Returning to the house that evening I expressed the desire to record the size and products of the *fincas*. Guillermo agreed to help. The following morning we began this task, interspersed with work around the house and other conversations. What follows is what I recorded; as far as Guillermo is concerned this is a complete listing of the *fincas* in La Piedra. (La Piedra is the name of the region between the Tucurinca and Majagua rivers in the highland area; it is also the name of the *vereda* in which Guillermo lives.)

Villa Rica has one hundred hectares in total; one hectare of sugarcane, two of yuca, five of maize. The five hectares of maize are broken down into three to sell in Majagua and two for the table. Guillermo is one of the few highland farmers to raise cattle. He refers to them as his cattle, but in actuality only 10 of the 63 are his. The remainder belong to the owner of Las Quince Letras, a store in Majagua which sells everything from soup to nuts. I did not get the name of the owner, but apparently he is a patron to Guillermo. Guillermo, then, runs a feeder lot. The owner buys the cattle and ships them to his *finca*, where Guillermo cares for them and fattens them. He then ships them back to the lowlands on the hoof where they are marketed by the owners. Guillermo's cattle are mostly for milk. He keeps careful records as to which cattle are his and which belong to the owners of Las Quince Letras, including those offspring born on his *finca*.

Guillermo's *finca* is typical. There is little variation upon the basic pattern, as will be noted. His *finca* includes several hectares of maize and yuca for the table, perhaps a few extra hectares to sell in Majagua, some *frijoles*, and perhaps a few cattle and swine and chickens. In addition are the *cultivos permanente* (crops that do not have to be replanted every year): fruit trees, plantain or banana, sugarcane, and pasture. Guillermo's son lives nearby, about a kilometer away in the same valley, with his young wife and baby daughter. They tend the bananas planted near their wattle and daub house.

Guillermo's house has a tin roof, but the cook shack or *cocina* has a thatched roof to let out the smoke. This is typical—all houses I saw had a separate building for the *cocina,* usually appended to the main dwelling. And most have more than one dwelling on the *finca;* usually a son or the parents who have grown old have a separate house a short distance away from the owner and manager of the *finca.* The sons help the father raise and market the cattle and crops. The daughters help in the kitchen, milk the cows, pound the corn kernels for *arepas* for breakfast, and care for the younger children. The boys also act as messengers, running between the houses to fetch items, and hiking to other *fincas* to deliver messages to neighbors (often several hours away on foot). When the father loads up a mule or burro with maize or yuca to take to Majagua, the younger boys walk on ahead early in the morning to the truck station, where they wait for their father to arrive. After he loads the sacks on the truck and takes off for town, the boys mount the mule or burro and ride it back to the house.

The center of the family life is the kitchen. They all gather there in the morning to clean up (consisting of brushing their teeth and combing their hair), talk, and have breakfast. They then disperse for the morning, to return again at midday for a large meal. In the early evening the men gather on the porch; the women are busy preparing supper and grinding the maize for breakfast the following morning. The family comes together again at supper, to remain in the kitchen for an hour and a half or more. The men again retire to the porch, this time to talk and smoke and perhaps have a drink if it is available (usually it is not—drinking is a town activity, I believe). While the mother and elder daughter clean the kitchen, the kids gather in the back room, where they listen to the radio or dance to the record player and one of their carefully protected 78s. (Dancing may have been for my benefit as it occurred every night I was present.) About 8:00 or a little earlier the family retires, all sleeping in the same room. The children sleep on a huge double bed; the husband and wife have a bed of three wooden planks covered with a straw mat and two pillows. The wife's father sleeps on two planks in the back room, alone. He passes the day sitting, for the most part. He helps out in the kitchen, feeds the hogs and chickens on the porch, and provides male companionship for the husband in the evening. In the evening the older son and his wife and baby come over to talk and visit, but they take their meals in their own house.

Guillermo has eleven children, three married sons, one of whom lives on his *finca,* four young boys, and four young girls (one of the latter of early adolescent age). The other two married sons live on other *fincas* of their own, one in a nearby *vereda* and the other some distance away in the department (equivalent to one of our states) of Norte de Santander. Guillermo is originally from Norte. So are almost all of his neighbors—he pointed out one person to whom I had been introduced (Angel), a *costeño*, as if he were an oddity. And he is. The highlands are populated by *cachacos*, as the *costeños* call immigrants from the interior (mostly Norte de Santander, Santander, and Caldas). (This would provide the basis for an excellent study of man-land relations, or the cultural persistence of a pattern of land use and tenure-settlement patterns. I may do this if I can.) Guillermo has lived on his present *finca* for only three years. Before that he had a *finca* in another *vereda* higher up in the sierra, where one of his married sons is today. Nomberto Bernal is another immigrant, coming to the highlands of Magdalena from the interior 14 years ago. Further down in the foothills Jorge and other *cachacos* have *fincas* where they raise the same crops raised on the highlands, but seemingly on a grander scale.

Thursday I visited the *fincas* Quita Sol, Las Mercedes, and Palistina. On the way Guillermo pointed out *jaragua, yaragua, genea,* and *elefante,* types of grass used for pasture. Only the former two are common in the highlands, the others requiring more water than exists. Guillermo has *jaragua* on his *finca* because it is more *permanente*. We talked about the methods of farming here and he explained that crops are usually grown in separate plots and are not rotated. He explained that in Norte de Santander they use a system of *huertas* or mixed gardening, growing several varieties of plants in the same plot. On the coast, here, this is called *"la roza,"* but is not a common practice in the highlands. He explained that yuca is planted in March and harvested all year long. Actually it can be planted anytime, except during the dry months of November, December, January, and February. Maize is planted in April and harvested in August. Rice is planted in April and harvested in May, then planted again in September and harvested in October. *Frijoles* are planted in October and harvested in December and planted again in April and harvested in July. With regard to kitchen gardens, I saw few; those I could examine usually consisted of a few herbs and onions. Guillermo's has hot peppers, but these are seldom eaten. A sauce is made from them that is sometimes used to spice up a diet consisting of maize, yuca, and rice.

13 September 1972

The intersection where the *tienda, alcaldía,* and Telecom office are located is an interesting site for observations. Each of these occupies a street corner, the back of the Catholic church filling the fourth corner of the

square. The intersection formed by these four corners is the site for meeting
and negotiation, discussion of politics, making of policy, buttering up
political and business influentials, keeping up on rumors and gossip, and
transacting official and private business agreements. Here groups of two or
three (seldom larger) men gather throughout the entire day, except during
the lunch hours of 12:00 to 2:00 when everyone is at home. They pore over
their deals in these groups, standing apart from the store and from other
groups. Conversations are initiated by one man shouting out a name or
greeting to another. The other may be walking along the street or engaged
in another conversation in the Telecom office or at the store. The shouter
makes a gesture rather like waving good-bye, but more rapid, with the
fingers curled inward and under the wrist as the gesture is completed. The
one trying to attract attention will do this several times. If he is of high
status, the gesture is enough for the one being beckoned to break off his
conversation and come over as desired. If the one being beckoned is of
higher status than the one calling, he puts him off. Another way to start
such a clutch of conversation is to grasp the arm of someone and pull him
away from one group to talk to him in private, making it clear to all
watching that the whispering pair have some important and secret business
to take care of.

Melo Luis is the municipal treasurer. He has responsibility for financial
reports, taxes, and the like. "Pancho" (whose real name I don't know yet)
is the *personero* or solicitor who is responsible for maintenance of roads,
public buildings, water systems, etc. Both of these men are frequently the
object of the wavers and arm-grabbers in front of the *alcaldía*, for they are
the mediators between the mayor and the people who want something from
the mayor. If the person who needs a paper signed can win the interest of
either Melo Luis or Pancho, they are practically in the mayor's office
already. Luis or Pancho simply walk in, whether business is in progress or
not, and interrupt the mayor, explaining their client's needs. Both men are
frequently employed in this fashion, bringing things to the mayor's attention.

Aside from such official business dealings in the street in front of the
tienda, private business (such as buying or selling) is conducted in similar
style. A man named Amin, a *turco*, is a businessman and farmer here in
Majagua. He owns some farmland as well as rental property in town. He is
constantly on the move in his Land Rover, moving from one problem to the
next. He will drive up the street in front of the *tienda,* hop out of his truck,
and drag someone by the arm to tell him something and then dash away.
When I am around he often stops for a Coke or an infrequent beer and
chats—he loves a joke, and loves telling them for the *gringo*. Jorge is

another arm-grabber and waver. He is the past master at getting people to come over and talk to him. He is constantly waving people down to go off somewhere and talk privately—about buying some corn or a cow, about selling a chicken, about getting some tin for his shack at the *finca*, about hundreds of different deals he has going.

GROUPS AND THEIR ACTIVITIES

During the exploratory phase of fieldwork the data are perceived mainly as a series of events. Careful description of these events permits analysis when taken together with other, recurring events of a similar type. The basis of the analysis includes the following considerations: the table of organization, including all the actors who participate in the event; the patterns of interrelationship that link the actors; the order of interaction among the actors as the events unfold; the setting and the use of space; and the sequence of activities by which the event is organized and structured.

Initially, however, not all actors are known to the observer. The description of the meeting among the household heads of the highland peasant families, which is illustrated in the selection from the field notes that follows, is sketched in detail but with little background information about the participants. It is not until after several such meetings, after months of study of the actors in other situations, and after a good deal of formal interviewing that regularities and patterns begin to emerge. Only then can generalizations be constructed about the analytical considerations mentioned above.

At the exploratory level the first concern of the ethnographer is to describe in as much detail as possible what actually occurs in the course of an event. As these events recur, the descriptions become more refined, permitting fuller analysis. Partridge's field notes contain his initial description of a meeting of highland peasants and a representative of Radio Sutatenza. During his fieldwork he was able to attend several such "meetings" in various locations and make comparisons among them. Over time, he observed that variations in the table of organization, the interrelationships among the actors, the order of interaction, the setting and use of space, and the sequence of activities appeared to be patterned. At a still later date these patterns were found to be reflections of subcultural forms of social organization by which many activities and events are structured. In short, interaction patterns observed at the meetings held by Radio Sutatenza in the highlands were found to be related to patterns of interaction governing agriculture, pastoralism, family life, distribution systems, and relationships between subcultural elements of the community.

9 September 1972

I traveled to Guillermo's farm, Villa Rica, today with the tired *comisión* from Compamento, arriving about 12:00. The *comisión* paused long enough for some *agua de panela con limón*, and long enough for the judge to inquire whether any *fincas* were for sale in this *vereda*. He wants to buy a farm about the size of Guillermo's, he said. Jorge and Guillermo explained that there were two or three for sale in the neighborhood.

What occurred next was most gratifying. Guillermo informed me that this afternoon there was a meeting of the neighborhood families to discuss Sutatenza, Acción Cultural Popular, a program of the Ministerio de Educación. He invited me to attend. Since I was beginning to come down with a cold (half the kids in the house coughed all night), I declined at first, but then reconsidered when I realized that this was an important event. It could become the focus of an analysis of social interaction. So I took off in the face of the rolling storm clouds gathering on the other side of the mountains.

The meeting was billed as *vereda*-wide. A person with the last name Arcila recently appeared at the house of Guillermo Castrillon. Arcila is an employee of Sutatenza, a *líder*, who goes about the countryside organizing the peasant *veredas* for the radio broadcasts from the capital. There is a regularly scheduled broadcast at 6:30 each evening by Radio Sutatenza. This meeting was to set the schedule for a special "course" for the *vereda* La Piedra.

[The following field notes were recorded several hours later at a meeting of the heads of families of several households of highland peasants. They had assembled to hear a proposal to sponsor a course offered by Radio Sutatenza, an educational radio program initiated by the Catholic church and addressed to the Colombian peasant.]

Acción Cultural Popular distributes radios to the peasants; each house receives one, marked clearly: "Sutatenza" and "Acción Cultural Popular." In addition, books are periodically sent by truck to the *veredas*: a shipment had arrived for a new *vereda* on the truck I rode last Thursday. The books deal with any conceivable subject. I examined one donated by the Red Cross of Belgium that was a reading, spelling, writing, and arithmetic primer—very fundamental. Another, donated by the Solidarité Liberal Internationale, was almost a small encyclopedia, covering everything: snakebites, first aid, units of measurements, how to organize a *finca*, dietary advice, water purification, care of sheep, goats, etc., poultry farming, child care, and on and on. One donated by the Banco de Bogotá contained information for agriculturalists about farming techniques, such as rotating crops, fertilizing, grafting, and transplanting. This one predictably contained the lyrics to the national anthem and articles on patriotism. Obviously, much of Sutatenza's work is donated through international organizations.

Arcila showed me the card identifying him as *líder*. He read it much like the Boy Scout oath. He is devoted to bettering the lives of peasants, but the wording is rather extravagant. He had called the meeting to accomplish several objectives, which he read from a notebook page taken from his pocket. The participants were assembled as follows: the family heads (wives were absent except for the wife of the host) sat in a tight semicircle on the floor; the *líder* sat in the center on a chair. Behind them and to one side, near the kitchen, were the families, clearly segregated except for some older daughters who sat near their fathers and Guillermo's daughter-in-law and a child. The younger males clustered together near the back of the circle on the side opposite the kitchen. Jorge and I were each given a chair upon arriving (Jorge is still called *Sargento* by the people here who remember his days as *alcalde*) and sat on the far side of the porch opposite the kitchen, behind the young men.

The leader opened with a few remarks about the importance of this program for everyone, stressing that there was no discrimination on the basis of sex, religion, or politics; all were able to listen to the program. His purpose as he told the group was to organize a *curso* that would last three days. He had called the meeting to talk with the *jefes* to set a date and make the arrangements secure. After much discussion, the group settled on 13, 14, and 15 October. Next the leader wanted to make the arrangements for food and a place to sleep to be provided for those who lived too far away from the site of the *curso* to return home each night. Guillermo said we should first choose the site. Guillermo Castrillon's wife (a large woman with the most Indian features I have seen in the highlands—with different dress she could easily be mistaken for an Arawak) laughed at this and said no, it was a concern of the women and they could take care of food and lodging whatever the site. It was then decided that lunch would be provided for everyone for three days; dinner would be provided for those who live far away and have to stay over.

Next the leader asked for women to assist in preparing the food so the burden would not fall on the host family or house. Guillermo Castrillon's wife immediately spoke up, volunteering herself, an aged woman beside her, and her oldest daughter (the aged woman I would guess was the husband's mother—very Spanish in appearance, unlike the wife).

Next on the list was the site itself (I expect it was put off to now to assure a sucker would bite). Guillermo volunteered elaborately. Then the leader briefly reviewed the date, the place, and the food and preparation arrangements. He covered two other points very quickly but with emphasis: first, there could be no drinking during the three days. This was not to be a fiesta. Guillermo assured him, "Of course not, we understand the importance of this." Then the leader mentioned pointedly that the programs would begin each day at 8:00 A.M. and run till 12:00 noon, at which time there would be a two-hour break for lunch. The programs would resume at 2:00 P.M. and run to 4:00 P.M. The assembly was consulted about this schedule and all agreed it was satisfactory. The leader made the point that the *curso* came from Bogotá and, once set, could not be altered. This meant no one could be late, and that the organization of the food, etc., had to be precise. All nodded gravely. After all, he reminded them, this *curso* is especially for the *vereda* La Piedra; the program is *your* program. Nods.

CONCLUDING COMMENT

The exploratory phase of Partridge's research was marked by an expanding orbit of activities accompanied by a growing self-assurance that encouraged a vigorous quest for information. He had begun to build a role for himself in the ongoing life of the town: he visited with the mayor, attended cockfights, frolicked with the young elites on picnics, and joined the males as they gathered in bars or elsewhere to conduct business or engage in conviviality.

Of equal significance were his journeys into the highlands and to nearby *fincas,* where he was introduced to a pattern of life that contrasted with that of the town, but which were nevertheless connected with the urban activities in ways not yet apparent to him.

But engagement in field research had other and less rewarding dimensions. There was the hassle over the flow of funds when the grants office in Gainesville capriciously (from the perspective of the field) changed the rules without informing him of what to expect. There was the unwelcome attack of *la gripe* that condemned him to bed rest (but which also elicited the tender care of new friends). And there were moments when Partridge missed the reassuring familiarity of his homeland. The imagery that this sense of separation evokes seems to be culturally based. Brazilians in the United States lament the absence of *movimiento* and comment on the individual coolness that pervades personal encounters. Partridge's discontent focused on the absence of American music.

The professional goals provided a constant incentive to keep driving ahead. Letters from his advisors affirmed the security of his professional connection. Their cautionary tone anticipated a changed tactic in research emphasis.

In all of these aspects we are witness to the subtle process of transformation. In the same way that the stage of guest merged with that of explorer, so also did exploration lead on to incorporation. As Partridge widened the range of his activities in some directions, he also intensified them in others. As he began to comport himself with the style of a native and to establish a reputation for responsibility, so also did he show himself worthy of others' trust; as a result, his opportunities begin to enlarge. Involvement cannot be achieved by merely desiring it; those who become accepted must earn that right. It is this double process of earning and claiming that is the subject of the next chapter.

If the reader feels that his grasp of the life of a Colombian community remains fragmented and incomplete, he is duplicating precisely the feelings of the fieldworker at this stage. Even with the authors' arrangement and selection of notes the sense of an apparently disjointed and haphazard progression is not dispelled. Through this method of presentation, however, we hope to have engaged the reader in some approximation to the actual experience.

4. Incorporation and Systematic Investigation

BEING a guest necessarily limits the degree of involvement permissible for the anthropologist. Like the man who came to dinner, fateful consequences befall the guest who overstays his welcome. Although as a guest one can engage in a limited amount of exploration, this is not entirely satisfactory for purposes of scientific investigation. The desired role provides participation or access to knowledge of the intimate world of family, neighborhood, and community. In this chapter we examine the process by which Partridge became incorporated in the community in a new social status with a new role.

The host-visitor relationship and its rituals assume that the stranger will soon move on. But Partridge did not leave the community after only one or two visits to various households; he stayed on for a total of 15 months. The conversation and interaction between informants and the anthropologist remained at the level of the host-visitor ritual until Partridge established himself in another role in the eyes of his informants. As he acquired a greater than superficial acquaintance with the community, he proved his right of acceptance.

The transition from visitor to what we shall call "observer" was made by Partridge in the months of October and November. No single event marks the transition. Instead a change appears in the pattern of his activities during these months. He was now actively engaged in seeking out various kinds of information about the community. From the notes recorded during this period we learn that he investigated the agricultural cycle, the legends and history of the United Fruit Company, the composition of the highland peasant households, church records, the educational program of Radio Sutatenza, census data on the municipality, and other areas of information. From visitor, bound by the etiquette dictated by the host-visitor relationship, Partridge has assumed a new role as a systematic investigator of the community life.

This change in role quite naturally was accompanied by a change in the nature of his relationships with various informants. He was now an accepted outsider busily engaged with his informants through interviews, questions, and visits. Partridge elicited a qualitatively different kind of behavior from his informants. It should be noted that this kind of behavior could not have been elicited had Partridge not first played the ritualized role of guest; nor would he have been aware of the variety of social groups, situations, and areas to investigate if he had not first played the role of explorer.

The observer role is usually very productive because it relies on the unique experience of the informants. The attempt to explain to a concerned stranger one's own behavior and that of fellow townsmen stimulates the interpretative capabilities of the reporter. The anthropologist cues and elicits appropriate behavior: he appears uninterested or excited by an answer, he asks for clarification, or he challenges an opinion with his own interpretation. In any case, direct questioning, interviewing, and probing the social field for data place the anthropologist and his informants in a different social status. As he walks the streets of town or rides his horse through the countryside, people are aware that his quest is information. Some consider him a pest to be avoided. Others seek him out, flattered by his interest in their social group and activities. But to everyone he is no longer merely an inquisitive guest or an explorer of the social field but a visitor with a definite, albeit unique, social role.

Kimball's letter of 9 October 1972, the response to the second field report excerpted in the previous chapter, marks the beginning of the new phase of the field research: induction and systematic investigation. We include this letter at the beginning of this chapter because it also signals the beginning of the exchange of ideas regarding the fieldwork—the dialogue—between the senior and junior partners. At the time Kimball wrote the letter his knowledge of the community was derived entirely from the field reports covering the period 13 July to 27 September. These early field reports provided no indication of any systematic plan of operation nor an emerging structure of the community. This helter-skelter phase is not unusual for the first few weeks or months; however, it did limit the specific questions Kimball could ask. Thus, the suggestions contained in his letter of 9 October were drawn largely from his considerable experience in similar research endeavors in other cultures of the world. He directed Partridge's attention to patterns of human relationships that are of significance in many other societies, asking, in essence, are these also significant in Majagua? Through his readings Partridge was familiar with these questions and directed his attention to the occurrence of like or unlike patterns in Majagua. For example, data on the nature of shopkeeping and credit in Majagua turned out to be quite important to an analysis of the social structure of the community, the relationships that unite and divide various subcultures of the community, and the economic cycles that are related to the cultivation, distribution, and consumption of cannabis. The stimulus provided by Kimball's query in this instance was quite important to the model of community eventually constructed. All of Kimball's leads were not so fruitful, however. In the case of his query regarding the cemetery of the municipality, for example, no important data could be discovered.

9 October 1972

Dear Bill:

Your letter of 27 September and the second of the field reports arrived on Friday, 6 October. I read the report over the weekend at the beach. Your letter regarding money had arrived two days earlier and, after checking with Margaret Johnson, the bank, etc., and learning that money had been sent to you on September 20 and that Johnson was writing to you, I decided not to answer that one because all the information (plus money) was by now there or on the way.

I thought that your notes on Radio Sutatenza were a good account of how a group gets organized. You should look for other instances and see if the same pattern is followed, or what the variations are. The description in your notes of 9 September of the interaction style and the pecking order was fascinating. Get more of this in a variety of situations.

Other thoughts evoked by reading:

1. How does credit work? How are debts discharged? How does one initiate a credit relationship, which in some sense is a dependent one?

2. Make a listing of all the connections between the outside and each locality. Include through whom and how often these connections are activated, and what the flow is (from outside in or from inside out). This should give you the institutional connections between lesser and greater localities and the institutional hierarchy in space.

3. Get someone to go to all cemeteries with you for purpose of getting information on succession of families, family status, and other connections. Remember in Vaucluse how the French village had a constant flow of residents in and out.

4. What is storekeeping like, what is the inventory of the various types of shops, who runs the shops, how are they obtained or established, what clientele do they serve?

5. Where are the assembly spots for drinking, what is the daily or weekly rhythm of gathering, and what clientele assembles?

6. Have you worked out a map of localities—from large town to smaller one, to smallest hamlet, to cluster of *fincas*? (This relates to number 2.)

7. I am not yet able to get any sense of the rhythm of life—daily in the household and related work (for different segments of the population); weekly or seasonal in relation to cropping activities and intensification of activity in the land, or in relation to centers in harvesting or selling crops and buying supplies.

8. I also have no sense of the spatial arrangements of Majagua. Are there a central plaza, barrios, major and minor *tiendas,* markets, residences, work areas? How are they arranged? Remember that there is a central tendency toward replicating a set pattern of humans in space and that larger and smaller settlements reveal the elaboration and the core elements.

9. When and where is shuttering done? In Ireland at time of death, stores are shuttered during funeral services, as are houses along the funeral parade route.

The answers to these questions all relate to the setting against which the drama of life is played out, in time and space, and from which the meaning of the examination of any portion of it becomes meaningful.

Best wishes,
Solon Kimball

The point to be made here is not that Partridge's research objectives, data collection methods, or his theoretical orientation changed as a result of Kimball's letter of 9 October; rather, the letter served two other important functions: it stimulated Partridge to make the transition from the explorer role to the observer role, and it initiated a dialogue between Kimball and Partridge that resulted in a change of focus from problems of a technical nature to those of an analytical kind. Each of these points deserves some elaboration.

The fieldworker who gains entrance into the private lives of others acquires obligations and debts. Out of this obligation-debt relationship comes the sharing of private information and, hence, the induction of the fieldworker into the community. As Partridge was received in the homes of informants, in their stores, or in the cock arena, and was treated to hospitality and kindness, he incurred an obligation to reciprocate in like manner on other occasions. A return of the courtesy—buying them a drink, for example—gave him the opportunity to establish a relationship of cordiality and encouraged his informants to reciprocate once again. Out of such relationships Partridge became incorporated into the community as an observer.

The change in focus from technical to analytical problems that was stimulated by the dialogue between Kimball and Partridge is reflected in the selections of field notes that follow. We have organized the selections under headings that are a product of rereading the field notes many months later, and several months after Partridge developed the model of community that is

presented in his dissertation. The headings represent kinds of social groupings, social situations, and social areas investigated by Partridge. These are
elements of the model that was eventually developed, but here they are
organized and presented in the manner in which they were recorded. This is
done so that the reader can observe the ways in which the model evolved. At
the time of the fieldwork neither Kimball nor Partridge knew what kind of
model would emerge eventually from the data. Certain priorities of relevance
were agreed upon, by virtue of shared methodological and theoretical orienta-
tions; but the elements of the model were unknown, since the data were still
incomplete. The notes included in this chapter, therefore, demonstrate in part
how the model of community was developed over time.

One final comment is appropriate at this juncture. We are saying that
systematic data collection can begin only when a preliminary model of the
social phenomenon under study has been postulated. The dialogue that began
with Kimball's letter of 9 October resulted in such a model. It was only then
that data collected in the field became scientifically interesting. Until that
point they remained superficial descriptions of the social field in which
Partridge was living.

INDUCTION AND EXPANDING NETWORKS

Extracts from Partridge's field notes included in this section demonstrate the
way in which a fieldworker begins systematic data collection activities. In
Partridge's case this marked the beginning of the stage of incorporation, an
induction into the community with a definite status and role.

Upon the trip to Bogotá and Barranquilla during which he conferred with
Colombian anthropologists, Partridge began seeking documentation of the
history of the community. He collected census materials for the years 1938,
1951, and 1964 in Bogotá. In Barranquilla and Bogotá he located several
reference volumes dealing with the north coast (Vergara y Velasca 1901,
Patiño 1965, 1967, 1969, 1970, 1971). In Santa Marta he found valuable
documentary evidence that traced the rise and decline of the banana zone
through an examination of production and distribution systems over the years
(Kamalaprija 1965). Each of these documentary resources provided important
information on the municipality.

Coupled with this documentary information, information obtained through
interviews with informants in Majagua contributed to the emerging picture of
settlement patterns and the role the United Fruit Company played in determining these patterns. Levels of wages and salaries, classes of workers and
employees, the administrative structure, prices of commodities, the organiza-

tion of work, the production schedule, and many other details of the United Fruit Company plantation system were collected from informants. The picture that eventually emerged from the documents and interviews constituted one of the elements of the model of community. This model will be described in detail near the end of this volume. Here we are concerned with examining the process by which the model was abstracted from the data.

Another important element of the emerging model was the manner in which production, distribution, and consumption systems were organized on the rice and cattle estates. On 16 November Partridge left town in the company of a representative of Radio Sutatenza who was to lead a *curso* in a rural lowland hamlet over the next three days. Partridge accepted the invitation to attend for two reasons. First, this would be his first formal introduction to 'a group of estate workers and peasants of the lowlands, providing entry into a new and significantly different social field from those encountered so far. Second, having attended (almost by accident) an earlier course among the highlanders conducted by the same representative, Partridge was intrigued by the opportunity for comparison between the two courses and, more important, the reactions of the two groups of participants. During the three-day course, Partridge gained information concerning the organization of a lowland hamlet, although this had not been his primary objective. However, these data, like data on the history of the municipality, later became important in developing the model of community.

Finally, isolated comments and incidents recorded in the field notes pointed Partridge in the direction of important areas of data collection. For example, a brief conversation with a highland peasant revealed the important factional divisions in the community. An offhand comment in a bar directed Partridge's attention to the existence of traditionally organized cattle estates that were located far from Majagua but operated as production, distribution, and consumption units of great importance in the lives of members of the community. Such leads were followed up in the months to come and eventually produced important information.

All of the examples discussed demonstrate that Partridge continued to expand his range of social contacts within and outside the community. Induction and incorporation into the life of the community occurred almost without Partridge's being aware of it. As he began systematically to seek specific information, such as that suggested in Kimball's letter of 9 October, he established himself as an investigator and recorder of data. As he did so certain members of the community stepped forward to assist him, to direct his attention to elements of community life that they thought important, and to offer their own specialized knowledge of specific aspects of the community.

8 October 1972

I have just returned from a journey to Bogotá, Barranquilla, and Santa
Marta; I have been reoriented as a result. Briefly, I went to Santa Marta
Saturday, 30 September, for a picnic with Carmen, Ramiro, Ruso, Hilda,
and some girls Hilda introduced me to. From there I went to Barranquilla to
catch the plane for Bogotá. This was Sunday night.

In Barranquilla I spoke with a Colombian anthropologist before catching
the 2 o'clock plane on Monday. He was most enthusiastic over my
progress, but strongly suggested that I do some digging into the history of
the region. He points out that the *Zona Bananera* is the context for
whatever I find, and he is right. He recommended that I dig up newspapers
from the 1920s forward and try and locate documents about the history of
the zone. Later at José's house his father, Don Pedro, told me the newspaper in Santa Marta at that time was called *Estado,* and that the owner,
editor, and publisher was still alive and living in Santa Marta. He knew of
no books, but suggested that the editor would know of some. José agreed to
accompany me and assist in locating people in Santa Marta.

In Bogotá I spoke with a Colombian anthropologist the first day. He
helped me locate the offices of the Departamento Administrativo Nacional
de Estadistica (DANE) where I made copies of the census for Magdalena
for 1938, 1951, and 1964. I was told that a new census for this year is
being readied for publication but is not yet available. A careful study of
these statistics should yield some interesting data on the *municipio* and the
department as a whole. The anthropologist in Bogotá was also enthusiastic
about historical data, emphasizing that it was particularly important in the
case of the *Zona Bananera* since the banana has figured so prominently in
the development of the coast. I spent some time at the Instituto Geográfico
Augustin Codazzi looking for a map of the town of Majagua (I have maps
of the *municipio*), but was largely unsuccessful.

I told him I had been advised to check the newspapers. He said I would
have more luck in Bogotá with *El Tiempo* because the national library was
required by law to keep all editions. He felt it would be hard to find
complete sets of the local paper in Santa Marta. He may be right, but on the
other hand I could hardly afford to live in Bogotá for the month or so it
would take to scan all those papers. However, if the *Estado* is truly
unavailable, I may have to find a way. He felt that everything would be
easier to locate in Bogotá, so it looks like I may have to spend some time
there in the library eventually.

My reorientation as of this date is in the direction of collecting historical
materials. This, I feel, is necessary, but I don't think it should become an
overriding concern. I would feel justified in spending one month reading

newspapers for such materials, as well as society pages to trace out the family alliances of the past, but more than that would seem to me to be too much.

A second phase of the historical perspective would be interviews with former employees of the company. These might take a little longer, but could easily be stretched out over the remaining months I spend here. I can travel to Ciénaga or Santa Marta or Sevilla to talk to specific people when I need to for this information.

Such historical perspectives on the current situation (which I will describe), together with statistical data, will form the context or conditions of my study of the contemporary culture. So, during the coming few weeks I will be seeking out these data, with an eye to setting up shop in Santa Marta for a while in order to obtain them.

On my return trip to Majagua the bus was stopped and thoroughly searched by five or six soldiers armed to the teeth. Papers were checked and baggage ransacked. All the males were lined up outside the bus; the females remained seated and were not checked. While waiting I talked with a passenger and learned that three men had robbed a bus early this morning in Ciénaga and then escaped on another bus about 6:00 A.M.

[No matter how well the anthropologist integrates himself into a community and commits himself to understanding another culture, events which are strange and different continue to stand out. This search of a public bus by military personnel armed with automatic weapons was one such event.]

11 October 1972

The Arawak Indian named Torres was in town today. He stopped to visit with me, to ask for the loan of 50 pesos (a significant request, as most mestizo peasants ask for twice that), and to report that there were many sick people in his town of Serancua. He is anxious that I visit him there with medicine for the sick.

Guillermo came to town as well, and we spent the evening talking in the cachaco hotel. It is the bar I mentioned earlier where Guillermo and I first spoke of marijuana. It consists of some ten rooms arranged around a patio, a store-front bar, and a common bathroom at the rear of the building. The building is of concrete block; unfinished and unpainted, it has a stark appearance. People from La Piedra and other highland regions stay the night here. The owner provides meals and a night's lodging for 20 pesos. Apparently the cachacos prefer to eat and drink here as there were about ten men sitting around drinking this evening. I was introduced to two cachacos who joined us. One is an Antioqueño migrant to La Piedra who is presently living in an abandoned building on the *finca* El Estación. He came to the *vereda* only three months ago and is working for others until he can buy his own *finca*. The other man, Guillermo said, was a loyal liberal party member. He has had a running feud with some conservative party neighbors in the sierra for several years. It was recently settled when the feud evolved into a fist fight. He had to pay some 400 pesos to the offended parties at the direction of the court.

[Contacts and friendships established during the stage of exploration matured in the following months into other contacts and other friendships. Friendships made in bars, in homes, and in offices led to introductions and visits to members of a social network. The process was quite a natural one, once Partridge made a commitment to the community and to certain of its inhabitants.]

12 November 1972

I spoke with Señor Ardila about the United Fruit Company days. He said the banana *fincas* averaged about 500 hectares. Each was divided into named sections; for example, Teremino was divided into La Cecilia and La Magdalena. Each section required four employees: a *mandador* (apparently in charge, carrying out orders of the company), a *selectador* (fruit selector, in charge of grading fruit), a *tanquepe* (responsible for washing the fruit and cleaning it for shipment); and a *capataz* (foreman or supervisor). In addition there were some 70 or so workers on each section. These were engaged all year round in cleaning the trees, cutting the weeds, etc., but on "cutting day" many more were required as cutting had to be accomplished quickly. All employees and workers lived on the *fincas* and not in town. The company provided individual houses for the employees and row houses for the workers. The work force on each *finca* ranged from 500 persons to as few as 150, depending upon the time of year.

Employees were provided by the company with a house; two or three mules; a *sirviente* to cook meals and a *casero* to take care of the house, wash the clothes, etc.; a *personero* to care for the animals; several cows for milk; a hospital fund, for which 2 percent of the salary was deducted (the hospital was in Santa Marta); and a salary of 250 pesos a month. Shopping was done on the *finca* commissary—each *finca* had one—and all needs could be filled there (clothes, shoes, farm tools, food, rum, etc.). Ardila says food was cheaper at the commissary than in town.

Workers made 1.50 pesos a day, but it was more common to contract with the workers for specific jobs. For example, to clean a lot (lots ranged from 10 to 25 hectares), 5 to 8 pesos per hectare was the common contract.

Cleaning included cutting weeds that grew between the trees and cleaning the trees of rotten leaves. This was a continual chore.

[The rate of exchange in the 1920s was roughly 1 peso for $1 U.S. Today the rate is 30 pesos per dollar, but at the time of this study it was 23 to 1. There are 100 centavos in the peso.]

The company owned a *ganadería,* or cattle ranch, in Majagua as well as in Sevilla and Santa Marta. Here cattle were raised and distributed to the commissaries on the *fincas* for sale.

The "cutting day" was organized at the time the train was to pick up the fruit. There were generally three trains: one for fruit shipped to the United States (the thickest or fattest fruit), one for fruit shipped to Europe (the youngest, thinnest fruit), and one for domestic shipment (neither fat nor thin). Often these cutting days would begin at dawn and last well into the night, workers using artificial light to continue past dusk in order to meet train deadlines. Ardila told me that during the United Fruit period the plaza was the site of the Catholic church, a wooden building with a thatched roof. The cemetery was located behind the church where the Catholic church sits today. For many years the new church faced an empty spot where the plaza and monument erected by Jorge now stand. This empty lot was the site of a festival sponsored by the managers of United Fruit each 20 July [Independence Day]. They would build a corral where for three days (19, 20, 21) bulls would be run. There was no bullfight proper, just ten or more bulls running around the ring. Men would test their luck at riding the bulls as well as horses. Horse races were held and people would get drunk and dance in the streets. The new cemetery has only a few old graves dating from this period. The bones or remains in the old cemetery were apparently lost and not transferred to the new cemetery. Ardila states that the old cemetery had only simple crosses with the name, date of birth, date of death on them. He claims that crosses were frequently moved and the remains lost; or new graves were dug and remains disturbed. Thus the earlier residents of the town are not to be found in the new cemetery.

16 November 1972

On our way out of town, Edgar Arcila, leader from Radio Sutatenza, pointed out that the barrio on the other side of Canal Tolima (which roughly bisects the town) is mostly *cachaco.* This is where he found lodging when he arrived here, not knowing anyone, much like me. He is *Antioqueño,* a *cachaco,* hence the location of his residence. Since my introduction here was through a *costeño,* I reside on the other side. The canal makes a rather neat line of demarcation between groups in the town.

We took a bus to the intersection of the road to the *vereda* Cauca and the

highway, getting off at the corner with our hammocks, food, and a change
of clothes. We arrived at Francisco's fields of African oil palm about 3:45.
Francisco came out to accompany us to the *campamento,* where Edgar's
students of Radio Sutatenza live. *Campamento* is the name applied to a
section of the administrative center of the Compañía Frutera de Sevilla.
The center is composed of a *quinta* (three large houses), a *comisariato*, row
houses for employees of the company, a warehouse, a building that housed
the generator (now in total ruins), and the row houses for the workers who
fumigated the banana plants to protect them from pests (see figure 4.1).

The contrast between the *vereda* Cauca and the highland *vereda* La
Piedra are obvious from the start. Cauca is in the middle of the rich and
well-irrigated soil of the now defunct banana zone; large tracts of pasture,

Empty shells of worker row houses, left after the departure of the United Fruit Company, stand
stripped of roofs, window frames, doors, and plumbing in a pasture near Majagua.

rice, African oil palm, and scrub dominate the land now. Settlements are
clusters of row houses abandoned by the company in its retreat and by
INCORA (Colombian Institute of Land Reform). The *compartimiento* or
work camps were built to house the banana workers, but now they have
either fallen into ruin or have been taken over by squatters (some are
former workers, some are emigrants from other parts of the department).

The *compartimiento* is the picture of poverty. Screens have long ago
been torn out. Tile and tin roofs have been removed to be used elsewhere
(notably for the refurbishment of the *quinta*). Doorjambs, windows, pipes,
plumbing, fixtures, hinges and anything else that could be pried loose from

the buildings have all been scavenged. Cooking fires inside the rooms have blackened the walls and ceiling—here the kitchen is not a separate building but is one of the rooms of the row house. The row houses originally

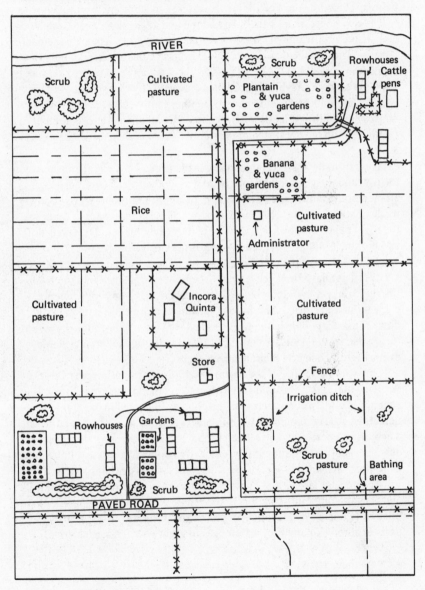

Figure 4.1.   *Finca* Cauca

consisted of space for two or three families, including a bathroom with shower, toilet, and sink, a bedroom, a living room, and a kitchen. The squatters use only the kitchen and one of the rooms to sleep in, the others being useless now that the fixtures are gone and furniture is minimal.

The row house nearest the road and the one adjacent to it are completely empty, their roofs, doors, windows, and fixtures gone. They are the hamlet latrines. The electrical generator building has been demolished; only the foundations are now visible. Likewise, the warehouse has been ravaged. Only the row house with the garden is occupied, by three families. The *comisariato* building is occupied by another family, and the two row houses behind the warehouse are occupied by an undetermined number of families. With the exception of one family, all the residents are day laborers (*trabajadores, macheteros,* or *jornaleros*).

Aside from the poverty, the setting is pleasant. The central area between the row houses is shaded by four huge mango trees. Each morning the women of the family sweep the area in front of their rooms with brooms made of sticks and weeds. Above the roof of the commissary one can see the royal palms of the *quinta* waving in the strong breeze. The sun is hot and the shade welcome. Potable water is obtained from the old water system installed by the company. Although there are no pipes into the houses (these have been scavenged), the women dip down into the main lines with empty cooking oil cans on ropes and bring up cool water and carry it into the house. Bathing is done almost daily at the irrigation ditch down the road; people bathe fully clothed, the women in cotton dresses and the men in cotton pants. Naked children up to the age of three or so play everywhere, tended by their teenage sisters.

[This was the setting of the Radio Sutatenza course offered by Edgar Arcila. This course was quite important to an understanding of the coastal subculture. When compared with the course conducted in the highland neighborhood, certain patterns of interaction were discovered to contrast. These differences could be related to the forms of social organization characteristic of each subculture, and had to do with contrasts of plantation agriculture and *hacienda* cattle ranching versus peasant subsistence farming, the nuclear family and migratory life cycle versus an extended family and very little mobility, and the nonkin male work group versus the bilaterally related male work group. The two settings provided an extremely complex pattern of differences of great significance.]

17 November 1972

For an understanding of the economics of the banana zone one needs to understand the organization of work. There were two kinds of *fincas*—those of the company and those of private individuals who had contracts with the company. Workers on the private *fincas* had no rights to shop at the *comisariato*.

The *fincas* were grouped into districts and employees of the company handled different districts. Employees who lived in Majagua ran the control stations or *espuelas* where the bananas were unloaded, cleaned of flowers, sealed with paint, washed, and packed in nylon bags for shipping to Santa Marta. They hired their own force of workers. Each of the districts had one such station. In addition there were fumigation and fertilization teams that worked the company *fincas* (and the private *fincas* as well when owners did not want to train their own workers).There were also the tractor drivers of the company and their helpers, who likewise were available to the private *fincas*. Finally, there was the work force on the company's *fincas* and the American residents of the quinta, all of whom were administrators.

Francisco was an employee of the company at the age of 17. He started out as a member of a fumigation team and worked his way up to *capataz* of a control station. His duties included keeping an eye on the *fincas* that he dealt with (both private and company). Thus, if the workers fell down on this or that step in the process he would contact the *mandador* or administrator of the *finca* and seek corrections. He also worked as a tractor driver.

Pay day for everyone was on Saturday, and they were paid weekly. Sunday was free, but double pay if one worked.

Francisco couldn't understand why the workers wouldn't work. They claimed they wanted more money. Someone would offer them a contract and they would turn it down. They had no vision of the future, he maintains. He worked his way through the ranks and became a supervisor. He concludes that for lack of foresight the workers chased the company away.

[The impact of the United Fruit Company on the lives of members of the coastal subculture of the community, residents of the lowland town and the hinterlands surrounding it was apparent from the beginning. Here Partridge set about constructing a description of that impact: the classes of personnel, the commissary system, the issues that united and divided Colombians, the wages, and historical events. Although the entire story could not be gained only from such interviews with informants in the community (much valuable data came from published accounts of the period), informants did provide much information that documents of the period omitted, such as prices at the commissary.]

FESTIVALS AND RITUALS

The lives of the people of Majagua are regularly punctuated with ritual and ceremonial events. Together with information gathered from documentary sources, from interviews with informants, and from listening to casual conversations among people, the anthropologist in the field observes recurrent events that structure community life. The rounds of daily, weekly, yearly, and life-cycle activities permit an analysis of society as "a system of meaningful acts commonly shared" (Warner 1959:452).

Event analysis as a technique of investigation yields a variety of information. The symbolic content of an event can reveal to an investigator the nature of beliefs, world views, and systems of meaning characteristic of a people. Turner (1957, 1966, 1969) and Peacock (1968) have demonstrated ways in which content analysis can be applied to such recurrent ritual and ceremonial events. Chapple and Arensberg (1940), Goffman (1967), and Kimball and Pearsall (1955) have, in contrast, pointed to the importance of analyzing social events as units of interaction. Such an analysis of the sequential round of interaction among the component elements of a community provides the observer with specific data regarding the relationship among people and groups. Kimball and Pearsall (1955) call this procedure "event analysis." The forms of assembling, the arrangement of actors, who participates and who does not, the frequency, rate, and order of interaction among actors— these are focal points of event analysis.

In the following examples from his field notes, Partridge recorded some of the recurrent and regular events that punctuate the lives of the people. Some of these have been mentioned earlier, such as the cockfight, but others are part of the yearly ceremonial calendar, including the celebration of the Immaculate Conception, the observation of the anniversary of a death in the highlands, or New Year's Eve. Still others, such as the farewell ritual for the visiting bishop, are part of a longer cycle, while the drinking in the local stores and the visiting of the beggars are part of shorter, weekly cycles. When taken together these events sketch for us the broad outlines of the organization of community life. Each event permits a detailed analysis of the social system as it is reflected in ritual and ceremony. The model of community that eventually emerges is constructed in part from data such as these.

20 October 1972

I typed until 10:00 or so when Cristina came and got me. She said there was to be a serenade for the bishop. I went with her to her house where about 20 people had already assembled, mostly her girl friends, the girls from the Ardila house, Guillermo, and some older women. Later several males joined the group. Bottles of *aguardiente* were produced by Carmen and we all drank and sang. The music came from the guitar played by the man who made the desk and chair for my room. He is Majagua's carpenter. He also made the guitars he and his partner played. The warm-up session lasted until about 12:00. (I recall that earlier today Ardila had told me that there could be a serenade tonight for the bishop. He said it would be a good time and I should go, that everyone drinks *aguardiente* and then goes and wakes the bishop up at midnight. He told me this as if it were great fun to wake the sleeping bishop. As it turned out, it was.) The group sang until about 12:00 and then at Cristina's direction set out for the priest's house where the bishop was staying. The carpenter stood directly in front of the window and he and his partner first played a guitar piece. It was hard to play with no chair to sit on, but the musicians did their best. When they finished we could hear the bishop inside clapping his hands in appreciation. But he did not yet open the window. Then the assembly proceeded to sing and play another song and the bishop came to the window and opened it. Standing there in green silk pajamas he clapped once more when the song was finished. He smiled as the people crowded up to the window to talk with him. Most of the assembly were young people. The nucleus of singers were from Cristina's house and the mean age of this group was probably about 35. But when the singing began the plaza emptied and all the young people came over to join in. In all there were over 100 people at the window. Two more songs were played. I felt at the time that they were working very hard to sing well and to please the smiling man in the window. After the second song Cristina's sister said they would sing another. The bishop said okay, but only one more. When the song ended the guitar players walked away, but the crowd stayed at the window, talking with the bishop. They apparently talked him into another song and they called back the guitar player. After that song Carmen called my name and told everyone I played guitar, and I was then forced to sing for the bishop. I was most uncomfortable, but did it anyway. After that the guitar players played a song called "Macondo" and the serenade was over. The crowd dispersed as the bishop thanked them all and shut his windows.

[Every seventh year the bishop from Santa Marta comes to the community and confirms the children in the Catholic church. He also determines the needs of the parish priest's house and the church building, authorizing expenditures for new paint, new vestments, or new ritual paraphernalia. He is hosted by the community's only religious society or *cofradía*.]

10 November 1972

I met Guillermo and Samuel at Las Quince Letras, the store across from the poolroom and bar, easily the largest in Majagua. They were in town to talk with Panteleón, the owner and their *patrón*. The meeting was to decide how many calves will be purchased for the coming year and how many will be ready for sale in December. Decisions were: (1) how many to sell at what prices, and (2) how many to purchase for the coming winter. Negotiations were conducted in the store, the negotiators sitting on sacks of salt and onions and drinking beer, which the owner paid for. This was also a sort of celebration of good business relations, and lasted until near midnight. Present were Panteleón, his brother who runs a store in Ciénaga, myself, Guillermo, and Samuel. The owner's two sons were also present. They usually handle the customers. They ran across the street to the bar to fetch beer when needed. Late in the evening the owner of the poolroom and bar across the street (he owns the store on the next corner as well) and his employee in the poolroom came in to join the group. It was rather like old-home week since the owner of the pool hall and Panteleón's brother knew each other well and were happy to catch up on gossip and stories. Guillermo and Samuel were very much strangers to this group of merchants and sat nearby, not taking part in the stories but drinking, talking between themselves, and laughing at stories told by the others. Panteleón is from Valledupar. He owns a new, quite modern house on the plaza adjacent to Señor Ardila's house. He is obviously doing quite well.

[The continual traffic of highland peasants into the town is particularly important in October and November, when sales of livestock (raised on a share basis by the peasants for the highland storekeeper) are arranged, and in March and April, when planting loans and new livestock sharecropping arrangements are made secure. The incident recorded above is only one of many similar events noted in these months. The storekeepers of the town are the patrons of the highland clients, extending to them credit and providing small cash loans. In turn the peasants sell their produce at these stores, shop only at these stores, and receive one-third of the proceeds from the livestock they fatten on their farms for the storekeepers. The storekeepers are also highlanders, from small towns and hamlets in the interior, who migrated into the town of Majagua about the same time that the highland peasants colonized the foothills of the sierra. Together they form a cohesive, endogamous, and interdependent subcultural unit of the community. They have successfully transplanted their subculture, described well by Fals Borda (1955), to the coast.]

22 November 1972

I left Majagua for the highlands in early morning in order to reach the home of Don Eduardo about 10:00. Last night I agreed to meet Jorge here this morning. He said he would be along later because he and Juan were to drive Señor Prada's cattle up to La Piedra. I arrived with a change of clothes, my hammock, and a few bottles of *aguardiente* as instructed by Jorge.

Jorge showed up almost as soon as I arrived, and together we set out, leaving the gear with Don Eduardo. We drove the cattle, 29 yearlings, up to the *finca* Escondido where there is a pen. Guillermo met us about halfway with his two older sons. In all there were five of us, three on horseback and two walking, a large number it seemed for that few cattle. The work consisted of keeping the cattle moving and together and from straying onto one of the many paths leading from the road off into the bush. One calf was dropped off at Juan's to be brought along later since it was too tired to make the trip (and a bit of a hellcat as well). Juan was paid by Señor Prada to drive the cattle up to Guillermo. Jorge went along to help Juan.

We got back to Don Eduardo's about 3:00 and were given *chicha* to refresh us. Then everyone took a bath in the stream that runs by the cluster of houses and changed clothes. Don Eduardo has three larger structures and two smaller ones; the three are the sleeping quarters and storage area built of planks and thatch, the kitchen of *caña brava* (bamboo) and thatch, and an open house (sort of like a Seminole chickee) of *caña brava* and thatch where Don Eduardo is usually found reclining in his hammock and where he receives visitors (he has an artificial leg and spends most of his time in his hammock). The two smaller structures are for the pigs and laying hens. The family and one hired hand live here. All are from the interior, Cundinamarca.

Refreshed and clean, we set out for Don Julio's *finca* on horseback, arriving about 5:00. Don Julio was at the gate to meet us and would not let us unsaddle the horses before having a glass of *chicha* at a large table set up near the kitchen. After the drink we turned the horses out for the night. Don Julio is no relation to Don Eduardo, but they are from the same town in the department of Cundinamarca and close friends. Present were the two family heads, myself, Jorge, Juan, Don Eduardo's wife (who had come earlier in the day to help cook), two of his sons (the oldest remained at home), Don Julio's wife, his four children, his brother and mother, and an older, unidentified man. The group had gathered to observe the one-year anniversary of the death of Don Julio's mother-in-law.

Several glasses of *chicha* were consumed and then dinner was served, consisting of *arepa,* pig, rice, potato, and more *chicha.* During the meal two men and a ten-year-old girl arrived from the *vereda* of El Bolante. They are coffee farmers and ritual specialists—very Catholic, said Jorge, friends of the priest in Majagua. They had come because they knew the ritual and were to lead it. Also arriving late was an old man from a *finca* near La Estación, a friend of the family. All were served and ate.

At 6:00 we gathered in a front room of the house, which had been prepared with an altar. The altar consisted of several boxes and tables piled together in a corner to form five different levels. Over these white cotton

cloth or sheets had been spread, forming a white background for the
various decorations. Hanging on the walls behind the altar were white
cloths, and the nearby doorway was covered with a fresh white curtain of
the same material. The following formed the decorations of the altar: four
poles bent in two and covered with red, white, and blue crepe paper were
anchored on the corners of the second level, forming arches; nine poles
bent into circles or hoops hung on the wall on the white backdrops, five on
one wall and four on the other; opposite the front door and at the level of
the top tier of the altar was a large square of blue cloth attached to the white
backdrop, and on this was tacked a silver cross made of paper; beneath the
cross on the top tier lay an open Bible with a crucifix lying over the open
pages; to one side on the second tier was propped a picture of angels
hovering about the Virgin and Child mounted on a burro; on the same tier
on the other side were pictures of the Virgin and Jesus in the same frame;
over the canopy formed by the arches of the four poles were two larger
poles, also covered in red, white, and blue paper and forming two taller
arches, at the front and back of the altar; the nine hoops were covered with
red, white, and blue paper as well; fresh cut plants, ferns, and other forest
scrub, as well as paper flowers, were held in newspaper-covered tin cans at
different levels of the altar; on all levels candles burned; in addition, there
were two large candles on the floor in candle holders made of wood; the
candles were lighted at 6:00 and burned through the night.

The ritual specialists had placed a woven fiber mat on the floor in front
of the altar, and on this had put a rug normally used to cover the seat of a
saddle. Upon this rug knelt one of the specialists and the little girl who had
accompanied them. The little girl recited the rosary, prompted at times by
the man beside her. The assembly and the man beside her responded with
the appropriate chant. The rosary was said rapidly and the responses began
before lines were entirely finished, forming a continuous hum of sound
punctuated by the changes in the speakers. The men sat along the other two
walls of the room on benches, with hats in hands; Don Julio stood to one
side of the altar, also holding his hat. As people entered the room during
the night, they removed their hats. The women and the little girl used no
head covering.

After the rosary the specialists left the room and all the participants
returned to the table where Don Julio served *aguardiente* and *chicha*. He
spent most of the night running between the kitchen and the table with
food, *aguardiente,* and *chicha*. The participants did not serve themselves
the *aguardiente*—it was poured for them in a shot glass by Don Julio.

The men drank until about 8:00 and then went to the altar once more and
the rosary was said by the other ritual specialist, his partner serving as the

main respondent in the assembly, his voice ringing loudly and strongly above the other voices.

About three or four minutes after this second recitation, the hired hand from Don Eduardo's arrived together with another man who appeared to be his relative, a brother or something, as they looked very much alike. The second man was striking in appearance in that the tip of his nose had been cut off, exposing the nostrils and giving him an ugly appearance. They were served drink and food. A little while later a friend from a neighboring *finca* arrived on a beautiful mare. At about 9:30 Arimiro, a storekeeper from Majagua whom I had met previously, arrived with another *cachaco* from the town. They had come in Arimiro's car, leaving it at a friend's house on the road and walking the kilometer or so to Don Julio's *finca*. All the new arrivals joined in the hearty drinking then in progress. (Several other *cachacos* from the town and other shopkeepers were expected to come, but they did not show.)

At 10:00 another rosary was led by the first ritual specialist. The arrangement and the procedure were exactly the same as at the 8:00 recitation.

Drinking continued until 11:00 when a second meal was served, consisting of soup, *arepa,* and turkey, all available in large quantities and seemingly pushed by the host family. I ate what I could, but had to turn down the seconds offered by Don Julio. We drank more *chicha* and *aguardiente* after the meal.

At 12:00 another rosary was said, led by the second ritual specialist, followed by more drinking.

At this point I sought out my saddle and, using it as a pillow, went to sleep. A little before 2:00 Arimiro woke me up, a glass of *chicha* in hand. I had a stiff drink and the next session was in progress.

Drinking continued after this session. Conversation centered on cattle, events of the past, horses, farming, and other shared experiences. Nothing was said of the deceased. Don Julio continued to pour the individual shot glasses of *aguardiente* and to fetch glasses of *chicha* from the kitchen.

At 4:00 the man who was missing the tip of his nose led the rosary. He did not know it very well and used a book brought by one of the ritual specialists to prod his memory.

Drinking continued. Arimiro slept through the last session at 4:00, his head on the table. During the session he fell head-first out of his chair. Jorge checked him and pronounced him all right and sleeping happily. The prayers did not cease during this interruption. One of Don Julio's sons was also asleep—he had confiscated my spot on the saddle.

At 5:00 Don Julio led the assembly, everyone now awake, in saying the rosary. After him, Don Eduardo's wife led the group. In previous sessions the women had stood at the door of the kitchen so as to see into the altar room. This was the first time one of them had come into the room proper and participated in the session (although throughout the night their voices could be heard from the kitchen, responding to the prayers).

Finally, the two ritual specialists, kneeling together on the fiber mat, led the assembly in the last recitation. This one was different from the others in that two songs were sung about six times each, in alternation. When this session concluded, drinking was once more resumed.

A breakfast of soup with two or three eggs in it, *tamal,* pork, blood sausage, rice, and coffee with milk was served at about 6:00. Those who could not eat because they were bloated with *chicha* and *aguardiente* were provided with banana leaves, in which they wrapped up the delicacies to take home with them.

Everyone departed soon after breakfast, after being made to drink several more shot glasses of *aguardiente* by Don Julio. His sons had gone out and retrieved all the animals while everyone else ate. We saddled our horses and burros and took off for Don Eduardo's, the line of participants stretching out over the trail. The ritual specialists accompanied us, carrying their woven fiber mat and a turkey given them by Don Julio in payment for their services. At Don Eduardo's they came in for a cup of coffee and then were on their way, with a four-hour journey by mule to their home.

Jorge and I headed off a little after the ritual specialists had left, Jorge complaining that his stomach was in bad shape. Mine, too. Three hours later we were back in Majagua to spend the day recuperating in our respective hammocks.

[The participation of the storekeepers in such sacred events as the wake in a highland household signifies the complete integration of this subculture composed of peasants and storekeepers. Their relationship is one of mutual interdependence and mutual respect. Similarly, at certain times of the year and during family crises, clients from the highlands attend ritual events in the homes of the shopkeepers.]

9 December 1972

The eighth of December is a national fiesta in Colombia. It is also one of the important celebrations in the town of Majagua. Others are 20 July (Independence Day), 7 August (Battle of Boyacá), Christmas, New Year's Day, and *Carnaval.* There are other fiesta days, but only these are celebrated in the town with special events.

The eighth is La Immaculada Concepción, but the celebration actually begins the evening of the seventh about dusk. People come to town from the outlying *veredas* and together with the townspeople fill the local bars, pool halls, and streets to capacity. Rum, *aguardiente,* and beer flow like water. The street vendors who sell soup, fritters, etc., from their portable kitchens do a booming business. Likewise, the kitchens in front of the market building are filled with travelers eating and drinking. Groups of men in the bars call out to their friends passing by, running out to grab and haul them in by the arm to have a drink. The records on the jukeboxes and record players are heard long into the night. Occasionally, for the benefit of his *compadres,* a man will call to a passing woman, teasing her and inviting her for drink or a picnic. One man shouts to a passing woman ''*Mi hija,* why are you crying so?'' and all the males look to see what she will say, if anything. ''Because I could not find you, Señor Castro,'' she shouts back, and all the men laugh at her response. ''Here I am, little one,'' answers Señor Castro. And he turns back to his drink and she passes on down the street, their interaction finished and the public joking a great success.

At the pool hall down the street from ''the four corners'' a group of men spends the entire evening drinking, playing pool, and singing. One among them is somewhat of a raconteur; as the evening wears on he is found singing song after song for the enjoyment of everyone present, accompanied by a friend on the guitar. His repertoire includes the favorite ballads, but he also is a master of the coastal art of making up lyrics to standard tunes—an art celebrated by Gabriel García Márquez in his novel through Francisco, the man who would come to the town and sing the latest news of neighboring towns and families. The singer weaves daily events, his audience, and the well-known people of the town into his songs, to the delight of everyone; they applaud and shout approval of his artful songs. At 5:00 in the morning a group of 20 or so men is still going strong.

They are not alone. Bars and kitchens up and down the streets are occupied by such groups. During the day an influx of peasants and workers has swelled the population. Like any other day they have brought their excess produce to sell to the owners of the large *almacéns,* and like any other day they have spent the afternoon and evening in the bars and kitchens drinking and eating. But unlike other days, today they drink more and buy more for their friends. This is a day for showing one's generosity and prosperity, a day to cement friendships and patron-client relations. The *cachaco* storekeeper Alcides is hosting some fifteen clients from La Piedra. They will consume three gallons of *aguardiente* this night at his expense. Señor Prada hosts his most important clients: not the peasants who trade their corn and services for credit and cash, but the other store owners who buy from him their small inventories. It is a day for forgetting the differences that separate and for celebrating the agreements that unite fellow travelers in the world. It is a day especially set aside for this purpose, a day given over from labor by "el Señor" and "nuestra Señora."

The women and children are not to be seen nor heard until early in the morning. During the late evening they went to bed while their men drank. The children awake early, about 4:30, with the anticipation that comes with the expectation of a unique happening. During the previous week explosions of fireworks shattered the early evening hours as boys in the plaza and up and down the streets play with their new toys. But this is only practice. At 4:30 the morning of the fiesta the boys awake to begin their demonstration in earnest. Sharp explosions come from over by the market, from the railroad station, from the plaza. The morning quiet is thus shattered as bands of young males run from house to house up and down the streets, waking sleeping residents.

The sharp reports build to a cacophony as more people awake. The band that has been playing at Señor Prada's party moves out into the street and spreads a blanket of music over the town. At 5:00 the bells of the Catholic church begin to peal, seeming to go on for several minutes. The priest lights some 20 candles in front of the parish house, and all over the town people decorate the sidewalks, porches, or dirt streets with columns of 15 or 20 candles. The plaza becomes a flaming square, and radiating out from it down the streets run parallel lines of fire, forming a perfect grid of flickering flames and bathing the houses and the people on their porches in an orange glow in the morning twilight.

The people come from their houses and the bars into the street to dance. Couples walk up and down to watch the spectacle of the candles and dancers. One group of men have painted their faces with white flour and dance wildly in front of the band at the four corners where the dancing is going on. The music, the explosions, and the singing in the orange glow of the candlelight is in itself intoxicating, but this does not prevent participants from passing around bottles of rum and *aguardiente*. The stores are all open and doing great business, together with the kitchens selling soups and fritters.

Drums, accordions, and voices join in song. It is the music of the coast that they are playing. It has a singularity and conformity that makes it instantly recognizable. The accomplished guitarist, the symphony orchestra, the smooth and lyrical ballad—all these are foreign to the coast. The music of the coast is rhythm and dance. Music is not music if one cannot dance in time, or clap hands and undulate hips and pelvis, or shout "huepa" in time. Subtle patterns are not the object; it is the technical proficiency of a good musician that is admired. Nimble fingers exercise in repeating the unchanging, restated, driving rhythm. All else recedes as this forceful and constant rhythm fills the morning and takes over the glowing town.

At 5:30 the bells of the church peal again, and again at 6:00 when a special mass is scheduled. But no one goes to the special mass, only a few old women dressed in black. Everyone is at the four corners, or the market, or the plaza, or watching the throng from porches. The bands of running boys, who have been startling the town as they light their *bombas* from the burning lines of candles, exhaust their supply of fireworks. They continue to run and jump in the streets, but the dragon has lost its teeth now. It is now that the twilight dissolves as the morning sun comes over the mountains. And with the light the people go back into their houses and the bands cease and the candles melt into hard puddles.

Little girls trail along the streets toward the market to buy milk to fill the pots they carry. Boys are hailed and the bands dissolve as they are drafted into the chore of getting meat from the market for the day's meals. The revelers return home to fall into bed. Only the women, the old people, and the young children rise today for coffee and breakfast. The men spend the day sleeping, recuperating from the celebration. At noon the town seems half dead. The usual groups of men at the four corners are absent, the stores are closed, and the pool hall's doors are bolted. The bank, the barbershops, the drug store, the *alcaldía* and municipal offices—all are closed. Only the market, which never closes its doors, remains open. And the ubiquitous fritter and soup vendors and kitchens near the market still peddle their foods. Otherwise life has paused momentarily in the town.

Saturday, the day after fiesta, seems to be a normal day in the morning hours: peasants leave for the fields, workers ride out of town on tractors, trucks come into town full of sacks of rice; people attend to the daily business of securing a document from the priest or the notary, visiting the doctor, shopping. But around 1:00 men can be seen with roosters in hand heading for the *gallera,* for today is the beginning of the cockfighting season. Men who raise fighting cocks come in from the various *veredas* for the inaugural event. Tomorrow they will go to Fundación for the first fight of the season in that town, the following weekend to another town or city, and so the fiesta season begins.

15 December 1972

Today Arimiro sold a milk cow to a *cachaco* farmer from La Piedra—the only description I could get out of him as to the location of his *finca* was *"arriba"* and near Samuel's store. The cow belonged to Arimiro and Señor Prada. The papers were made out over several beers at Ramiro's *cachaco* beer and pool hall. Then the contract was celebrated at two other bars before the two men parted, some six hours after they visited Arimiro's *finca* where the cow was inspected and the bargaining begun. Until the deal was struck (3,500 pesos, 200 paid now, the rest by 6 February), we each bought rounds of beer for the others. After the papers were signed Arimiro, the seller, purchased round after round for the three of us and for other friends who would occasionally sit down for a minute. The man who bought the cow is Juan's brother-in-law.

[November is the time that cattle are sold before the long dry summer begins, which lasts from November until April. Irrigated land or a farm high in the sierra is the only insurance against huge losses in calves and yearlings. In the incident above the shopkeeper Arimiro is happy to supply one of his highland peasant clients with a milk cow; this reduces the size of his own herd and gives him cash to purchase calves when the rains begin in April. The peasant will have to see to it that the cow and any calf she may have make it through the dry summer.]

2 January 1973

New Year's Eve Jorge invited me to a combination New Year's party and birthday party for his oldest daughter. About 11:00 I found the party well under way. All present were important people in the town, the majority being employees of IDEMA that I had met before at the party with Cristina (the first party I went to here). Food was served, as well as *aguardiente* and beer. I wondered at the time what had become of the *chicha* Jorge had been touting yesterday when I met him—he had said that he had a full batch. About 11:45 most of the guests departed, the IDEMA group in a beat-up but nonetheless status 1959 Chevrolet. At least nine people crowded into that car. At midnight Jorge, his wife, the children, and I welcomed in the New Year with *abrazos* (embraces) all around and several more beers. The children were permitted (even encouraged by Jorge with jokes and invitations) to drink beer this evening; never before have I seen him offer alcohol to his boys. A few minutes after 12:00 people began to arrive. The first was Señor Escorcia, a peasant client of Jorge who helped us search for a stray cow one day on Jorge's *finca*. Escorcia was offered a glass of *chicha* (which Jorge had spiked with *aguardiente* and rum, he told us later, laughing). He drank it and gave each one of us an *abrazo,* saying *"feliz año nuevo."* He had barely arrived when another peasant I have met (but can't place where) arrived with his wife. They also offered New Year's greetings to all; he was given a glass of *chicha* and she a glass of sweet vermouth. For the next hour the same pattern was repeated by several other peasants, friends and clients of Jorge and his family. With each arrival the men drank the *chicha* and women were served a glass of vermouth. After about an hour I left and walked to the business area of town, where people were milling in the streets, giving each other *abrazos* and greetings for the new year.

[During many festivals and ritual events clients pay visits to the homes of their patrons and wish them well. This is particularly true of the New Year's Eve celebration. Patrons generally host parties at their homes for friends, and toward the end of the evening clients of the host pay short visits to the home. Clients, and their families if they are with them, are greeted, invited in, and given food and drink by the host. The visit is short and the clients soon move on to visit other friends. Maize beer or *chicha* is traditionally served on such ceremonial occasions by the highland subcultural groups, but members of the coastal subculture prefer the more prestigious contraband, Scotch whisky.]

EXPLORING ALL AVENUES

Systematic data collection includes investigating all possible sources of information in the community. In this section we have included samples of the field notes that illustrate the ways Partridge followed some of the suggestions offered in Kimball's letter of 9 October 1972 and the ways he investigated sources of data that presented themselves in the field.

In working out Kimball's suggestion to investigate spatial arrangements linking the town to outlying hamlets, Partridge discovered the work of Radio Sutatenza in a highland neighborhood. Invited to attend one of the sessions they sponsor, he recorded the activities in detail. Weeks later he attended a comparable presentation in a lowland neighborhood. From his comparison of the two sessions the contrast between the interaction behaviors of the two subcultures became apparent.

Similarly, examination of local historical materials, church records, and the town's cemetery provided other data that helped him to understand the development of the community and its contemporary organization and cultural divisions.

8 October 1972

This afternoon I talked with the priest about the church records. He said I could look at them whenever I liked, so I began right then. The records consist of two sets of books. One is the series recording *bautismo* in the parish of Majagua, which includes Rio Frío, Sevilla, Fundación, Orihueca,

Buenas Aires, and small hamlets. Majagua was apparently the central town of the parish where the records were kept initially, for entries for the towns of Rio Frío, Sevilla, etc., are in the hand of the priests from those towns. Entries for Majagua are in the hand of the priest for Majagua. The second set of books records marriages celebrated in the same area. Both sets begin around 1912 and run up to the present. There are a few missing volumes that the priest says can be found in Pueblo Viejo, or actually Ciénaga, since the former has been absorbed by the parish of Ciénaga in recent years.

While looking over the books I found a note written in 1928, but recorded in the book for the years 1917–19. The priest, Don Francisco C. Angarita, gives a very brief history of the town. He says that the region was originally devoted to *haciendas* and this remained the case up until about 1908. There was a small settlement at a place known then as the old plaza or *placita vieja,* which today lies about three blocks from the park in front of the house where I live. In it is a small monument to the original settlers. These are described by the writer as "ruined families" from "the old town of Fundación." The settlement did not become a *municipio* until the coming of the banana and the intensification of migration into the region.

[These observations on the origins of the community are valuable. But equally important is the priest's testimony that the strike on both Colombian-owned and United Fruit Company estates was put down in 1928 by the Colombian army in a bloody massacre. The soldiers were from the interior provinces, and the coastal people in 1972 and 1973 still view the highlanders as violent and dangerous people. Novelist Gabriel García Márquez, who was born in the banana zone, describes the coastal memory of the highland army:

Then he went out into the street and saw them. There were three regiments. . . . The snorting of a many-headed dragon filled the glow of noon with a pestilential vapor. They were short, stocky, and brute-like. They perspired with the sweat of horse and had the smell of suntanned hide and the taciturn and impenetrable perseverance of men from the uplands. Although it took them over an hour to pass by, one might have thought that they were only a few squads marching in a circle, because they were all identical, sons of the same bitch . . . (1970:280).]

13 October 1972

Guillermo set out at 7:00 with us, dropping off at the *finca* Sepulveda to head for Majagua while we continued on the other trail to the house of

Señor Raul Valencia. The location for the *curso extensión* had been changed, I was told by Guillermo, because Raul's wife was sick. She has been running a temperature for several days. Thus, since she could not make the journey to Guillermo's *finca,* they simply moved the location to her home. I noted, by the way, that Guillermo crossed himself before starting out from the house.

Arriving at Raul Valencia's we (Guillermo's oldest boy, wife, and baby, the next two youngest boys, and I) were greeted by those who had already arrived. Señor Edgar Arcila, the leader I had met at the previous meeting, was there to greet us, as he was staying the three days with Don Raul and his family. He invited me at once to another course in the *vereda* Cauca, explaining that this one would be different in that it is more advanced. I accepted since I was interested in visiting Cauca, a *costeño* neighborhood in the lowlands near Majagua, about 40 minutes on foot according to Edgar. It is the *vereda* in which Manuel's *finca* is located (and the *costeños* referred to will be those workers that Francisco sees following the rice harvester to scavenge the stray grains). In short, it is distinctly different from the La Piedra peasant neighborhood. This course will take place the evenings of 16–19 November since the peasants must work during the day, Edgar explained. This also leads me to believe that the residents are workers rather than peasants.

The course began late, about 8:30 A.M. Present were Guillermo's family and I, the sons of Sepulveda, the family of Raul Valencia, and Señor Acosta and his boy. Edgar began with a lecture on comportment during the course. We were all to ask questions and participate in a civilized manner. He outlined the following themes for the three-day course: (1) *La Dignidad de la Persona Humana,* (2) *Relaciones Humanas,* (3) *Grupos de Opinión,* (4) *Plan de Vacunación del Ganado,* (5) *Dinámico del Grupo,* (6) *Desarrollo de la Persona,* (7) *La Escuela Radiofónica,* (8) *Nutrición,* (9) *¿Qué Es Acción Cultural Popular?,* and (10) *Como enseñar la Poder de Vivir Mejor.*

He began by reading from the Bible, drawing the conclusion from the reading that the Bible was a great book, not just for Protestants (he himself is Catholic), but for everyone. All listened intently. I got the impression that the greatest effect of this act was that he could read; more important than what he said, it was the sign of an educated man.

(All pull out notebooks at Edgar's direction, except Raul Valencia, who does not write.)

(Edgar writes "Dignity of the Human Person" on the board.) "We are persons placed on the earth by God," he says. "Genesis, chapters 25–26, tells us that we are just a little less than God. We have qualities, natural potential, each of us." (Then he writes "*potencial*" and "*inteligencia*" on the board.) "We also have natural intelligence." (He asks Raul Valencia what he will be doing Sunday.)

(Raul sputters and does not answer; Edgar reminds him he will be here with the course. "Yes," Raul answers, somewhat shaken.)

Edgar continues, "We all have intelligence. Like the record storing a song, our brain does the same." He says that President Pastrana and his father were born the same day, and asks, "Which was more intelligent?"

(Silence.)

Edgar answers, "Both were equal. Which is the more important now?" (The elder Acosta says Pastrana.)

"Right," says Edgar. "But why? Because he had an interest in developing his intelligence. My father is a peasant in Antioquia, a good person. But everyone can't be president. The point is that we must all develop our intelligence, to live better, to make more money, to produce more." (Next he writes "*voluntad*" on the board. He refers again to Genesis, saying that man has dominion over the lower animals.) "Who of us does not want to progress: some want to be Bobby Fischer, some to have 180 cows. The secret is volition; we have to want to progress," he says.

(The elder Acosta adds "*práctica*" and Edgar agrees, but repeats his theme—"*voluntad*.")

(He writes "*libertad*.") "All of us are born free; it says so in books about the rights of man. But freedom ends where the next person is." (He demonstrates this by putting his hand in the face of Raul's son Pablo.) "Freedom ends there. God created us free; but a cow is not free. The world is a *medio* for us—a tool for us to use like chalk. It is the same for trees and rivers; they are servants of man." (Edgar uses me as an example.) "The *doctor* is far from his home because he is free to go; he has liberty. The tree does not."

(He writes "*Imagen de Dios*.") "Man can believe in God. The rock is also made by God, but it doesn't have a soul, yes or no?" he asks.

(There are various answers, some positive and some negative.)

Edgar says, "Yes, it has a form, a soul of form, but man has an immortal soul." (He draws on board.) "The tree is born, grows, reproduces, and dies; for these reasons the tree is more perfect than the rock. The animal feels, and makes sounds; thus it is more perfect than the tree. But all serve man; man dominates them all. This hierarchy is the order of creation. Man can learn and remember; the animal can only become accustomed, like learning the trail to Majagua."

[The notes continue in this fashion for another two days. Only a portion has been included here, concluding with the final hours of the three-day meeting.]

15 October 1972

. . . Edgar says, "Alfredo and I want to thank everyone for their participation. There are not words to express our gratitude. If we were not all poor here, we would pay Don Raul and the señora for their work for us and this course. But God repays those of us who help others and they will be rewarded up there" (Edgar points heavenward).

Don Raul rises and apologizes for his poor contributions to the course. Likewise, his wife apologizes.

At this point everyone gets up and begins shaking hands with the leaders. I make it a point to shake hands with them, as well as with Don Raul and Acosta. People pick up the chairs, the benches, the blackboard, and the leaders' books and materials and head toward the house. At the house the guitars and *tiples* are again produced and the men play four or five songs. They play the first song on the porch, but the afternoon sun is hot and so we move into the room where the tack and grain are stored. There the men perch on sacks of coffee and corn and listen to the music. Two boys are playing chess in the corner at a table with a radio on it. The girls are in the next room, sitting on the señora's bed with the señora. The room is occupied only by the boys and me. Edgar interrupts the chess game in order to fill out certificates of appreciation for Don Raul and Acosta, saying they have been instrumental in arranging for this course. Finally Acosta gets up and hands the guitar to Alberto. The music stops and all leave the room.

The pattern of interaction revealed through close study of the notes taken at this course in the highlands contrasts markedly with the pattern of response to the course in the lowlands. In each instance the local people gathered to hear what is essentially a sales pitch by representatives of the nationally sponsored Radio Sutatenza, which has as its goal the teaching of reading, writing, and arithmetic over the radio. The behavior of the two local groups was different, and the differences were systematic and profound. In the sample of notes taken at the La Piedra course, the reader can study the interaction between the two outside representatives and about 15 highland peasants. The variation in numbers of peasants attending the meeting did not alter the pattern of interaction. In almost all cases, only the heads of families, the adult males, responded to questions asked of the audience in general. There are few exceptions to this rule. Adult sons and daughters of these elders said little or nothing, and certainly their adolescent offspring said nothing. The leaders, Edgar and Alfredo, responded to this by addressing themselves almost entirely to the household heads.

A second characteristic pattern of interaction has to do with the frequency and rate of interaction. In the highland example only once during the entire three-day period of the meeting did the leaders and the household heads debate any point among themselves, and here they were briefly joined by some of their adult offspring. But as a rule there was no argument, no debate, no disagreement.

A third characteristic of this pattern of interaction has to do with the consequences of the meeting. Near the end of the course the leaders called for the election of a committee responsible for ensuring that the highlanders did participate in the program of Radio Sutatenza. The household heads responded that one man could do it, and each of them proceeded to place the other's name in nomination. No vote was taken. At the request of Edgar, Raul Valencia accepted the burden of office and all seemed satisfied.

This pattern contrasts with that observed in the lowlands, a portion of which is reproduced below from the field notes. In this instance we see that, in terms of the order of interaction, many different individuals participated. While a few people dominate the discussion, they are not the heads of large extended families. Rather, they are in all cases either labor brokers or managers of estates. Francisco is the administrator of a nearby African oil palm and cattle estate, and Don Ramon is the *capataz* or administrator of another cattle estate. These two men were quite influential, but then so was Señor Villazon, who is merely a day laborer on the cattle estate of Don Ramon. Villazon is, in fact, an older worker who functions as a labor broker. He recruits laborers for the work crews needed by Don Ramon, providing Don Ramon with a steady supply of dependable laborers and providing the laborers with steady work. In addition he directs the daily work activities of the labor crew, even though he himself works in the fields like any other. Thus, in contrast with the highlands, those who dominate discussion do so not by virtue of being older household heads but by virtue of their positions in the estate systems.

Another contrast occurs with regard to the rate and frequency of interaction. While Francisco, Don Ramon, and Villazon are each treated with deference by the leaders and participants in the course, these men do not exclusively retain control of the meeting. In fact, discussion and debate were common throughout the three-day course. Young men, adolescents, and respected household heads all joined in the disagreement. As often as not, this called forth a pronouncement by one of the leaders or from Francisco, Ramon, or Villazon. But the pattern is in marked contrast to that observed in the highlands.

Finally, the consequences of the meeting were different. When the leaders called for nominations and voting for a committee to encourage the work of

Radio Sutatenza in the lowland hamlet, the response was immediate and impressive. Nominations followed quickly, ballots were torn from sheets of paper and passed out, and people elected a president, vice-president, secretary, and treasurer of the committee. Predictably, Don Ramon was elected president, and a group of workers from his estate, including Villazon, were chosen for all of the other offices. However, the elections were held with little difficulty and the officers chosen ranged from 23 years to about 45 years of age. This too is in marked contrast to the highlands, where elections did not ever take place: the household heads in the highland *vereda* already constitute the committee that determines what will be accomplished and what will not. There is no need to hold an election. In the lowlands different groupings assume different tasks and responsibilities. A new responsibility demands a new grouping, which is created by forming a voluntary association of a type learned long ago, probably before the days of the United Fruit Company.

Compare now the following selection from the notes of the meeting in the lowlands that occurred the following month.

16 November 1972

Edgar asks, "Can the rock grow?"

(Someone says, "yes." Two others agree.)

"No," says Edgar, somewhat disturbed. "The rock doesn't have life." (He moves rapidly to the next point.) "The tree has life; it can grow and it dies. The rock doesn't die; it turns into dust. This picture (on the board) is a ladder of perfection. As you go up things are more perfect. What are trees for?" he asks.

("Fruit," says one man. "Wood," says another.)

"Good, what are these for?"

("To eat," says one man.)

"Yes, they are for man. Man is more perfect. The animal is more perfect than the tree; it can feel, it can hear, it can make noise. One can't call to a tree, 'Mango! Come here.' "

(All laugh.)

"But the animal is at the service of man. Man dominates all these. When a man mounts a stubborn burro what does he do? He hits it or yells at it to make it move. What is this?"

("*Voluntad*," says a man in the rear.)

"Good. Man can use his intelligence and volition and animals can't. Man dominates animals, rocks, trees, all things in the world. Man is the center of creation." (Draws a picture of man). "He has all the qualities we spoke of. What are the qualities?"

(Francisco recites, *"Inteligencia, voluntad, libertad, imagen de Dios...."*)

"Man uses all of these qualities to dominate the world. He is superior and closer to perfection than all the others. Man is the center of creation. He can better himself. You must pardon me, but we must speak the truth now; *campesinos* live in the country and often don't work to progress. Many people live on only bananas and plantains. But they can better themselves. How many people don't have a chicken to eat?" (Edgar pardons himself again.) "This is not criticism, but the truth!"

(Man in rear speaks up, saying, "No, this is not criticism. It is the truth.")

Edgar says, "Each day man has lots of ideas. He can create, he can work and better himself, because he is intelligent. Another thing, he can plan. Animals can't make plans. Man can buy *panela* for six days. He can think, 'Next week is the meeting. Let's go.' We can decide to plant rice, cacao, etc. We can plan for the future. What is the future?"

(Two men give answers.)

"Good," says Edgar. "He has to think of his sons. Why? Because he is the center of creation and can better himself. Another thing. Man is divided into two parts." (He writes *"cuerpo"* and *"espíritu."*) "Spirit is like soul, it is immortal. The soul does what we think, what we do. Man has to better both parts. He can't just develop his body. This is bad, because the body dies. He needs to develop the spirit also. Intelligence, volition, etc., are of the spirit. They have to be bettered to improve life."

(A man arrives and sits in back against the wall with others. I notice that children peer in the windows, and doorways are occupied by children.)

"Does intelligence grow in the body?" asks Edgar.

("No," answer several persons in unison.)

"Let's continue with the second theme," says Edgar. "It is *'desarrollo de la persona.'* " (He writes.)

(Danielo asks the name of a woman in front row, she answers, and he records it in his roll book.)

Edgar draws man with a pea-sized brain. "This is intelligence."

(Danielo asks the name of a man in back, while Edgar draws.)

"This man can grow. God gave him dominion of the land. Each day he grows a little bit more."

("He develops," a man in the rear volunteers.)

"Yes," says Edgar, and repeats the phrase. (He draws a stick figure and calls it a boy.) "This is Colombian President Pastrana." (He draws another boy, amid laughter and general comments and conversation among the assembled.) "Here is Pastrana as a boy, and here is Don Francisco as a boy. Which is the more intelligent?"

("They are equal," says a man in the rear.)

("No," says Francisco, "Pastrana is clearly more intelligent.")

"They are children," says Edgar.

("Okay, they are equal," says Francisco. Several echo, "Equal.")

"Who knows more now?" asks Edgar.

(At this point discussion is loud and verbose; everyone in the room seems to be talking at once, arguing the point. Edgar regains order by shouting that Francisco is right.)

"Pastrana is the more intelligent now." (He excuses himself to Francisco.) "Pastrana developed this grain of intelligence here," says Edgar, pointing to the stick figure with the pea-sized brain.

(Many persons comment, "*Verdad*" and "*Claro*.")

Edgar adds that Pastrana also had more money, more opportunity to learn, but he also had *voluntad* to do so.

[Here again we will skip ahead to the final hour of the meeting, after Edgar has called for and conducted elections.]

(. . . Someone nominates Villazon. Another is nominated. They vote. Villazon wins by two votes. Much talking and laughing follow as Edgar and Danielo confer in the front room.)

Edgar then says, "These officers of the *junta* have a great responsibility to better the people, but each of us here has the same responsibility; it is a thing of all the *vereda*."

THE EMERGING MODEL OF COMMUNITY

During October and November, Partridge began to sketch the broad outlines of community through systematic investigation of the neighborhoods of the town, the outlying estates, census materials, satellite hamlets, and the flow of produce from the countryside into the town. Partridge's training and the stimulus of Kimball's letter of 9 October directed him to seek the locus of community in the interconnections among component elements: the markets, the estates, the peasant farms, the peasant cooperatives, and the storekeeper farms. The nature of these interconnections and the interdependencies that they foster provide an empirical definition of the social and economic system of community.

Clearly the town of Majagua is properly considered an urban area. Its population of 5,300 (1964) far exceeds the minimum of 1,500 required to qualify as an urban area in the national census (Departamento Administrativo Nacional de Estadística 1959, 1971), a minimum that Dix (1967) employs as well. Even the more conservative criteria of the *Statistical Abstracts of Latin America* (Latin American Center, UCLA 1968:74), which uses 2,500 as the criterion of urbanism, would include Majagua. But population is perhaps not the significant index of urbanism. Wheatly (1972) points out that Sweden, Denmark, and Finland accord a mere 250 people urban status, while Canada chooses the figure 1,000, Venezuela 2,500, Ghana 5,000, and Spain and Switzerland 10,000. Rather than numbers, urban functions that stem from nodal centers are the important features of urbanism (Arensberg 1968).

TABLE 4.1   Census Data for Municipality of Majagua

	1938[a]	1951	1964
Population			
Total	15,861	12,713	22,202
Urban (over 1,500)	8,159	4,336	12,984
Rural (under 1,500)	7,702	8,377	9,218
Cabecera of Majagua	3,898	4,336	5,304
Buildings			
Total	2,796	2,156	3,785
Urban (over 1,500)	1,355	764	711
Rural (under 1,500)	1,411	1,392	3,074
Cabecera of Majagua	630	764	711

a. In 1938 Fundación and Majagua were a single municipality. This figure includes the population of Fundación, at that time a *corregimiento.*

The community composed of Majagua and its diverse component elements is part of an urban system. This has been true since its founding, not merely since the incursion of the United Fruit Company, for the community form is old. The political form is the *municipio,* found throughout the lowland tropics of South America, Central America, and parts of the American South (Arensberg 1955). In the *municipio,* we find the diversity of settlement forms which represent the nexus of different subcultural traditions: the cattle estates and plantations of the great landowners, the small shopkeeping tradition of the coastal merchants and their coastal clientele composed of estate workers and peasants, and the highland counterpart of small shopkeepers and their peasant clients scattered on dispersed family farms throughout the Sierra Nevada. This diversity of subcultural form, however, achieves in the *municipio* tradition a unity which permits us to classify it with other community forms that are more homogeneous. Community does not require homogeneity, although in the popular writing on the subject this is often the naive assumption. Community implies complementarity and congruency, a system of linkages among diverse parts, which creates a pattern of social life. It is from the linkages and the complementarity that this particular community emerges. Out of a diversity of subcultural forms the functions of the *municipio* kind of community weld a cohesive whole.

The *municipio* form and function are surely ancient urban phenomena in

Majagua. Since the sixteenth century its cattle and dairy products have fed the city dwellers of Santa Marta and Barranquilla on the coast, as they do today, together with the rice estates and newly emerging peasant cooperatives. Each are urban functions located in the countryside. Landowners frequently live in the cities of the coast, and the workers from their estates have been migrants to these same cities for generations. Similarly the resident Catholic priest brings the rites, record keeping, and rhythm of life of the national religion into the community. The mayor is appointed from Santa Marta, yet is one of the members of the founding families of the town of Majagua and an integral part of the community. Finally, most residents of the community are linked by blood to other towns and cities of the coast. Majagua is an agro-pastoral community in the countryside, but its form and function are urban phenomena. Politics, economics, family life, religion, and other institutional functions of community life are centered here in the *municipio cabecera* or the county seat. Here we find the powerful families linked to the national political parties and government; here also are the wealthy cattle and rice producers and merchants; here too are the residences of representatives of national religion, administration, and police. Through these nodal functions the diversity is made whole, and the whole is related to the larger societal unit of which it is a part.

Selections from the field notes that follow demonstrate the first outlines of this urban community tradition that is so widespread in the American tropics. Not until after many months of fieldwork was the model of this community achieved, and a complete picture of the peculiar way in which the *municipio* community form welds a diversity of subcultural traditions into a whole is probably not yet visible to the reader; but the steps leading to an understanding are traced through the field notes reproduced here. Census data provide a broad sketch of the development of the community during the founding days and the days of the United Fruit Company. Descriptive and historical information on the neighborhoods of the town demonstrate the growth pattern that occurred as well as the spatial arrangements among the various subcultures of the community. A survey of one of the regions of outlying estates and peasant cooperatives provides an overview of two important production units that characterize the community. A short discussion of the drinking habits and haunts of the working men indicates some of the different and distinct ways in which the town of Majagua is utilized by various elements of the community. By following the steer from slaughterhouse to the table we observe the manner in which locally grown beef is distributed and consumed. Finally, we examine through several short descriptions the round of local life as it is experienced by the town storekeeper and the manager of a distant estate.

These are only a few of the elements that Partridge used to formulate a working or preliminary model of community. This model will be considered in the following chapter. Here the reader will gain an understanding of the kinds of data on which the emerging model of community was based.

3 December 1972

I looked at the census data today. Most of it is rather useless for purposes of municipal-level analysis. For example, for the year 1938, occupation, age, schooling, place of birth—in general all data—are broken down to departmental and municipal levels. For 1951, however, only age, sex, and literacy are broken down to the municipal levels. One problem is that totals are likely to be inaccurate. Still another is that different things are counted each year, such as the designation of various buildings as residences, stores, jails, etc. The definitions used are another problem. For example, in 1964 there were 404 hovels in Majagua. A "hovel" is not a very precise term; by some standards most of Majagua could be considered a hovel.

Nevertheless, the following patterns exist: (1) the *cabecera* of Majagua, or the town proper of the municipality, has grown very little since the 1930s; (2) growth has occurred mainly in rural areas, areas with population clusters of less than 1,500; (3) the town of Majagua has actually decreased in size when number of buildings are counted, but increased when population is considered (see table 4.1); (4) the town loses from death and emigration almost as many people as it gains from birth and immigration.

From the 1938 census it is apparent that Majagua was the second largest of the "banana-railroad" towns. Other important centers of banana production and transport were Sevilla (2,680 inhabitants), Rio Frío (2,941), Orihueca (2,305), Guacamayal (2,161), and Fundación (4,261). With the exception of Fundación, these towns are the product of the banana-railroad complex of forces, each being originally built on the railroad and not the highway that usually lies at least a mile and sometimes several miles away from the town. Fundación is a true crossroads town, located where the railroad and the paved highway meet and cross the River Fundación. All of the others are combinations of embarcation centers, residences for workers, and small-scale merchandising centers. Today they can be described as residential centers for farm workers and centers of small-scale merchandising, the banana trade having disappeared from all but Sevilla.

10 December 1972

Sunday I observed further evidence of the difference between subcultures. I went to several bars in town looking for either Jorge or José to rent a horse for Señor Ardila. On Monday we plan to go to some of the outlying estates where he has worked in years past. He was quite eager to go as he gets bored sitting around the house all day with the women. Likewise he prides himself on his knowledge of horses and immediately agreed to my proposal that I rent him one for our educational field trip. While going around the town looking in each *tienda,* bar and poolroom, I perceived that the drinkers were divided into two cultural groups for their Sunday drinking.

Transportation between coastal estates and hamlets or towns is provided by ancient vehicles converted into brightly painted buses called *chivas*.

Alfonso's *tienda* on the corner of the market building is a *cachaco* drinking place; so are Ramiro's poolroom, Señora Alvaro's bar, the *tienda* of Alcides in the *cachaco* barrio, and the hotel in the *cachaco* barrio. The others (La Brasa, the poolroom around the corner from it, Manuel's store, and the other bars and *tiendas* in *el centro*) are all *costeño* drinking places. Now I realize that every time Jorge has invited me for a drink it has been to Señora Alvaro's, Alfonso's, Alcides's, or Ramiro's poolroom. Guillermo has uniformly taken me to Señor Restrepo's or Alcides's. When with Melo Luis or Pedro Pertuz it is always to Manuel's *tienda,* to the poolroom around the corner from La Brasa, or to La Brasa.

11 December 1972

I went to the outlying estates on the other side of the River Majagua with Señor Ardila. We visited the following estates: La Andalusia, El Cacao, La Colombia, La Bogotana, La Zacapa; and the following hamlets: La Colombia, San Isidro.

The purpose was to acquaint the workers and managers with my presence and reasons for returning various times in the coming year to their estates. We spent most of our time traveling rather than interviewing people so I could get the lay of the land. La Andalusia is estimated by Ardila at 300 hectares, but he didn't know for sure, producing mostly rice, cattle, and, having a palm processing plant, African oil palm. The *administrador* (Spanish) lives in a *compartimiento* with several other employees. The *compartimiento* consists of four buildings, a shed for tractors, and a commissary. The truck from Majagua was being unloaded at the commissary when we returned for lunch; supplies for a week or so (no alcohol) were laid in. Workers can buy food here and the families of the employees live off these supplies. I spoke with two workers here. One lives in the barrio San José Majagua. I met him at the end of the day as we were going home—my horse is kept in this barrio. He commutes to work at the estate from his home by *chiva*, their name for a broken-down truck that has been converted into a bus and runs between Majagua and Fundación. Most of the passengers on the truck are men and women like this worker. They go to work on it, ride it to town to buy supplies if they live on the *finca*, or take it to run errands to a neighboring estate or hamlet. There are a number of these *chivas*: at least eight or nine different ones passed us during the day on the road to El Retén.

The other worker (a *costeño*) lives in the foothills of the sierra and owns a *finca* there where he grows rice, maize, yuca, etc. During the dry season in the foothills (which is now), he comes down into Majagua and works as a wage laborer. In March or April, planting will resume and he will return to his *finca*.

The estate La Zacapa is where Señor Ardila worked during the years of the United Fruit Company (all the estates listed above were company-owned and planted in bananas). La Zacapa is about 400 hectares in total, 300 planted in rice and about 70 in sugarcane. There are about 50 head of cattle on the remainder. The manager is named Felipe and the owner, who lives in Fundación, is named Martinez. The manager also worked for the company and is *compadre* to Señor Ardila. Earlier in the day Ardila estimated the departure of the company in 1936. Felipe gave the same date when asked. He says they came back again later, not as owners, but as buyers, and left for the second time in 1956. First they left El Cacao, then La Colombia, and then La Zacapa, he said.

I asked about planting and harvest times. He said there are two harvests a year: rice is planted in July and harvested in February, then planted again in February and harvested in July. This is in contrast to the highlands, where only one crop can be obtained a year. Felipe says the estate is a little dull now, but around 15 February the workers will be coming in. About 80 are hired on the estate of La Zacapa for the harvest, plowing, and planting in

February. He says these workers come from all over. Some live in Majagua, some in Fundación, while others come from as far away as Valledupar. The workers go where they can find work, he explains. The cotton harvest is concentrated on other estates in Valledupar. Rice is grown mainly in the former *Zona Bananera* around Majagua. When these crops are ripe workers migrate to these areas. The rice harvest has already begun, he explained, on Señor Perez's estate near El Bongo (which he estimates at 1,000 hectares). Each day six or seven truckloads of rice pass by the front of La Zacapa. He said about 40 workers are needed to cut, plow, and plant the sugarcane. The estate has a *trapiche* on the grounds, a modern plant with eleven vats for making the *guarapo* into raw sugar.

We spoke some of the *colono* (squatter) problem. It is pronounced on his estate, Felipe claims. He spends a lot of time chasing them off for the owner. Felipe feels the problem is that owners too frequently pay bad wages, 15 or 20 pesos a day. A man needs a minimum of 50 pesos a day to live and feed his family, he says. He can't live on 20 a day, so he looks for land to invade and colonize.

The hamlets of San Isidro and La Colombia are former *colono* invasions. When the United Fruit Company left these lands in 1936 the *colonos* quickly moved in. San Isidro is a hamlet of about 30 homes, laid out in the standard grid pattern, with three *tiendas* and a restaurant. Ardila dates their invasion from 1936. I suggested 1930, before the company pulled out. But Ardila said no, definitely after the company left. The same, he continued, applies to the *colonos* of La Colbia, another hamlet next to the estate of the same name. Here about 15 homes are clustered along the sides of the road where it forks off to La Bogotana to the southwest and to Fundación to the southeast. All along this road are to be found *colonos*, sometimes living in houses sitting by themselves alongside the road, but more often in clusters of homes forming a little node. The whole area along the road from the paved road (which passes by La Andalusia and La Colombia) to the estate La Bogotana is a single *vereda* called San Isidro.

Also on this road is a rambling old mansion (the kind one finds in Windsor or Melrose near Gainesville, sitting off alone in the woods), which belonged, says Ardila, to General Herrera during the "war." (When Colombians refer to the war, it is to the War of a Thousand Days at the turn of the century.) The mansion is two stories high and made of wood, with a veranda and shuttered windows. It is a lovely old building, but fallen into ruins and not inhabited. The general's estate was also sold to the company at the turn of the century. The general later became a senator and wrote (I believe) a history of Colombia. The old home is located about a kilometer from San Isidro.

The hamlet of San Isidro has an adobe factory (an enterprise of one of the *colono* families). One can see evidence of its work up and down the road, although most homes are of wattle and daub. A few have been notably improved in recent times, concrete block being added to the basic wattle and daub construction. The two *tiendas* and a few other houses are of concrete block and wattle and daub, mixed. Kitchens are, as usual, separate little shelters with thatched roofs. Some kitchens are simply a table and fireplace at the rear of the house, pots and pans and cooking utensils hanging on the wall on nails.

The *trapiche* powered by a mule grinds sugarcane and produces *panela* (raw sugar), a dietary staple and a cash crop, which the highlanders market at stores in Majagua.

Up and down the paved road to Fundación is evidence of the company's presence. *Compartimientos,* like the one described for the *vereda* Cauca, dot the landscape. And like those at Cauca most have been ransacked, their roofs, doors, windows, and fixtures stolen. Now they are grisly, raw concrete block hulls. A few are occupied by workers, but most house only weeds and guava trees, their branches and leaves poking out through the skeleton of the building.

Ardila explained that when he worked here in the twenties and thirties the road did not exist. It was then a railroad spur, all the way to El Retén and beyond, linking the banana estates to the main line at Ciénaga and Santa Marta. Workers, employees, and bananas were hauled by train from town to town. The road was built around 1940, after the company pulled out, by the government and some wealthy landowners, he said.

The general pattern in the outlying district seems to be: two major towns, Fundación and Majagua, linked by two paved roads; several hamlets such as San Isidro and La Colombia locked in by the large estates and located on the dirt and gravel roads that run between the boundaries of the large estates to the major settlements; several isolated houses built during the United Fruit Company days in which estate managers and current employees of the estate owners live; several *compartimientos* sparsely occupied by the estate workers.

8 January 1973

During the morning hours I took a walking tour of the barrios of the town with two objectives: first, to delimit the barrios and, second, to count the neighborhood *tiendas* in the town. Attached is a scheme [figure 4.2] depicting the general arrangement of the barrios, the central business area, IDEMA, etc. This is taken from an earlier map I had made of the town, which is too large to copy, that also shows the locations of each business, store, garage, funeral parlor, gas station, and pool hall. The schematic drawing is a by-product of my walking tour today, since it was the first time I had consciously set out to cover every street in the town.

The barrios labeled "old" are those that date from the construction boom when the United Fruit Company came in, approximately 1900. The barrios labeled "new" are so called because the older townspeople have distinguished them as "nuevo"; that is, they were not here during the heyday of the *Zona Bananera*. General descriptions of the old and new barrios follow.

Old barrios.—El Carmen and Loma Linda are *costeño* barrios of original migrants who built the town during the banana zone period. In them one finds some concrete block houses of modern design that replaced the original house of wood, adobe, and palm thatch when the family became wealthy. Here the high-ranking employees of the United Fruit Company lived, as well as some property owners and cultivators. The plaza area has only two of these modern concrete block style houses, one belonging to a *cachaco* store owner and the other one belonging to one of the remaining wealthy *costeño* families who have holdings in the area devoted mainly to cattle. Likewise, the business district is an old settlement area. Here, as in El Carmen and Loma Linda, one finds that the older style of building predominates, with the thatched palm roof, perhaps replaced in spots with galvanized tin, and the heavily buttressed walls (stylistic holdovers from the peasant practice of thickening the walls at the base to bolster the adobe

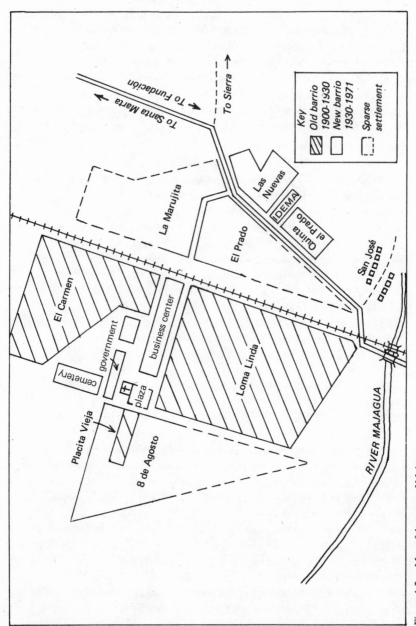

Figure 4.2.   Map of the town of Majagua

wall and prevent erosion of it). Thus, while many of these older buildings from the 1900s forward are of adobe and clay plaster, sometimes with a stucco finish, they retain stylistic features of the peasant wattle and daub house.

New barrios.—The barrios 8 de Agosto, Las Nuevas, and El Prado are for the most part the result of squatters and rural migration into town as the days of the United Fruit Company came to a close. They consist of cane, mud, and thatch structures in the first phase; later additions are built of adobe, concrete block, and galvanized tin to make a square, squat, block-house kind of structure, with sloping roof tapering back in lean-to fashion. The barrio La Marujita was settled by an invasion of *cachaco* families. *Cachaco* families are also mixed in with the recent growth of Las Nuevas and El Prado, but here they are the majority. Here also all the *tiendas* are *cachaco* owned. The barrio 8 de Agosto, in contrast, is a working-class *costeño* barrio with (to my knowledge) no *cachaco* residents.

The individual neighborhoods can be characterized as follows:

El Carmen and Loma Linda.—Old barrios from the heyday of the United Fruit Company; inhabited by *costeño* families, many of them well off in those days; construction dating from 1900–1920 period, but interspersed with "improvements" and modern construction by the few better-off families; original residences have adobe construction, thickened walls, thatch or tin roof, patio facing the center of the block; people sit on front porch and in living room to socialize and live mainly in the house and front porch area; indoor kitchen with gas cooking.

8 de Agosto.—Recent migration and invasion of *costeño* working-class people and some peasants, which occurred sometime in the 1930s (probably late thirties): houses uniformly of thatch and mud construction, with the few exceptions made of wood or cane; patio is an area of family living, the kitchen table and cooking area being located here; cooking is done over charcoal or wood fires in the open, usually on a hearth built on top of a table with brick, sand, and clay (often another fire on the ground for large pots of water, soup, etc.).

La Marujita.—Product of *cachaco* migration of the 1950s into the town; lies along the road to the highway, although highway did not exist when town was built; this barrio was literally "the other side of the railroad tracks"; today it sits on the important highway, where workers gather to catch buses, families to travel to the city, and shoppers for the stores.

El Prado and Las Nuevas.—Mixed settlements of *cachacos* and *costeños,* grown up during the 1950–70 period; these areas are the main areas of growth of the town at present as they are not yet filled to capacity; houses range from simple mud and thatch shack to modern concrete block, but the latter are quite rare. Living pattern is mixed, as is the population.

Business district.—Most all the stores owned by one of three *cachaco* families or one of three *turco* families (latter are of Arab descent, but all were born in Majagua and speak fluent Spanish). Several of these families live in refurbished, modern concrete block houses either in the district or in Loma Linda. One *cachaco* family lives on the plaza.

Placita Vieja.—Original site of the town of Majagua before the coming of the United Fruit Company and the railroad. The homes of the town founders and several of the old land-owning families are in this area, but the plaza has been given up to weeds and the old families have dispersed.

Plaza.—Located on the site of the cemetery of the Placita Vieja. Plaza itself (benches, lights, landscaping, trees, etc.) was not built until 1954 with the administration of a military mayor.

Quinta El Prado.—Site of the plantation-style homes of the American employees of the United Fruit Company; today a cattle *finca,* the owner of which rents homes to managers and employees of IDEMA (government cotton gin).

My count of the stores is not yet complete; however, I have been able to differentiate two types.

Tiendas.—These I've defined as neighborhood stores that are differentiated from *almacenes* by the presence of the following characteristics: a small stock or inventory; serve only a local (neighborhood) clientele; family of owner lives in same building; usually the *tienda* is the front room of a house converted into a store by the addition of a counter, chairs for clients, and a refrigerator for making ice and keeping beverages cold. There is generally at least one *tienda* per block; usually there are two and sometimes three. In the barrios of El Carmen, Loma Linda, and 8 de Agosto there are 41 *tiendas.* They generally stock the following items: *panela,* refined sugar, coffee, herbs, salt, candy (homemade), cookies, bread, laundry detergent, bath soap, rice, noodles, beer, colas, fruit juices, toilet paper, matches, cigarettes, thread, kerosene, aspirin, Mejoral, Metholine, rum, *aguardiente,* onions, ketchup, hot sauce, eggs, tomatoes. Some *tiendas* have larger inventories and carry a variety of toiletry items like toothbrushes, hair creams, first-aid ointments, toilet bowl brushes, nails, etc., whereas others have an inventory of only the most frequently used items such as rice, *panela,* rum, toilet paper, salt, coffee, cookies, soft drinks, beer, and cigarettes. The range is great, but the characteristics described above put them in a class together.

Almacenes.—There are only seven or so in the town, all located in the business district. They range from Las Quince Letras, which has the largest inventory and stocks everything one could possibly need, to a hardware store, two clothing-shoe-hat stores, and a drugstore. The owners of the *almacenes* live in homes separate from the store building itself, but often close by (within the same block). All *almacén* owners are also landowners, usually operating *fincas* devoted to cattle or cash crops. They are either *turcos* or *cachacos*. They maintain elaborate systematic relations with clients who market their produce at the store, shop for their family needs at the store, and work for the owner on the latter's *finca* or through share-cropping.

In all cases *almacenes* are places of business solely. *Tiendas* are more complex from a cultural point of view (not economic). *Tiendas* serve several functions: they provide a small income for the family and a residence; they sell household necessities; and they serve as a meeting place for friends (all have chairs for clients to sit and pass the time of day), as drinking sites for clients (chairs again), as distribution points for milk, *plátanos*, eggs, and other products the peasants market in small quantities. *Tiendas* near the market building are also distribution points for meat and fish, but only these *tiendas;* the others in the town have no meat or fish for sale. Meat and fish are obtained through the market by *tienda* owners.

10 January 1973

At 6:00 in the morning the streets are full of people going to the market. The stores are open on all the main streets, and the women who run the kitchens in front of the market are brewing coffee, making *bollo* (a corn dish which is like cold grits wrapped in a corn husk), frying breads, etc., for sale. Small children go to nearby *tiendas* for milk. The meat market is open this hour too, but meat (like milk) is only available at certain stores. Whether a store sells meat depends on the owner's relationship with a large man (name not noted) who today is wearing a yellow shirt and who sells meat in large quantities. A store owner with a freezer can buy a steer and arrange to have it slaughtered for sale. But this is not a common practice. Most stores buy from this specialist, who arranges for the permits and taxes and inspections of the meat (actually the steer, on the hoof, is examined for signs of illness). The signatures of four officials are required to kill a steer for sale to the public: *inspector de la policía, alcalde, secretaría de hacienda,* and *inspector de sanidad.* The owner writes up a note saying how many steers are to be killed for market, their descriptions, brands, etc. The four officials then sign the paper. Ardila says only the police and health inspectors actually look at the cattle—the *alcalde* and the secretary of the hacienda merely sign the sheet after the others have signed. Jorge told me the police can usually be bribed with about 200 pesos into approving a thin or sick steer. Once the authorization is secured, the large buyer then takes the cattle to Señor Francisco Pastrana at the *matadero público* where they are slaughtered and cut up into chunks (the word "pieces" implies more precision than Señor Pastrana uses). Pastrana kills the cattle with a rifle early in the morning and has them at the market by around 6:30 ready to deliver to the fat man who buys them all. The fat man then sells chunks to the storekeepers—10 pounds, 20 pounds, etc.—who market it to the public during the morning hours. Around noon the storekeepers pay for the meat that they received that morning, after having sold it or the best part of it. A few, like Juan, who have freezers buy a larger quantity than they know they will sell in a single day. Often, according to Pastrana and Jorge, Juan will buy a steer himself, obtain the permits, and have it slaughtered. But he participates in the system described above as well, thus avoiding the problems and complications of paperwork, bribing, slaughtering, etc. Pastrana makes 40 pesos per head of cattle he slaughters, according to Ardila and Jorge. Pastrana says the most he has slaughtered in a day has been four animals.

At 7:30 and on into the morning people continue to frequent the market. Some come before each meal to buy a tomato, a piece of meat or fish, a banana. No one appears to shop for a week, or even a single day, entirely at one time. Ice, tomatoes, onions, bread, meat, Cokes, fish, etc., are examples of items that are purchased daily and sometimes before each meal. Items like rice, potatoes, and cooking oil are purchased in larger quantities and last several days to a week. Corn products, like *bollo*, bread, and meal for *arepa*, are purchased daily as needed. All vegetables such as cabbage, onions, peas, and beans, and bananas and other fruits are purchased as they are used.

Storekeepers generally go to work before breakfast, returning about 8:30 or so for the morning meal. Workers leaving early for the fields will have coffee and some *bollo* or rice, or they will carry food with them for breakfast in the field. Almost everyone returns home at noon for the large midday meal and the two-hour lunch-siesta time. They are back at work about 2:30 or so (often 3:00) and continue until 5:00 or later. The evening meal is eaten between 6:00 and 7:00. Work crews are rarely picked up by the manager or owner of a *finca*. They walk to work along the numerous dirt roads cross-cutting the lowlands. Some ride their burros if they plan to bring home a load of wood, charcoal, or hay. Often, however, a manager or owner will bring a load of workers back into town at the end of the day, dropping them off either in the plaza or near his residence where he parks his tractor or jeep. The men returning from the fields often carry *mochilas* (knapsacks) which rattle and clank with empty aluminum pots in which they carried breakfast or lunch.

The few peasants who live in town leave early in the morning—6:00 or so—returning only at the end of the day. They most frequently ride burros and return laden with produce for the house.

5. Midpoint Assessment

PERIODIC stock-taking is a deeply engrained aspect of Western civilization, perhaps of all societies where changes in activity segment the round of life. Except for those who experience conversion, such interludes seldom bring much change in either tempo or direction. Such a casting up of accounts, however, should be a standard operating procedure in all scientific enterprises; it possesses special merit for field studies in anthropology.

It was not merely a coincidence that Partridge and Kimball independently and almost simultaneously arrived at the decision that the time had come to *assess* the situation by formulating a model of the community from the data and by planning future activities. One cannot assume that some powerful ESP wavelength connected Gainesville, Florida, and Majagua, Colombia. Yet it is significant that on 2 January Kimball composed and posted a letter reaffirming the context and objectives of the research and listing the specific areas of community life about which information was needed. On the following day in Majagua Partridge prepared a progress report explaining a tentative model of the organization of the community.

The length of time that elapses between entry to the field and the production of the first working model of community structure varies. Formerly, no attempt was made to arrive at tentative syntheses while in the field. Instead time was spent in the frenetic gathering of ever more data to be sorted and analyzed after return to home base. And for many researchers, then and now, the description of community as the setting of the problem under investigation was not considered essential. Those who investigated such topics as child-rearing or property rights counted their success entirely on the completeness of their coverage of the subject with little concern for its relationship to other aspects of the social life. In Partridge's research, however, the conceptualization was of a different order and hence his emphasis upon community as the gateway to understanding cannabis. Thus there was the need for an early comprehension of the structure of community.

The empirical model that Partridge prepared as of 3 January is relatively simple. He describes it as ''a community differentiated into segments on the basis of subcultural traditions, forms of organization, and control of resources.'' There are the *costeño* hamlets of the coastal plains associated with agricultural estates; the *cachaco* settlers on the separated homesteads of the highlands; and the urban center with its complex arrangement of *costeño* and *cachaco* segments together with the governmental intrusion of INCORA. Present-day arrangements reflect four recent influences: the influx of the *cachaco,* the departure of the old land-owning families, the new agricultural technology, and the government-created INCORA to control the use of the old banana lands and the irrigation system. Within this framework some of the detail of the production, use, and distribution of cannabis had begun to accumulate.

A comparison of the Partridge summary of 3 January with that called for in the Kimball letter of 2 January reaffirms their remarkable agreement on objectives and methods. The specific requests of the Kimball letter add up to those aspects of behavior necessary for constructing an empirical model of community. These include past events, settlement pattern, table of organization, social structure, types of assemblage, and the organization of work and economic patterns. That there was no mention of collecting data about cannabis is evidence that Kimball considered this to be of secondary significance at this stage in the research. Partridge, in contrast, was quite explicit about the deficiencies in his knowledge of this area.

The Partridge summary of 3 January differs from his earlier ones in the order of presentation and in the greater amount of detail. It is this type of analysis that indicates the direction for future efforts. Not only does it reveal deficiencies, but it signals areas that are likely to be highly productive through more intensive research. In effect, the plan of operation for the succeeding months is a natural consequence.

The specific areas that Partridge indicates deserve in-depth examination are almost identical in both reports. In the later one (10 January), however, they are more precisely stated and their connection to the overall objective is clearer.

The material that follows includes correspondence and field-based reports. The former illuminates conceptual problems while the latter provide the first full view of the structure of community.

2 January 1973

Dear Bill:

It seems to me that the time has come for you to spend whatever days are necessary to assess the information that you have amassed to date and to make a plan of operation for the future to complete those areas where there are gaps. Your notes are quite adequate in revealing what you are doing, but they are not giving us clues about the situation you are in. This may well be because you are continuing largely to record what happens in diary form rather than developing a plan of research for gaining knowledge of the community.

Is it not the objective of your research to specify the nature of the community in which you work and then to understand, if possible, the economic, social, and other aspects of the cultivation, distribution, and use of cannabis? The latter is going to have to be done in the context of community—that is, to see both its functions and its place in the social ecology—if it is to be meaningful.

As yet, we are not certain what kind of town Majagua is. Is it the seat of the *municipio?* What are its relationships to the countryside and to other towns in the *municipio?* To answer these questions you need to do the following:

1. Make or obtain a map of the area that shows the settlements and any variety in the type of landholding, agricultural practice, origin of population, types of agrarian systems, etc. This is all inventory material. (If possible, get a soils map, because oftentimes there are real cultural and economic differences related to soil and topographic factors.)

2. Work out a gross (preliminary) sketch of the status differences of the population. Use such factors as ethnic distinctions, town and country people, social class, etc. Perhaps these should be treated separately.

3. Develop a table of organization. This is the actual listing of the types of individuals in the community related to their specialities, e.g., officials, teachers, clergy, commercials, laborers, etc. Think of this as the community counterpart of a kinship chart. Then consider which ones you already know something about and which ones you don't.

4. Work out an inventory of the types of assembly, including the setting, time, and frequency. This would include households, bar drinking groups, schools, and churches.

5. Make a preliminary typing of the kinds of agricultural operations—in terms of not only the technology of the activity, but commercial and subsistence dimensions, the complexity of the organization (family versus larger operations), etc.

6. You are gaining some historical evidence about the sequence of activities and of farming operations and settlements, and migrations. This information, placed in the context of some of the items mentioned above, should begin to show you the bases for change and the dynamics of the situation.

7. Once you have the information assembled that I have indicated, you should begin to see some pattern emerge from what you are working with,

a pattern that is only vaguely apparent in the notes you send us. It should indicate the direction of the research effort and indicate those places in which you need to do both observing and real interviewing, because now you have the basis to ask questions about the way things are and how they have come about.

8. Try to get some life histories. These are often very revealing of the intersection of segments of the community.

9. At times you are doing all right on getting in the ethnography, but not at other times. By this I mean the detail of the situation in which events occur: the furnishings of a room, the clothing of the participants, the food items. These eventually become the diagnostic items of situations that will clue you as to the kind of behavior that will occur and the kind of people that will be there. Once you have done it for a few hovels, then you can say in your notes that things are the same as elsewhere, or note the variations.

This may sound like a big order, but it is order that we are urging you to insert in your activities, even though the pursuit of the main fox seems most elusive.

Happy New Year,
Solon Kimball

P.S. Please send us your plan of operation for future work.

4 January 1973

Dear Dr. Kimball:

I was pleased to receive your letter and holiday greetings just before Christmas. I was feeling frustrated about then, after getting the runaround at the government archives office in Santa Marta. They told me to come back later, with *permission* to use the newspaper collection. Your thoughtful wishes were quite welcome.

Another set of field notes accompanies this letter. Contained in them are complete lists of house owners and *finca* owners in the *municipio*. I will be using these to interview older residents of the *municipio* in the coming months. Also contained in the notes is a listing of marriages from the church records for the period 1914–25 and the period 1957–68. A comparison of the two lists is revealing.

I have attempted here for the first time to compose a model of the organization of the community. It is accurate to the present state of my knowledge and data, but far from complete; I will be filling in the gaps as I go along. But I think it touches upon the major points of difference among the groups composing the community. I have indicated with arrows the major interaction networks among the component elements. These include goods, services, wages, farm products, etc. A major gap is the organization of life in a coastal subculture hamlet. I was planning to spend several weeks studying one of these this month, but my key contact in the hamlet has been jailed for molesting a fifteen-year-old girl! This has caused me to change my plans for the moment. Despite his incarceration he should still be useful when he gets out of jail. Members of the hamlet have taken in his wife and she continues to bring him his food at the jail each day. So apparently the infraction is not cause to expel him from the community.

Things are going well here, and I feel the study is progressing at a steady if not spectacular rate. I have other materials for which there are not copies—notably, maps of the town, photocopies of historical notes, newspaper clippings, etc. I will mail these toward the end of the study rather than risk losing them, because I am still using them right now.

I am going to begin a series of directed interviews among the several component elements of the community as soon as I can make the arrangements. These will include the *costeño* hamlet of laborers, the *cachaco vereda* La Piedra, and selected older people of the town's upper crust. I will record the interviews on five-by-eight-inch sort cards for analysis later.

Best wishes,
Bill

3 January 1973 [enclosed with the above letter of 4 January]

The New Year seems a good point at which to assess the progress of the study. Attached is a working or tentative model of the organization of the community [figure 5.1].

Outlying Neighborhoods

Costeño hamlet.—Made up entirely of workers on large- and medium-sized *fincas* and *colonos* or squatters who may own from one-half to two (maximum) hectares of land, but who also work on the large *fincas*. Migration to the city is frequent, indicated by the dotted lines. Significant credit-wage-work relationships exist with the manager (*capataz, mandador, administrador*) of the *finca*. The owner lives either in the town or city and simply provides the capital for the daily operation of the *finca*. The manager is the one with the technical ability and contacts among the workers; the manager makes things go. The workers buy from commissaries on the *fincas*, although they also shop in town when cash is available, but this is a rare circumstance. (Gaps existing at present: marriage patterns, incidence of migration, life cycle, developmental cycle of the family, marijuana use, land use practices.)

Cachaco vereda.—Occupied entirely by *colonos* or squatters from the interior of the country who fled *la violencia* in the late 1940s and settled in the foothills of the Sierra Nevada. They own from 50 to 200 hectares of arable land and are true peasants. There are few if any landless laborers

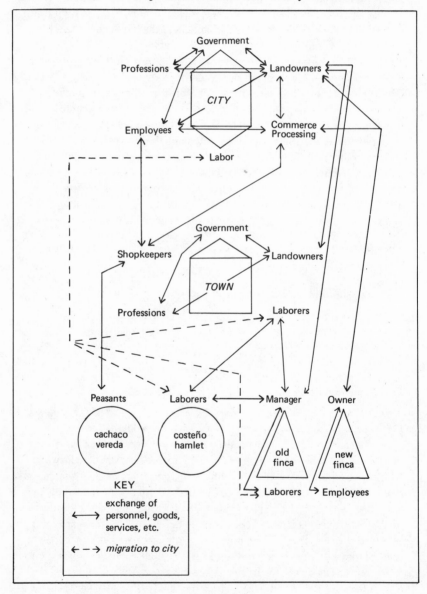

Figure 5.1.   Organization of the community (working model)

living here. The settlement pattern is the dispersed individual family homestead. Family members form the work force. Older people past productivity migrate between relatives in the *veredas*. The *veredas* are linked by marriage and kinship ties—highly endogamous. Slash and burn pattern prevails. Here are located the feeder lots for cattle of storekeepers in the town; thus there are strong exchange relationships with individual *cachaco* storekeepers for credit and goods. Credit is also obtained from the Caja Agraria, the national agrarian bank. The agricultural base is mixed, but staple crops are manioc, rice, and corn, depending upon availability; manioc is the most plentiful. There is some cultivation of marijuana for merchandising.

Old finca.—Organized and operated almost exactly the same as those of the United Fruit Company between 1896 and 1964. The owner lives in town or city, investing capital through his manager; the manager is responsible for hiring workers, for the technological tradition used, for all daily decisions, for paying wages, and for stocking and distributing supplies from the *comisariato*. It is not uncommon to divide these tasks among additional employees (recruitment pattern of managers and employees is unknown). The managers are active in the cockfight circuits and prominent at the town fiestas. They live on the estates or in town. Laborers sometimes live on estates, but more often in the hamlets.

New finca.—Owner lives on the *finca*, but frequently spends time in the city; manager is in charge of employees and the few laborers used (loading trucks, etc.). Mechanized farming: plowing, planting, harvesting all mechanical. Airplanes hired in Fundación dust crops for weeds and pests. Land is sometimes rented from INCORA; water is purchased annually and workers are used for cleaning irrigation canals. Credit is obtained from the Caja Agraria. Manager and employees also live on the estate, but outbuildings for workers (left over from United Fruit Company days) are frequently vacant since few workers are needed.

Town Residents

Shopkeepers.—Most of the large *almacenes* (huge versions of country stores, stocking everything from food to farm supplies and tools) are in the hands of *cachacos* who migrated here about the same time that the old "*crema*" or wealthy families of the *Zona Bananera* days were migrating out. Their business relationships are with the *cachaco* peasants, a few employees on their cattle *fincas*, and with buyers in the cities. Several are married into the *costeño* subculture, but their social contacts remain centered on their regional origin and in the *cachaco* subculture through their business contacts and ritual life.

Landowners.—Few of these remain in the town proper today. This is especially true of the large landowners, who in the days of the *Zona Bananera* lived in town; these have fled to the city. Whether in the city or in the town their relationship to their land is a formal one. Rarely do they live on the estate; rather they constitute an urban upper class in the feudal pattern. They are, or were, active in the professions and politics. The large holdings are now broken up into smaller parcels, the lush family *quinta* lying in ruins. Today this group frequently overlaps with the shopkeepers. Together with the estate managers and employees of the *Zona Bananera* days they dominate the government, a vestigial form of the older system of organization.

Professionals.—I have little data on this group. What there is indicates that they are the offspring of estate managers, employees, and shopkeepers from the days of the *Zona Bananera*. I know this is true of the physician and the majority of schoolteachers, but data are lacking for others.

Government.—The dominant group is that consisting of old families from the days of the *Zona Bananera* who were employees, managers, and shopkeepers. Now that the landowners of those days no longer live in the town, this group forms the *"crema"* of Majagua. Only one *cachaco* serves on the *consejo municipal*. However, petty landlords in El Retén and Buenas Aires are represented, as well as several owners of large estates in the El Retén area (old style *fincas*). Government employees (treasurer, tax collector, judge, *personero*, etc.) are all *costeños* from the dominant group.

General Overview

Several processes have combined to influence the organization of the community at present. These are (1) the influx of the *cachaco* subculture in the 1940s; (2) the exit of the old and important land-owning families from the heyday of the *Zona Bananera;* (3) the spread of mechanized technology and green revolution and the creation of the *"new finca"*; and (4) the creation of INCORA and the available irrigated lands for rental property, which have cemented the new *finca* into the municipality as a permanent element.

These, then, constitute the important elements of the community as I perceive them now. I have not yet located the contractors for the growing of marijuana in the *cachaco vereda,* but suspect them to be found among the former elite. However, this is just a guess, since I have only one lead at the present and it points in that direction.

What emerges from this model is a community differentiated into segments on the basis of subcultural traditions, forms of organization, and control of resources. The four processes mentioned above have created a rapidly changing situation in the lives of my informants. Marijuana may be interpreted as an effort of the *cachaco* peasant to gain a foothold in the community which he has adopted, but which has not yet fully adopted him. The *cachaco* subculture is very much a part of the economic life of the community, but politically, socially, and ritually it remains a subculture apart from the dominant *costeño* group. Ironically, the dominant group today is composed of those leftover from the days of the *Zona Bananera*— the fringes of the dominant group from the old days, since the truly powerful families have disappeared to the cities. The arrival of the new *finca* on the scene creates competition for the traditional elite, or what is left of it, and spells its doom. The new *finca,* both in form and function, bypasses the town completely. It is an urban function pure and simple. With the floundering of the old system of organization, symbolized by the failing fortunes of the old *finca,* the labor class from the banana zone days has adapted in two ways: they either have become *colonos* and invaded the land of former *hacendados* or have migrated to the city and become part of the unskilled industrial worker ranks.

Thus the urban influx of former farm laborers provides the market for marijuana production. The rural influx of *cachaco colonos* provides the production mechanism itself. The marketing mechanism as yet eludes me.

My future plans for activities include: (1) in-depth interviewing of a *costeño* hamlet (either Cauca or San Isidro) and a house survey of the entire hamlet; (2) further study of the *cachaco vereda* La Piedra to fill in the many gaps; (3) a study of selected *tiendas* and stores in the town, after a complete count has been made of the number and variety of these; (4) interviews with old people of the town, who will be asked to identify the names that appear on the church register (the landowning families, the employees, the workers, etc.) as well as the names that appear on the land register from the *alcaldía;* (5) complete listing of the trucks used to transport produce to the city, their owners, and drivers; and (6) comparison of the annual cycles of an old style *finca* and a new style *finca* (Zacapa and Camito, respectively).

13 January 1973

Dear Dr. Kimball:

I think the idea of a midpoint report is excellent. Earlier (3 January of current field notes) I attempted such an assessment, but it is not as extensive as that which you indicated would be ideal. Apparently both of us saw the dawn of 1973 as an appropriate time to assess the progress of the study. I went to Barranquilla the tenth of this month to mail the field notes and found your letter of 2 January, and I have since taken a few days to write a short report that covers some of the ground you outlined.

As you noted in your letter, with a working model of the nature of community organization I can go about the task of specific data collection on a specific problem. I intend to do this by directed interviews (which I will record on index cards for easy handling later). Arrangements were made before I left Majagua to begin these in a coastal subculture hamlet. I intend to initially cover all the families of the hamlet, then return to interview specific ones with whom data collection on cannabis use seems possible, and finally to collect life histories where these seem most useful in view of the other data I collected.

I have left the earlier attempt at assessment of the study in the field notes so you might get an idea of my thinking at the time, together with the earlier letter I wrote to you on 4 January.

I have made a copy of the report for Dr. Carter and included it with the field notes and this letter. Would you forward it to him, together with the field notes?

Paying greater attention to ethnographic detail is the only point you raise that I have not addressed in the report. This I will try to do, particularly for variations in family life in the town, where only recently I have become aware of significant differences in the coastal subcultural group (namely, barrio differences).

Whether I can complete all my plans remains to be seen.

Best wishes,
William L. Partridge

MIDPOINT REPORT

10 January 1973

To: Drs. Kimball and Carter

As a midpoint report, the following will be a summary rather than a discussion of specific data emphasizing patterns known to exist. The report ends with a list of specific items to be worked out in the coming months. The outline form is drawn from headings used by Dr. Kimball in his letter of 2 January 1973.

General Description of Region

Majagua is the *cabecera* or county seat of the *municipio* of Majagua, an area embracing varied terrain and populations. Contained in the *municipio* are vast swamplands and the highest peak in Colombia, and the population is accordingly various. Arawak Indians occupy the snow-rimmed valleys of the sierra, highland immigrants from the mountainous interior occupy the foothills of the sierra, and the lowlands are populated by the coastal mix of Negro, Indian, and Spanish races called the *mestizo*. The *municipio* has around 20,000 inhabitants, about 7,000 of whom live in the *cabecera*. The rural areas of the *municipio* have recently received more migrants than the urban area, but the urban area continues to grow, if only slightly.

Historically, Majagua was the second largest of the complex of banana-railroad towns in the *Zona Bananera*. Its inhabitants are well acquainted with modern industrial forms of exploitation and social organization. With the departure of the United Fruit Company from the area (beginning in the 1930s but not fully completed until 1964) two processes began: first, both elite and labor families migrated to the cities; second, squatters took possession of portions of land abandoned by the fruit company. In the 1940s these processes dovetailed with a third process: highland immigrants moved into the *municipio* and its seat in significant numbers. Thus, many of the merchandising units were taken over from fleeing coastal families by enterprising *cachaco* families. The rural highland migrants merely colonized land that was unattractive (no roads, services, etc.) to the coastal people, i.e., the highland areas.

The town of Majagua has responded to these processes in its recent growth pattern. In the 1880s the town was a cluster of houses (*aldea* or *caserio*) founded by a family from Fundación. Fundación has a long history as an early Spanish settlement on the road from Valledupar to Salamina and has long been a market center. In the past century it was the distribution point for goods shipped from Ciénaga on the coast, across the Ciénaga Grande (a large freshwater lagoon fed by six rivers that flow out of the Sierra Nevada), and up the River Fundación. The town of Fundación faded during the banana days and became the *corregimiento* of Majagua, but with the decline of the banana industry it has regained its former centrality in the region and Majagua has faded in its turn. With the railroad and banana industry Majagua grew, mainly along the railroad line: a new church was built, the town became the seat of the *municipio,* and its residents prospered. The barrios of Loma Linda and El Carmen are products of this period, constructed mainly of adobe, palm thatch, and wood. Today they remain the prominent residential areas. Prosperous families have replaced thatched roofs with tile and tin and mud walls with concrete block. The banana industry faded and left Majagua in this form, about 1940.

Growth slowed after 1940. The barrios Las Nuevas, El Prado, and La Marujita grew up when the highway to Fundación was completed in the 1950s. It brought new life to the little town as trucks rolled out with produce that previously had been shipped by train.

But it was not until the 1960s that a second great change swept the region. The banana cooperative formed in the wake of the United Fruit Company departure also sold out. The townspeople and rural workers had entertained hopes that the banana companies (and the heyday of the 1920s that they all had heard about from their parents) would return. But in 1964 the banana cooperative transferred all efforts to Sevilla, a town to the north, and the remaining United Fruit Company lands were given over to INCORA. INCORA thus became the largest single landowner in the *municipio,* dwarfing the remaining coastal elite both in size and economic resources.

Today the landscape of Majagua is a product of these changes. INCORA rents land to a sizable number of entrepreneurs, many from outside the *municipio,* who with mechanized agricultural technology are quickly taking over the economic life of the *municipio.* Alongside the modern estate (which is the product of INCORA) exists the traditional estate, with its absentee landlord, *capataz* or supervisor, and the crew of wage laborers. It is a system doomed to extinction, but it exists today. The *cachaco* colonists and storekeepers exist as another system entirely, one drawn entirely from their subcultural origins in the interior. They form a tight social and economic unit of peasant-patron, the former scattered in endogamous, highly homogeneous *veredas* made up of dispersed individual family farms, the latter clustered in the town where they operate large stores, pool halls, and bars and run rice and cattle ranches.

In the town the *cachaco* storekeepers form a group apart from the principal families. The latter maintain all political power of the *municipio,* occupy the government posts, dominate the professions, and outnumber *cachaco* representatives on the municipal council eleven to one. The mayor, appointed from Santa Marta, is of the town *crema,* the best families, but many of the other government officials are recruits from families of lesser distinction—former managers and employees of the United Fruit Company rather than land-owning gentry. The gentry is largely gone now; although *haciendas* can still be found in the hinterlands, they are overgrown with weeds and squatters. Pretenders of the same subcultural heritage have taken their place. The police stationed in town are a national institution, but most of the force in Majagua hail from the coast. The only *cachaco* mayor the town has ever known was imposed by military rule in Colombia during the years of Rojas Pinilla; he is as unpopular today as he was in those years in the fifties, in keeping with the federalistic, anti–central government sentiments typical of the coastal subculture.

Majagua today is a center of residence, ritual, entertainment, govern-ment, and everyday commerce for the *costeño* subcultural members, the estate managers, the *tienda* operators, the landless laborers, the marginal peasant day laborer, the professional, the bureaucrat, and the aging survivors of a past full of boom and bust. The town is a tedious and dusty little necessity for the entrepreneur with his modern technology and knowledge. He buys his groceries there, but not much more. It is a challenge to the *cachaco* invaders, a challenge they are meeting by following a centuries-old way of life. But it is only a grisly reminder to the old people that life was once much better, much richer when bananas blanketed the lowlands as if they had been spilled out of a great cornucopia up in the sierra. These people still debate among themselves whether the company will return.

Maps

Maps of the region are in abundance; I have plotted the locations of the major population clusters, the estates, and the networks of transportation, both major and minor (see figure 5.2). Topographic features play a genuine role in the distribution of the subcultural groups. The *cachacos* have clung to their natural habitat, the lower-altitude valleys of the sierra. The *costeños* stick to the lowlands; even though land pressure would seemingly push them into the mountains, few coastal colonists have settled the lower-altitude valleys. A very slight trend toward barrio segregation can be seen in the development of the town plan in that a few new barrios (post-1940) are largely inhabited by *cachaco* immigrants. The older barrios remain enclaves of coastal families. I have constructed a detailed street map of the town showing each business, government office, garage, store, church, funeral home, park, school, etc. This proves useful when overlaid with the schematic drawing of the barrios.

The soils map suggested by Dr. Kimball has eluded me, although I have tried to locate one. The Instituto Geográfico Augustin Codazzi in Bogotá and Santa Marta has such maps for some of the interior departments but not for the coast.

The town of El Retén is the only other town in the *municipio* of Majagua. It is a farming community totally dominated by the influence of residents of the county seat. Buildings, land, and so on are all owned (generally) by either persons or groups in Majagua. Analysis is not yet complete so far as home ownership is concerned, but preliminary analysis indicates that homes in El Retén are frequently owned by landlords in Majagua—more frequently than homes in Majagua are owned by landlords in, say, Fundación or Santa Marta.

Important hamlets include El Bongo, San Isidro, La Colombia, Cauca, Buenas Aires, Sampues, and Teoremina, inhabited by landless day laborers or marginal peasant laborers. Such hamlets are all products of squatters moving in along the roads constructed by the United Fruit Company (except for El Bongo, which is a river port dating from days of commerce on the River Fundación), and date from the 1930s and 1940s. Although

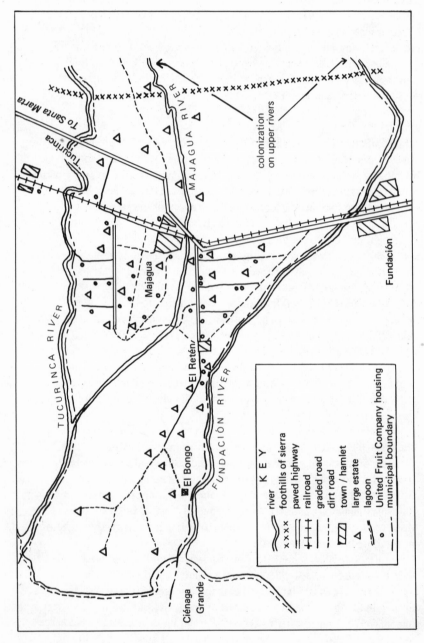

Figure 5.2. The *municipio* of Majagua

KEY

	river
××××	foothills of sierra
	paved highway
+++	railroad
	graded road
	dirt road
▲	town / hamlet
◿	large estate
○	lagoon
▨	United Fruit Company housing
	municipal boundary

TUCURINCA RIVER

MAJAGUA RIVER

FUNDACIÓN RIVER

To Santa Marta

Tucurinca

colonization
on upper rivers

Majagua

El Retén

El Bongo

Ciénaga
Grande

Fundación

today they are established hamlets, then they were *colonos* and *invasores,* fought much the same as INCORA colonists are fought today by the landowners.

Fundación is the important commercial center of the region, the town of Majagua being merely a production and consumption center. Parts for autos, tractors, and trucks, fertilizer, seed, farm tools, and appliances are purchased in Fundación. Santa Marta and Barranquilla are the important destinations of the trucks that roll out of Majagua loaded with rice, cotton, millet, corn, palm oil, and chickens. Of these only cotton is not a local specialty. It comes in from the estates near Valledupar and Aguachica to be ginned in the government-owned IDEMA plant in Majagua. The others are grown on local plantations and shipped to the city by locally owned trucks. Cattle and cattle products are the only other important produce, and these follow the same routes. Cattle account for over half the arable land in the *municipio,* and are the main crop of the traditionally organized *fincas.*

Status Differences

The following list represents categories used by the residents themselves to divide the population. In all cases the differences are not yet clear in my mind. I have indicated where information is lacking. Subcultural affiliation is indicated if relevant to a particular status.

(1) Peasants (almost always *cachaco*)—migrants from rural areas of *municipios* in the interior departments (notably Norte de Santander); extended three-generation family; concentrated in endogamous, homogeneous *veredas* consisting of dispersed individual family farms; mixed agriculture base with manioc and corn as staples; variety of cash cropping including coffee, sugarcane, cannabis, corn, rice, and manioc, all of which (excepting cannabis) are marketed to *cachaco* storekeepers in Majagua; travel to town frequent during growing season, infrequent during dry season; no wage labor reported or observed.

(2) Storekeepers (*cachaco* and *turco* or Arab)—migrants to Majagua from other towns and cities; owners of all town businesses of large scale; Arabs tend to control clothing and hardware stores, *cachacos* control the general stores; both groups also own large tracts of land; Arabs own a large number of trucks used to move produce to the city; family and business ties to other towns of the coast such as Ciénaga, Fundación, Maicao, Barranquilla, and Santa Marta; the *cachaco* peasants buy from and sell to the storekeeper *patróns* and graze cattle for them in the highlands.

(3) Wage laborers (wholly *costeño*)—employed by the job, they live on the edge of, if not in, poverty (20 pesos a day or about $1.00); live in nucleated hamlets colonized in the 1940s along roads of banana estates;

stem family organization (according to sources); frequently occupy row houses abandoned by United Fruit Company; strong evidence of frequent migration to city and other *municipios;* no subsistence or cash crops; work for estate managers cleaning irrigation ditches, clearing and cleaning fields, caring for cattle, running farm machinery; possibility of seasonal migration.

(4) Peasant laborers (wholly *costeño*)—identical to group (3), but they own from one to three hectares of land planted in subsistence crops such as manioc, plantain, and corn; no cash crops.

(5) Estate managers (mixed group)—a significant number are drawn from the town population, but several are immigrants; majority are of *costeño* subculture; live both in town and on *fincas;* travel frequently to cities for interaction with estate owners; run day-to-day operation of the estate, being responsible for all aspects of that operation; well integrated into social and ritual life of town, often having family in the town; frequently called "*patrón*" by workers, they form a minor elite in rural hinterland.

(6) *Tienda* owners (*costeño*)—the large number of *tiendas* in town are primarily *costeño* institutions, but there are a few (I've counted four) *cachaco tiendas;* sell household necessities on a daily basis; very small inventory, ice, soft drinks, cookies, and liquor being major sale items; little studied at present, but their stores are neighborhood gossip centers, drinking sites, and places to relax; always located in the front room of a family house.

(7) Elite (*costeño*)—called "*la crema*" or cream of Majagua, half in jest, they represent old families of the town; few in number, but socially important; links to coastal cities and towns in other *municipios;* formerly land-owning, but not now as economically important; contribute members to two subgroups: (a) professionals, including teachers, doctors, college-trained agriculturalists, and agronomists; frequently these are from similar families of other *municipios,* but just as often they are from local elite (little studied); (b) government employees, such as clerks, secretaries, treasurer, tax collector, and *personero,* all drawn from elite (not studied).

(8) Local government employees—mayor is appointed in Santa Marta but drawn from the elite of the town; judge is a *cachaco* appointed by national government, but secretary is *costeño* and recognized as more influential; municipal council is elected and composed of eleven *costeños* and one *cachaco;* the council chairman is a *costeño* elite; police are part of the national police force, but most come from the coast; police chief is a *cachaco*.

(9) Students—sexes are segregated in schools; girls wear uniforms each

day, identifying which school they attend; boys dress regularly; elite
children complete 11 grades; college students drawn wholly from children
of elite and Arab storekeepers; peasants do not send children to school, but
wage laborers frequently do; *cachaco* storekeepers' children usually work
in store; plaza is center of adolescent life, where parties are held and
invitations given.

(10) National government employees—includes staff of IDEMA, Instituto Colombiano Agricultura (ICA), railroads, etc.; usually much
more wealthy than local people, living in *quinta* or grand houses occupied by Americans during United Fruit Company days; socially and
ritually separated from the town population, although occasionally
buttered-up by special invitations; usually from the interior departments; referred to as *"técnicos"* or *"empleados."*

(11) Landowners of mechanized ("new") estates—live on the estates and direct their day-to-day operation; employ a supervisor and
several workers as well as domestics; origins not well known but
many bear coastal names; most have houses in town or city; little
studied.

(12) Landowners of traditional ("old") estates—live in the cities; daily
operation of *finca* in hands of *capataz* or supervisor who hires and fires,
directs operations, pays salaries, purchases needed supplies, and runs a
commissary for employees and workers; same system of organization as
the banana estate of 1920; running battle with INCORA over efficient use
of the land, since INCORA supports invasions in cases of underproductiv-
ity or inefficient or idle land; little studied.

Inventory of Assembly Patterns

Information here is scanty and uneven. The following is a list of common
assemblies. I have data on those marked with an asterisk (*). The others
represent gaps in my data.

(1) Front Porch Visiting*—family unit and, in the evening, neighbors;
costeño pattern in the old and new barrios.

(2) Kitchen Activity—family unit, differences expected between the
barrios and between *costeños* and *cachacos*.

(3) Shopping and Market Going*—members of family unit shop before
meals for individual items needed.

(4) Plaza Promenade*—young people of town; courting as well as
sex-segregated gossiping; "cocacolas" or younger boys tease and taunt the
older ones.

(5) Funerals*—general pattern known, participants known in detail for
only one though four have been observed; *costeño*.

(6) Wake*—detailed data on *cachaco* wake, none on *costeño,* which occurs on the ninth day and on the one-year anniversary of death.

(7) Baptism*—data on only one.

(8) Special Masses*—data on only one.

(9) Regular Mass—no data.

(10) Fiesta Day Mass—no data.

(11) Fiesta Day Drinking among Males*—good data on sites, participants, choice of liquor, conversation, subcultural segregation.

(12) Post-Bargaining Celebration*—good data on ritual sequence, choice of site, subcultural segregation.

(13) Travel to Town*—data on *cachaco* interaction, modes of transportation, frequency, purpose, activities, contacts in the town.

(14) Private Parties and Dances*—some data on private parties among *costeño* and *cachaco* subcultures.

(15) Cockfights*—good data on assembly pattern, activity, participants, frequency, betting, drinking, organization.

(16) Protestant Church Activity—no data.

(17) *Costeño* Male Work Group—data incomplete.

(18) *Cachaco* Family Work Group—some data but on only one example.

(19) Schools—indirect observation only.

(20) Work Groups on New *Finca*—data spotty and random.

(21) Work Groups on Old *Finca*—data spotty and random.

(22) Everyday Assembly at *Tienda*—some data, but many gaps on frequency, participants, activity, etc.

(23) Seasonal Migration of Farm Labor—no data.

(24) Special Fiesta Activity*—data on Feast of Immaculate Conception, Christmas, New Year's; others expected to be important include 20 January, 3–7 March (*Carnaval*), 20 July (Independence), and 8 August (Battle of Boyacá).

In summary, assembly patterns are only superficially known at present. Significant gaps in the areas of church and work group organization are particularly serious. Schools, family, market, bars, travel, fiestas, cockfights, funerals, wakes, baptism, and business negotiations are variously known, but data are not complete for any one of these. No marriages have been observed.

Kinds of Agricultural Activity

Agricultural practices correspond to the two subcultural and regional divisions in the community. The *cachacos* live in a region greatly affected by seasonal variation in rainfall and their activities are markedly different from other community members', although the crops are basically the same. The *costeños* occupy the lowlands where the United Fruit Company irrigation system is still in operation under the supervision of INCORA. Activity in the lowlands follows a different schedule, with several variations. The following is a listing in summary fashion by subcultural and regional area.

(1) Lower-altitude valleys of sierra (*cachaco*)—peasant extended families work the land, children being a major resource for this purpose. Holdings range from 50 to 200 hectares. Farming is mixed: everyone grows subsistence crops such as corn, manioc, and plantain for family use; some grow cash crops such as rice, coffee, cattle, cannabis, and sugarcane; some sell subsistence crops, particularly corn, in town. The cycle of cropping runs from March or April (beginning of the rains) to November (beginning of the dry season), with generally one or sometimes two (depending upon location) crops each year. Many gaps exist in the scheduling, the work groups used, the technology, etc.

(2) Lowland irrigated land (*costeño*)—devoted to three kinds of agricultural activity:

(*a*) peasant subsistence plots, belonging to squatters owning from one to three hectares of land, usually planted in subsistence crops such as manioc, corn, and plantain for family use. No cash crops have been observed. Cycle unknown at present. Work group expected to be the family. Males work as wage laborers on larger lowland estates.

(*b*) old style *fincas,* which are usually devoted to cattle. Manager lives in town or on estate, owner lives in city; few workers. Cycle is unknown at present, as are the organization of work and participants.

(*c*) new style *fincas,* characterized by mechanized farming. Owner lives on estates, land can be rented from INCORA, minimum of labor used. Cropping cycle runs from January or February to June or July, or the "first semester." A second crop runs from June or July to January or February, or the "second semester." Fields lie fallow for one year after three semesters of planting and harvesting. Significant labor is required for cleaning and maintenance of irrigation canals; otherwise all activity is mechanized and only five to six laborers are needed. Cash crops that conform to the "three semesters of planting and one year of rest" cycle are rice, millet, sugarcane. Crops that are "permanent" and do not conform to this cycle are pasture and African oil palm. Significant gaps exist in area of marketing and transportation of produce; planting, harvesting, and processing of palm products; irrigation arrangements with INCORA; and organization of work and participants for cleaning canals. An important further gap is the number of renters (as opposed to owners) of these estates.

Historical Materials

I am accumulating historic documentation at a satisfactory rate. At this point I feel that I know the early history of the region well, including the original population distribution, the effect of the United Fruit Company, the coming of the railroad and paved highway, the regional history, and important events. Still, I need more data on the origin of the town of Majagua, although church records are helpful to an extent. Likewise, I want further information on the founding families, the original owners of banana estates in particular. At present I have data on only one of these formerly all-powerful, prestigious families. A search of the newspapers in Santa Marta as well as interviews with selected older persons in the town should provide the information I need. The sequence of events is rather well known, and further investigation of the United Fruit Company is probably unwarranted.

Working Model

The pattern that emerges from this summary is anticipated in my 3 January assessment. There I constructed a working ''model'' of the interconnections among various elements of the community. The model is a product of consideration of the following factors: regional divisions; appearance and disappearance of the United Fruit Company; ruination of large, old family holdings and breakup of these units; urban migration to coastal cities; colonization by interior peasant peoples; and creation of INCORA in the 1960s.

The result of these factors is the present organization of the *municipio* and town. The two can very definitely be seen to be tightly interconnected, the fortunes of the hinterland directly affecting the composition of the town.

From the working model I conclude that the following elements warrant in-depth, detailed examination (intensive observation, directed interviews conducted among participants, life history collection):

(1) The coastal subculture hamlet—wage laborers, marginal peasants (consumers of cannabis).

(2) The *cachaco* subculture *vereda*—true peasants (growers of cannabis).

(3) The coastal subculture *tienda* owners—petty merchants (no known relation to cannabis).

(4) The mixed group of estate managers—new and old style *fincas* (no known relation to cannabis).

(5) The old people of the coastal subculture—history of families that were once powerful (suspected relation to the marketing of cannabis).

(6) The coastal subculture professionals—descendants of formerly powerful families now slipping in economic, but not social, status (suspected consumers and marketers of cannabis).

These six points, then, constitute my work plan for the coming months. Arrangements have already been made (work to begin 20 January) for the directed interviews and intensive observations among the coastal subculture hamlet residents (1). These will be carried out in the *vereda* of Teoremina (hamlet named Cauca) with the assistance of two contacts in the *vereda*. Likewise, arrangements have been made (but a specific date not yet set) for the work on the *tienda* owners (3) with the assistance of two store owners in the town.

I plan several weeks of directed and informal interviewing and observation in the hamlets and *veredas*. Life histories of selected persons will be sought only after the interviews are completed.

I plan to conduct a complete survey of all *tiendas* to assess their number and variety, to interview the owners of selected *tiendas* considered representative, to conduct an in-depth observation of at least two days of activity in several different *tiendas*, and to complete a listing of typical inventory of the neighborhood *tienda*. The in-depth observation will be accomplished by sitting in the store for two days and making notes on all activity that occurs.

Among the old people of the coastal subculture I plan directed interviews and life histories if they are willing. I also plan to interview coastal subculture professionals. Information on cannabis will be sought only after the interviews have been completed. It is expected that I will receive some information in the processes of interviewing, but the bulk will be collected by returning to the hamlet or *vereda* at a later date after arrangements have been made with the residents for specific interviews on this topic. I do not intend to participate in the cannabis-using rituals, but only to collect information about them. In the event that I am invited to participate I will do so.

Life histories will be sought from persons with more than ten years of experience with cannabis, as well as from persons fitting a typical sociocultural profile (as determined from interviews, observation, and general knowledge of the larger community, migration patterns, work and subsistence activities, family organization, etc.).

If I may make an assessment of my progress thus far, I believe that, through careful delineation of the variations in status, activity, subcultural affiliation, history, and economic alliances found in the community of Majagua, I have constructed a controlled data collection situation. This has been the objective as indicated by Dr. Kimball in his letter of 2 January 1973. Thus, information gained from informants can be accurately placed in the ongoing life of the community. Efforts to interpret the significance of this information can then be made against the background of the social and cultural ecology of community structure and organization. I anticipate that the interview data will be richly rewarding in this context.

24 January 1973

Dear Bill:

Your last batch of notes and summation arrived a few days ago. Either the material you are getting seems richer or else the context within which I can now place what you are recording has become somewhat clearer. In any event the notes and the summary both look good. I think you are now on the trail of the social function of cannabis, which will show it to be an artifact of a social process, much as Scotch drinking is for a particular social group. You are on the way to liberating its use from the purely physiological, idiosyncratic, and individualistic chains in which the thinking about it has been throttled. You are about to anthropologize the behavior as one item making up a complex pattern—or so it seems, and so our experience with behavior would lead us to believe.

The other items in this letter will be mostly helpful hints, since at this time you seem to have the larger picture in mind and to know what you need to do to make it clear.

You can take an a priori position that the family and household are primary social groupings and organizations of social space. Hence, pay close attention to getting the variations in these among the classes and the subcultural groups, because they should reflect the heritage of the past as well as the distinctive aspects that lead to understanding the present and predicting the future. When placed in context of type of activities (economic, religious, etc.), your knowledge about the primary social groupings, together with age and sex divisions, should give you the forms of organization that each subgroup learns and may reveal why cooperation across subgroups is either possible or difficult. This naturally leads then to the distinctive patterns of reciprocity associated with activities and with subgroups, and perhaps to why certain kinds of activity such as drug use can be penetrated easily or with difficulty. How about those old men beggars—are they derelicts? What drugs do they use?

Here are two possible techniques. First, follow some person through his day and record the variety of contacts, forms of behavior, etc. You have already done this in effect, but not with the specific purpose of seeing the social realm of the daily round. Second, select a few spots and check them at certain time intervals to see who the participants are at each time period.

On varieties of types of shopkeeping: how does a person get involved in such activity? What is the source of his customers—locality, relatives? What happens to a business when the owner and operator dies? Does it go to an heir, his wife? What credits come from where? What are the roles of the people such as salesman, etc., who distribute goods to such centers? How is all this related to family and social class? What kind of credits are given and how are they repaid?

Migration—you have the types and sequence of migration in, but only that for upper-group outmigration. What about other groups? Do excess or wandering members of family go elsewhere for work, to settle, etc.? Do you have the displacement as you want it?

The church bell is a signal for all types of events. Go to the sexton and find out when he rings and under what circumstances: funerals or other rites of passage, mass, hours of day, etc.

Type of relationships—sexual teasing is permitted across age levels, but when else is teasing used? When besides New Year's do the clients come to the patron—any reciprocation?

It seems to me you have an implicit theory of change, of dissolution and replacement related to economic activity affecting technology, migration, social class, etc.

At some point soon now you need to get away for a few days and have a vacation. When you come back you will find yourself in a new relationship with people and at a deeper level of involvement and access. It looks like you have acquired some people who are trying to help you understand what it is all about. That is good.

Two last items. Your book is out, but Zandy Moore (who praises it) is the only one in Gainesville who has a copy. If you have not done so you need to write to your publisher and give him a list of all the people who should receive complimentary copies; also ask why free copies were not sent, as with other books in the Spindler series. Next, your "Annual Review of Anthropology" arrived with the wrapping three-fourths off. I rescued—or appropriated—it from the mail room. What shall I do with it? (I'll be happy to keep it.)

Best wishes,
Solon Kimball

P.S. Work out reciprocity chart(s) for all major areas of activity—the actors, situation, manner of obligation accrual and discharge, etc. The comparative study of this may hold *the* key to entire system. On death, interview all functionaries, the undertaker, grave diggers, priests, etc., to get variations. You may also find a *key* here to reciprocity and family and age and sex and status.

There's a mild student stirring in the department among new graduates, this time demanding (?) a stronger program in applied anthropology—will wonders never cease?

Kimball's letter written in response to Partridge's report reflects his theoretical position. The model of community organization outlined by Partridge resolved Kimball's earlier complaint that it was impossible for him to offer any effective advice since he lacked a sense of the whole. Now that the pattern of contrasting rural *cachaco* and *costeño* subcultures (with Majagua as the point of fusion and connection between them and to the outside) had emerged, the major remaining ethnographic problem was one of filling in the detail. Kimball's questions about shopkeepers, which alerted Partridge to what may be a significant aspect of the detail, stemmed from his own fieldwork in Ireland. So did the items about the tolling of the church bells and request for information about beggars. But Kimball raised the questions for another purpose. There is always the danger that the deeper the fieldworker becomes immersed in the new culture, the easier it is for items such as these to escape his conscious attention and become part of the accepted landscape. The insistence upon attention to detail, even when there is no apparent significance, has always been the precept of the natural scientist. From careful observation have come such principles as those of evolution and natural selection, the dynamics of valley glaciation, and the meaning of the dancing of bees.

The letter also reflects the nature of Kimball's continuing concern with the varied and specific structuring of groups as revealed through reciprocal exchanges. Partridge's description of the custom of visiting patrons on New Year's prompted Kimball's suggestion to seek out all other occasions of a similar nature. The postscript on the significance of reciprocity was added as a reminder to Partridge, who had received the admonition frequently as a student and had utilized the concept in his earlier analysis of hippie culture.

Other portions of the letter referred to data collection procedures. The reference to the occurrence of sexual teasing was intended not only to alert Partridge to look for additional detail but to remind him of a basic anthropological principle, namely, the importance of context. The suggestion about accompanying an informant through his daily round and of systematically checking out gatherings in time and place were based on implicit theoretical considerations of time and space in social behavior. These unstated aspects of Kimball's letter were meaningful to Partridge because of the conceptual understanding they had established over their long period of working together.

In his letter Kimball suggests to Partridge that he take a short vacation and also comments favorably on the efforts of some of his informants to explain how the society works. Both points merit some comment.

The accumulated wisdom of field research holds that a vacation is not only salutary for the researcher but beneficial for those being studied as well. Many an anthropologist returning from a few weeks or months in the boondocks will attest that what initially appeared to be an exotic crudity now takes on the warm glow of a familiar haven. The transformation is truly one of perspective, because the same effects occur among those who have chosen the quiet towns of mid-America as the locus of their research. But the transformation is a double one, for the return to the place of study takes on something of a homecoming.

There seems to be an analogous process at work among those who have been the willing or unwilling subjects of study. Some of the diffidence, hostility, or reserve that they have shown toward their resident anthropologist becomes modified during his absence. Upon his return there is often the desire to recount what has happened during his absence; areas of behavior that seemed off limits before now become more open to discussion or observation (Berreman 1962). Furthermore, subsequent absences seem to intensify the process of deeper incorporation.

Kimball's cryptic reference to "some people who are trying to help you understand what it is all about" deserves some comment. A number of anthropologists have reported encountering one or more individuals who have helped immensely in interpreting the social behavior of their group. Warner gives such tribute to Mahkarolla among the Murngin; Nancy Lurie found John C. among the Winnebago; Anthony Forge and Twasmung in New Guinea worked out the details of the social structure together. In Majagua, José Martinez and Jorge Durán proved to be competent guides to the social system. Among these and all other individuals who have been so indispensable there has been a common characteristic: they have all had some cross-cultural experience that has had an impact on their lives. Although we can only speculate on the intellectual processes, it seems that the contrasts that they have observed have helped them to see the routines of their own societies in deeper perspective; they have begun to ponder the meaning of the differences. When a like-minded stranger comes along they have an opportunity to communicate insights that are of little interest or unintelligible to their compatriots. This is why they become such valuable informants.

3 February 1973

Dear Dr. Kimball:

Thank you for your letter and excellent suggestions. In the coming months I will be working to implement them.

January has flown by. I have all but completed the formal interviews in the coastal subcultural hamlets that I mentioned in my last letter. The results thus far are striking in that perhaps only 1 percent of the residents of the hamlet were born in the *municipio*. They make up a highly mobile working lower class with a work history stretching across the entire coastal geography (including some five departments ranging from the Venezuelan border to Panama). I am reminded of Whitten's (Jr.) report on the coastal Negro of Ecuador.

In addition, I have discovered that my "sketch" of status differences must be modified. The coastal subculture hamlet is a more complex societal organism than I had thought. Thus, in addition to the day-wage laborer and marginal peasant (which I already knew about) I've discovered that a distinction is made between these and individuals known simply as *"empleados"* of such-and-such a *finca* or so-and-so the *patrón*. The individuals have relatively secure positions in the economic picture, characterized by long-standing relationships with a patron, use of several hectares to plant for subsistence purposes, and usually a multitude of livestock. They play the role of client to the patron or landowner in the city, and the role of patron to the wage laborers. They rank lower on the scale than a *capataz* or supervisor who lives in town and runs a huge *hacienda*, and they frequently are drawn from outside the *municipio*.

I also managed to tie down the credit-obtaining and credit-giving mechanism. While tracing shopping patterns and asking questions about these I found that two systems are in operation for the coastal subculture: (1) a new employee or worker is given credit at the *hacienda* commissary as part of the hiring contract, or (2) the wage laborer or employee is "sponsored" by another who has credit in the stores in town, the latter accepting responsibility for his bills for several months until the former proves his ability to make regular payments on the balance, at which time he is granted credit of his own. The *empleados* play this role of patron-sponsor for the wage laborers in the coastal subculture hamlet; the patron of the *empleado* plays it for the newly settled *empleado*.

During February I hope to finish off the coastal subculture hamlet and move on to the highland neighborhood. The first week of March is the *Carnaval* celebration, and I would like to have the initial interviews completed by then so I can watch the interaction during this all-important festival through informed eyes.

Probing has produced several important contacts for interviews about marijuana use and cultivation. Several of these are located in the coastal subculture hamlet and several in the cities and towns of the region. I shall devote the remainder of March to tracing them down and by April I hope to have initial data on cannabis use.

My younger brother is coming down here in a few days for a visit. This will provide me with the excuse to take the vacation you mentioned. In showing him around I will also have the chance to reexamine some earlier impressions—through his eyes—and steal some of his observations as well.

Having discovered through the interviews the tremendous range of geographic mobility here on the coast I will necessarily have to readjust my focus. I suspected it before, as is indicated by the dotted lines on my chart of the "model" in the last set of notes, but only now do I have firm evidence of it (i.e., work histories of the residents of the *vereda* Teoremina). Note also that the event analysis I conducted of the two *cursos* corresponds to the two rural *veredas* where I am conducting interviews (Cauca and La Piedra). With the interview data I hope to reanalyze the data collected at that time and see if anything of significance comes out.

I will proceed to an in-depth analysis of family forms after the interviews are completed. The interviews will of course play a role in putting together the patterns of family forms.

Your suggestion regarding reciprocity charts is a valuable one. I will try this during the coming month, since I already have enough data to make a start. I will modify them as time passes and more information comes in.

Finally, in response to some of your specific questions, I want to mention how helpful this exchange of letters is to my perception of significant data. For example, you asked where else sexual teasing is permitted (besides across age levels). Until you raised that question I was unaware that I had seen it elsewhere, namely among drinking males and the women who sell vegetables, soups, and fritters at the market. It also occurs across class lines—*patrón* to females of client's household (laundry women, cooks, etc.). There is also an elaborate joking relationship established among classes during the *Carnaval* celebrations. The young people from the poorer barrios form groups to support and advertise their candidate for *Carnaval* queen. During the early evening hours they come to the plaza homes (those of the *patróns*, storekeepers, and elite) singing the song of the cayman or crocodile, the symbol of *Carnaval*. On 20 January they carry a *papier-mâché* and wood replica of a cayman and dance beside it to drums and rasps. They all sing the chorus together, and then the song leader steps out (often with the words written on a sheet of paper) and sings the verse alone. These verses are invented each *Carnaval,* and are improvised as the festival goes on, to tease and joke about the important figures of the town. Thus, they come to the mayor's house and sing several verses in which they insert his name. He laughs and goes along with the joke, and the dancing line proceeds to the next house to ridicule that important family. Likewise, on another occasion the dancers and their candidates for queen go from house to house singing a mock mass. Men dress as women and women dress as men. The lead singer wears a rosary constructed of donkey feces (which come in neatly rounded balls anyway). The assembly replies "Amen" to the teasing verses chanted by the singer; and they sing the cayman song as they come, only now holding lighted candles instead of the effigy.

Thus, your questions set off a chain reaction in my mind and I begin to see things I have noted but not yet fitted into the model. Needless to say, I am quite grateful for your suggestions and questions.

More later.

Best wishes,
William L. Partridge

P.S. I am discovering that the cockfight is probably one of the more important ritual events. Several *empleados* and estate managers have told me of meeting their patrons or landowners for whom they work at these events. And when one examines the composition of the assembly three groups predominate: the patrons who sit in the front row and are addressed as *"doctor"*; the estate managers who own, train, and fight cocks (often the cocks of the patron); and adolescents and young adults from the town who drink, raise hell, and bet. Significant groups not represented are the storekeepers, the *cachaco* peasant, and the town elite. Thus, one is tempted to conclude that the cockfight is an important mechanism in the maintenance of the patron-client relationship in the realm of estate management. Here is a place (and the only one I have found so far) where both owners and workers congregate and mix.

6. The Search for Cannabis

SINCE mid-August, when Partridge informed the mayor and several key informants of his interest in cannabis, he had collected little useful information regarding its cultivation, distribution, and use. In part this long period of silence about cannabis was a product of the warnings contained in Kimball's and Carter's first communications with Partridge in the field, warnings that advised against pushing for information too rapidly. Equally significant, however, was the reaction of informants to Partridge's initial inquiries. Rumor and hearsay are not evidence, although they are valuable indicators of social dynamics in a community. Responses to his initial inquiries were invariably couched in denial of any firsthand knowledge of or participation in cannabis-related activity. Lastly, the long period of silence was a product of Partridge's own ignorance regarding the life of the community. Information—even hearsay—can be followed up and investigated when one knows where to look, whom to approach, and how to phrase a question in the local vernacular. In mid-August and on through November Partridge was simply unable to pursue information about cannabis because he did not yet understand the nature of the community in which potential informants lived.

Of these three explanations for the lack of information on cannabis up to January 1973, perhaps the first two are easiest to understand. But it is the last reason that holds most interest for us and for this analysis, because it is most profoundly related to the collection of data on a specific topic in a community context.

The structure of community life is not merely the setting in which some scientific hypothesis can be tested. It also includes the processes that account for the intricate intermeshing of groups as individuals engage in the cyclical events of life. Thus, factual information about any aspect of behavior must derive its significance from within the social and cultural process that produces it. Consider for a moment the relationship between cannabis smoking and geographical migration. Scientists have noted that among prison inmates studied these two variables are correlated, that they evidence covariance that can be clearly demonstrated by simple statistical operations (Ardila Rodríguez

1965). Presumably, other scientists might investigate causal relationships that account for this covariance: they might seek explanations of geographical migration in the effects of cannabis on neurological functioning, upon economic motivation, upon changes in social group membership, and the like. But the perceptive reader will have already noticed that this procedure assumes that the statistical correlation expresses significance and may properly be considered "data" from which a testable hypothesis can be constructed. We have a different perspective: the correlation is meaningless; it is essentially an example of what C. Wright Mills called "abstracted empiricism," or the property of statistical measures to reorder data in ways that do not reflect the natural world.

Establishing correlation among variables is a key scientific operation, however, when those variables are selected by systematic observation of naturally occurring phenomena. It becomes a doubtful scientific procedure only when variables are selected by the measures used, rather than from their observed association in nature. Migratory life histories are easily collected, especially from prison inmates; thus, they can be conveniently examined for correlation with cannabis use. Moreover, a strong correlation between a variable such as crime and cannabis use can be found, using a prison inmate population. This is what is meant by measures determining choice of variables. The prison population is highly likely to exhibit a correlation between *any* variable and migration or an action defined as a crime. If the sampling procedure, the heart of the measurement process, leads the scientist to study crime in prisons and migration in migratory populations, then the results will be trivial in the extreme.

Correlation among variables is important scientifically only when the sampling procedure is grounded in natural, social, and cultural reality, the ongoing processes of social life that give rise to the variables in the first place. When we are concerned with distributional problems we can ask, for example, whether a migratory life history is characteristic of cannabis smokers in a natural community. Is the correlation applicable to all or only some of the community members? If the correlation is typical of only some of the members, we can try to identify the social processes in which they engage that are related to cannabis smoking. Are these same processes present among other members of the community who do not smoke cannabis? If the answer to the last question is *yes,* then we have focused on the wrong social processes. If the answer is *no,* then we may have discovered significant data. But when a population is being statistically sorted, it is only in the context of community that a trait acquires meaning.

On 31 December 1972 Partridge attended a New Year's Eve celebration at Jorge's home. In the course of the evening several of Jorge's "clients," the highland peasants with whom he traded, for whom he had signed notes on loans, and for whose children he had stood as godparent, paid the traditional New Year's Eve visit to the home of their *patrón*. Jorge took the occasion to introduce Partridge to an older peasant named Escorcia and told the farmer of Partridge's interest in cannabis. At Jorge's encouragement, Escorcia promised to assist Partridge in gathering data on the subject.

Following this meeting Partridge did not see Escorcia for several weeks. His conversations with Escorcia later in January, which are reported in the field notes, continued in much the same vein as earlier attempts to gather information. Informants continued to view Partridge as a buyer of cannabis, and to propose elaborate plans for growing a crop and transporting it to the United States.

The situation changed on 22 January 1973 when Escorcia journeyed from his home in the foothills of the sierra to announce to Partridge his willingness to cooperate in gathering data on cannabis. Escorcia was a commercial cultivator of cannabis, planting each year several hectares of the crop and marketing it through middlemen in the lowland towns of Majagua or Fundación. He agreed to teach Partridge how to grow cannabis in this manner. He did not really understand what exactly Partridge wanted and no doubt held ideas roughly similar to the then popular notion that Partridge was a buyer. He agreed to cooperate for two reasons: first, he had been requested to do so by a man he respected and trusted, his *patrón*, Jorge; second, Partridge was willing to pay a nominal fee for the information. With the passage of time Partridge and Escorcia grew to be friends and share a mutual interest in the project, which added an even greater incentive.

Almost six months had elapsed since Partridge made his first inquiries, with few results, about cannabis, but now the flow of systematic, firsthand information began to increase. Partridge received visits and instructions from Escorcia throughout January, February, and the remainder of the dry season. In March the first batch of seeds was planted and by then Partridge was paying frequent visits to Escorcia's farm in the highlands. Knowledge of Partridge's activities spread, of course, to other people in the community, and it was soon apparent that Partridge had been accepted by a portion of the highland growers. Informants who had previously contributed only rumors, tentative promises of cooperation, and proposals for selling cannabis now changed their view of the foreigner. Data became easier to collect as the people of the community tried to find out more about him. Meanwhile, the normal data collection activities in other areas continued; and when an interview or an introduction was requested, the people of the community were cooperative.

There is a good reason for the increased flow of data at this time. Partridge had entered another stage in the fieldwork process, one we shall call the stage of sponsorship. This stage illustrates an important general point first developed in chapter 3 where we described the involvement in community life brought on by expanding obligations of reciprocity. The stage of sponsorship is significantly different, however, even though it is based on the same principle of reciprocity between a fieldworker and his informants.

Fieldwork is much more than the mere accumulation of data; at the most profound level fieldwork requires incorporation into a social structure. As the stranger progresses through a series of stages he is given access to more and more information about the lives of his informants. But access to the private world of esoteric or sensitive information is not granted to strangers, nor even fully disclosed to those who merely reside within the geographical boundaries of the community. Admission to the private lives of informants is granted only to those who become incorporated inside the social boundaries of the community and who acquire a status and role by structure and definition. When the outsider becomes insider he can be controlled and manipulated according to native expectations, native rules, and native understandings of the social situation. Such a position opens the doors to the inner workings of community. Partridge at this stage became a virtual member of the community; others could now judge his behavior on a familiar basis and sanction and control it according to familiar standards of conduct. In short, the community could now observe Partridge and judge how well or how badly he behaved with the new information he possessed, how closely he would guard it and keep it from outsiders. Partridge was fully aware that the observer was being observed, and during the months of April, May, June, and July he was careful to discuss cannabis with only the few trusted informants who shared the knowledge of cannabis production, distribution, and consumption in the community. By establishing his trustworthiness Partridge gained access to the entire field of social relations related to cannabis in Majagua.

But this access was predicated upon successful incorporation into the social structure. As other anthropologists have noted, incorporation is facilitated by a very special type of individual who becomes crucial in the anthropologist's field career. It is an individual who for some period in the past has lived apart from his community or who has had contacts with the outside not available to others. Such an informant views the world differently than his fellows. He has developed a degree of detachment and objectivity and responds to the anthropologist's questions, for he too has wondered about the order and the variation of the world in which he lives. He is interested in the questions to which the anthropologists seek answers, and in the anthropologist who stimulates him to think about them. Jorge was such an informant, and he provided the means of incorporation into the social structure which made Partridge's passage to the stage of sponsorship possible. Casagrande (1960) and Warner (1964) have documented the special kind of relationship that evolves among the anthropologist and such informants. Our interest here, however, is not in the relationship itself but in the manner in which it was achieved and implemented.

Incorporation into the social structure, which we called sponsorship, entailed establishing an appropriate role for Partridge to play. This Jorge provided in the traditional and socially appropriate Latin patron-client relationship. Jorge accepted Partridge as a client, receiving in exchange the considerable prestige that close friendship with the foreigner brought (not an uncommon experience among anthropologists or other social scientists). In reciprocation he sponsored Partridge in the network of cannabis cultivators by introducing him to Señor Escorcia and by "requesting" Escorcia to assist Partridge with his endeavors. Of necessity Partridge came to play his new role in the social structure very much like a Colombian in a similar position would have played it. Partridge now became Escorcia's sponsor. This was the only way in which Escorcia could deal with Partridge, and it was a ready-made role into which Partridge stepped by virtue of his incorporation into the structure. For what has been called a patron-client relationship in Latin America is in reality a series of relationships, a network of obligations in which a man stands as patron to those below him in the structure and as client to those above him. The successful Latin learns that his obligations are defined in these terms by his position in a fluctuating and shifting series of patron-client ties. He assists his dependents and is assisted by his benefactors. The new position in the structure opens an entirely new stage of the fieldwork process. Now Partridge could unravel the entire production-distribution-consumption cycle by utilizing his own personal network as well as those of other participants in the system.

Contact with the highland growers led to his introduction to distributors in the lowland towns, and these in turn led to interviews and visits with consumers. He had met some of these individuals previously, during earlier months of data collection on other topics. As the research progressed, it became apparent that Partridge had collected a wealth of valuable information on cannabis without knowing it. He had studied the work crews of the large estates; recorded the information on the yearly economic cycle; observed the progression of the ceremonial calendar. He had studied the composition of social groupings in bars, stores, and poolrooms; investigated the structure of the various production units that made up the community; and examined the composition of households, hamlets, and town neighborhoods. The new data on cannabis became meaningful in these contexts, and successive interviews added to the emerging picture.

But these consequences anticipate the content of this chapter. Although the pattern began to emerge in the months of May and June, it was not apparent to Partridge earlier in January when he made the first breakthrough. This is where we now begin, with the progression of events that eventually led to an understanding of the role of cannabis in community life.

14 January 1973

I broached the subject of marijuana with Ardila in the late evening (9:00 is late for him). At first he perceived an opportunity to get involved in a good business deal. He discussed the need for caution, and said he could help me locate a "*tipo serio*" (serious person) to do the growing. I explained several times over that I did not want to buy any, but to ask some questions of some *viejos* (old ones) who knew a lot about it. He continued to stress the need for finding someone who "does not talk when he is drunk." He warned me against Jorge, saying that he talked a lot when he was drunk. The best plan, he said, would be to find a spot to plant a hectare in marijuana surrounded by *puro monte* or scrub and weeds. In this fashion the plot would be hidden from view on all sides. The path used to get to the plot could be covered with cut brush. He advised the same concealment procedure for making an airstrip to land a plane to pick it up (!).

He said he had a friend in Valledupar, an Antioqueño, who had been in this business for several years. He grows and sells it. He said this man could help me get information. I said that this was important, since I suspected that there were at least two different varieties of the plant, one good and one bad. I would have to talk with several different people about this to find out which was which. I emphasized the need to talk with old people who used or grew the plant. He understood and said he would help me find some of these.

He said his friend in Valledupar used beans to conceal the marijuana when he harvested it. He would grow a field of beans and pack the marijuana in the sacks of beans, tie them on a burro, and walk into town with no one being the wiser. (He also told the story of a friend in Antioquia who had brewed moonshine *aguardiente* and brought it into town in bamboo cut near the river. He made several trips and then later used the bamboo for building a house—no one suspected him.)

15 January 1973

I showed Ardila the letter about cannabis from the Instituto. He was very much impressed and said he would work on this and would help me. He doesn't know anything himself, but he knows everyone in town and can tell me who is among the users.

[By 15 January Partridge had become anxious about the lack of information on cannabis and he began once again to bring up the subject with a few trusted informants. Ardila was one of these who had provided useful information on other topics but who contributed little to the research effort because of his response to Partridge's interest in cannabis. If such reaction continued, Partridge suspected that he would gain very little information on cannabis.]

22 January 1973

Señor Escorcia came to visit this afternoon at about 6:00. He had spoken
to me earlier (on New Year's Eve) about marijuana and we had agreed to
talk later. I asked him first if there were different types of marijuana. He
replied there were three: *mona* is the strongest, *negra* is the weakest, and
rella is in between. He said they all come from the same plant—it is a
matter of when and what part of the plant you harvest. I told him I was very
much interested in his teaching me how to grow the plant. He said he
would, but that we would have to find the seed now, because if we waited
until April it will be very expensive. In April, when everyone wants to
plant it, a pound of seeds sells for about 500 pesos. He said he could get it
from the *cachaco* growers. He told me about one *cachaco* who planted 3
hectares and sold it for 3 million pesos in Fundación: "Brought it down on
a burro and came back with 3 million," as he put it. This *cachaco* lives
"*bien arriba,*" almost to the Indians, said Escorcia. Any of those
cachacos who have a lot of money, he said, are cultivators of marijuana. I
explained to him that I did not want to engage in the marijuana trade but
that I was interested in learning about the plant, customs, etc. I suggested
that we plant 20 plants so that he could teach me how to grow it. And he
said this was okay, but it was not the way it was done. Usually, he said,
those that grow it plant three or four hectares. I said I had no use for this
much. Okay, he said, we will plant just a little, but it is usually safer to
plant a lot. The reason is, according to Escorcia, if the police find out you
have a little they will put you in jail. And the person who only plants a little
usually doesn't have the money to get a lawyer and get out. But the person
who plants a crop of three or four hectares can pay off the police, because
he has a client who will advance the money. I told him that we need not
fear the police because I had permission to do this, so we agreed on 20
plants. Escorcia said he would find the seed now. I asked him if he smoked
and he replied that he did not. He doesn't like to because "it affects the
brain." He thinks that the plant makes one go crazy. I told him of my
desire to interview some experienced users, and he said he could help me to
find some. He offered to bring them to my house to be interviewed, but I
suggested that I visit their homes in his company. That is better, he said. I
suggested the month of March for this interviewing. We parted after I
found out where he lived. This is where we will plant in April.

[From the conversation recorded above it is apparent that Escorcia still
had not discovered to his own satisfaction what it was Partridge was doing.
He too perceived the possibility of a good business deal. But he was willing
to let Partridge negate that possibility while continuing to cooperate.]

13 February 1973

I visited Señor Escorcia today. He is ready to plant the marijuana crop
we discussed some time back, so I rode up to the highlands, to see the site
and firm up the deal. I gave him 100 pesos and said we needed to talk in
Majagua later on about how much I was going to contribute to his operation. He said he needed a little money while he was preparing the land,
getting the seed, etc. He would come to town Sunday and discuss it with
me. We again discussed how much was to be planted. I repeated that I
wanted no more than 20 plants and that my purpose was to study the
growing process, not to sell. He replied that this was not business—if he
was to get arrested it might as well be for a ton as for 20 plants. I agreed
that it was unusual, but repeated that I had no use for a lot. He suggested
that we plant a hectare or more and sell it in Majagua. I told him that if he
wanted to plant more than the 20 plants he could do so, but I didn't know
who to sell to, so I couldn't sell. "No problem," he said. He knows people
that will buy. He has sold it in the past and has "*patrones*." I finally
agreed and I said I would pay for the seed and give him a little money to
live on and such. I will take only a few plants for my study, and the rest
will be his to sell in town. The only condition is that I be allowed to take
photographs, ask questions, watch him work, and generally learn the
cultivation and selling process. To this my client readily agreed. I asked
who he had in mind to sell to. He named one Enrique Barro (this name and
my client's are false), a wealthy owner of an estate in the *municipio* and a
cattle baron. Escorcia and his patron are apparently well acquainted, since
he named the buyer immediately.

[Tracing out Escorcia's contacts and his growing and distribution networks yielded much important data. This visit and similar visits throughout
the remainder of the period of study cemented the friendly bonds between
Partridge and Escorcia, and communicated to others in the community that
an alliance had been formed and Partridge was gaining the information that
he had sought.]

17 February 1973

Señor Ardila brought to my room this evening a man he has found who is
willing to talk about marijuana, a grower from the highlands and a friend. I
was surprised and grateful. I did not ask his name. He told me that the
growing season is nine months. First, you plant the seed in a small
germinating box (such as used to grow herbs and onions in the highlands;
often on four legs above the ground). The seeds germinate there and are
thinned out. Two months later the plants are transplanted to a plot that has

been well doused in aldrin, an insecticide used against ants and crickets. I asked how much salable marijuana a single plant generally produced. He said it depends upon the soil and water conditions, but that 10 plants about 2 meters in height would produce 80 pounds of marijuana. A good plant should give 20 pounds if all conditions are ideal. I asked him about varieties of the plant. He said there were two. *Patagallina* is an ordinary variety, with larger-than-normal leaves, and though not preferred, it is still sold. *La mona* is the finer variety, with smaller leaves of more potency. The only visible difference in the two varieties is the size of the leaf. I asked him what parts of the plant were used. He listed the following: *la hoja*—leaves from the most inferior part of the plant—they bring on the market about 100 pesos a pound; *la negra*—leaves of the plant that have darkened (due to a lack of good ventilation, he explained)—they sell for about 200 pesos a pound; *la mota*—flower, seeds, and leaves around the flower—they are the most valued part of the plant, selling at 500 pesos a pound; leaves are yellow-orange in color.

He explained that *la hoja* can be harvested after the third month; *la negra* is also ready for harvest any time that such leaves appear. *La mota* takes a total of 11 months to grow—2 months germination and 9 months in the field. Only the female plant of the species produces the flower called *la mota*. The female and male plants both bring out flowers and they are identical, except for the wide petal-star shape of the male flower. Although the male plant is generally inferior, both sexes are marketed; but the finest grass comes from the female flower and the yellow-orange leaves around it.

I requested samples of *patagallina* and *la mona* from him so that I could describe them. He agreed. I also asked if I could take some pictures of each variety of the growing plants. He hesitated at this, so I dropped the subject. I simply said I had a great interest in learning how to grow the plant. He said we could get together and he would teach me.

[Following successful interviews and visits with Escorcia, Partridge's status in the community changed. Other informants now came forward with information they could communicate. Volunteered information and positive responses to requests for interviews accelerated from February until the end of the period of study.]

18 February 1973

Searching for pasture today I spoke with the *técnico* who works on the experimental farm of ICA. Alfonso is his name. Black, good-natured, always smiling, always wearing his cabbie cap and sunglasses to hide his bad eye from view, he looks like a 1950s jazz musician. He accepted my horses to be kept on his experimental farm where there is good water and some pasture. He agreed right off and, being pleased to have solved a troublesome problem so easily, I invited him to share a bottle of rum. Over the third glass he asked me, "What are you really doing here? The townspeople all have various stories. Most think you are FBI or CIA." He laughed, but in a questioning fashion. I explained my study in very general terms. Then he asked if I was interested in marijuana as some people said. I replied that it was an important part of my study and asked if he knew anything about it. He said he did and then confided that several people were saying I was a dope dealer. He asked me bluntly, "Are you?" I said no, and reiterated my role as observer. (Technically, I am not a dealer—yet. Planting is not until April and I am acting only as *patrón* to a peasant grower.) The subject broached, we went on in this vein. I asked if many people used the drug here in town. He said there were many. I explained my earlier difficulty in getting information from known users. He said they thought I was FBI or CIA or something. I asked if he could tell me when people generally use it. He said there were many different customs. For example, a friend of his who works at the railroad station uses it only on weekends and not while working. Others use it when working with a machete. Still others use it not as a tobacco but as an ointment mixed with rum (*ron cana,* from the department of Magdalena, he specified), which they apply to painful joints. He told me that Americans who come to Colombia, like the agronomist with whom he once worked, frequently use the drug. The agronomist was particularly fond of cocaine (which he used while working), but also used marijuana. When we finished the rum I left, promising another visit about marijuana.

[This informant actually brought up the topic of cannabis and began to interview the interviewer about his well-known interest in the topic. Such events during the latter part of the period of study were not uncommon as more people attempted to find out for themselves exactly what the anthropologist was seeking. Thus did many interviews that began on different topics eventually turn to cannabis.]

14 March 1973

I left on horseback early this morning to arrive in Cerro Blanco about noon for an appointment with Señor Escorcia, my client in the great marijuana venture. I had lunch at Jorge's house and spent a few hours scouring the hills for two lost yearlings that his employee, Lucho, had only recently reported, but that had been missing for about a week. We put in about three hours looking, but had no luck with the yearlings.

I left Jorge on the trail near an isolated corral back in the hills, agreeing

to meet him at a mutually known spot on the trail at 5:00. From there I set
out for Escorcia's farm, located back behind the hills and hidden from all
normal traffic. Escorcia had been right. In approaching his farm the
traveler's beasts are of little use. It is very isolated, and the paths leading to
it all are steep and dangerous. I tethered my horse on the top of one of the
hills that surround the farm and descended on foot to the house in the
valley.

Escorcia is indeed a poor *cachaco* farmer; his house is made of the same
upright poles as were the Indian homes in Serancua. The wind whistles
through the unplastered uprights at will. The only major difference between his house and those of the Indians was the presence in Escorcia's
house of rooms: pole partitions differentiated the sleeping area from the
kitchen. No central fire was present, but there was a *fogon* or hearth as in
the other peasant homes. An attic was built over the living area; there corn
and other foods were stored. Escorcia was at home and we shared a few
shots from a bottle of *aguardiente* I had brought (and left with him upon
my departure). He was quite glad I had come and immediately produced a
fique sack wrapped around a brown paper package. He undid the package
and showed me perhaps two pounds of good cannabis seed. I examined it
and knew instantly that it was authentic seed. Where did he obtain it? From
a friend in the *vereda* of La Piedra who grows marijuana and who owed
him a favor, he said. A few more words about the quality of the seed, and
we were off to plant them.

We walked out from the house up a dry creek bed (from which Escorcia
still draws his water—he digs a hole in the sand in which a good quantity of
water accumulates rather rapidly, although its color is milky and silty).
Slightly beyond his water hole in the creek bed we turned uphill and
walked into very high weeds. About five minutes into the weeds, or half
way up the hill, we came to a dead tree stump blackened by many years of
burning off the brush on the hillside. There at the base of the stump
Escorcia had prepared a germination bed. It was an area about three feet by
five feet. The dirt had been leveled on the uphill side of the stump and all of
the weeds cleared from the stump on that side. This had been done in the
last two weeks, Escorcia explained. Then he had constructed a germination
box, building a small retaining wall on each side of the stump so that the
soil could be built into a considerable pile and would not be washed away
by the rain. The soil was then mixed with cattle manure (*abono*) about 15
days ago, and each day since Escorcia had come up the dry creek bed to his
water hole and carried a bucket of water up to the germination plot. This
was done daily, he explained, so that the fertilizer would break down and
mix with the soil.

Escorcia then commenced the planting activity. He first stirred up the soil with his hands, churning it up and breaking up clods of earth that had formed. Then he sprinkled the seeds in handfuls from about two feet above the plot. The seeds covered the surface of the ground, perhaps four or more to the square inch in places, one or two in other places. He made no effort to form rows or to be neat about it—just to cover the surface with seed. Then he fetched a bucket of water and with a half gourd dished water out, splashing the water over the seeds. He did not cover the seeds with a layer of soil. He then picked up the small bag he had carried to the site and

Germination plot constructed in the highlands with cannabis seedlings about six weeks old.

removed two boxes of aldrin, an ant killer. He spread a thick layer of aldrin in an unbroken line about two inches wide around the entire germination plot. This is essential, he explained, because the ants were the greatest pests. He then fetched another bucket of water and repeated the watering, followed by more aldrin to patch up breaks or thin places in the barrier. When he was finished, I took a series of photographs of the germination bed.

As we left he predicted 15 April as the transplanting date. He said he would water the plot each day and put on more aldrin as a barrier to the ants for the first 8 to 10 days. After that the risk would be less, and the plants would have germinated. He explained that he would transplant them to his *roza* or mixed garden, where the soil would likewise be prepared in advance with cattle manure. We still had some of the seed left and I asked what he would do with it. ''Plant another germination plot,'' he responded.

Between the two plots we would obtain enough plants for 2 hectares of marijuana . (My investment in this venture, the proportions of it, grew larger in my mind. I was impressed.)

The marijuana would be planted in the center of the *roza,* he continued. His regular crops, maize, yuca, beans, etc., would be planted around the outside, thus concealing for a while the crop within. He expressed the need for a pistol, not right away, but when the plants were about four months old. Then they could be marketed for the leaves. At that point he would

Seedlings are transplanted from the germination plot to the *roza* after the corn is tall enough to hide the cannabis plants. Manioc is then planted between the cannabis plants.

need a weapon to keep thieves away. I told him this would be difficult since permission from the police would be necessary. I was reluctant to purchase a weapon. But he was convinced it was a necessity. Otherwise, he said, people would rob us before the crop is ready (i.e., before the plants flower, producing the most valuable grade of drug—five times more valuable than the leaves of young plants). I continued to express reluctance, saying that we had some three months to think about it. He agreed there was time.

[Partridge was at this time elated with his progress. Finally the preparation was beginning to pay off. The planting of the crop represented the opportunity for firsthand observation and the beginning of a period in which data began to mount and the number of informants to grow.]

13 March 1973

Dear Bill,

Your last batch of field notes and letter arrived last week just before the Florida contingent took off for the SAS meetings at Wrightsville Beach, N.C.

In regard to your major objective or, I should say, your objective in relation to its place in a social system, it appears that your careful preliminary efforts are now beginning to yield some results. Obviously there are some dangers and you can never be too prudent. Even though the au-

Cannabis plants attain a height well over six feet in the highlands. Fields are located in places that are difficult to reach.

thorities know what you are doing and have granted you an immunity, even a written assurance would be worthless under a situation of stress. From your reports it seems to me that there are some powerful people who know how to act on the behalf of others to protect their clients. In the event of the worst possible circumstance, do you have such a person you can turn to who will intercede and quiet the trouble? Always expect trouble from a direction you least expect—someone you unknowingly threaten, or who can exploit you, or who is actually mad. Never let down your guard.

As to helpful hints: public ceremonials are simulations of a total system;

so also are private ceremonials the simulations of private and smaller systems. Pay attention to the private rituals as they are acted out in the variety of situations in which you participate. To put it differently, look upon the behavior you observe as ritual expression of the relations among persons, expressing their values and their positions. From this perspective total behavior is the ritual of life—what some call ''culture.''

Sincerely,
Solon Kimball

9 June 1973

Señor Benjamin Alceves of DAS (National Secret Police) from Fundación showed up at my house about 8:00 A.M. this morning. He was on his way to Santa Marta and apologized for missing our planned meeting yesterday.

He began by answering my request for the arrest records of DAS for the past ten years on the charges of possession, cultivation, or sale of marijuana. He said that his chief in Santa Marta had refused permission to open their archives to me. Then I asked him if he would be willing to help me with his personal knowledge of the situation. He said this he could do. He has worked in narcotics for the past 15 years, 12 of them in Colombia. The other years were spent in the United States, Mexico, Canada, and Panama. He feels that the problem has grown tremendously in the past 12 years. He estimates a fivefold increase in the incidence of marijuana use. I asked in what sector of the population this increase was taking place. He said in the middle class, among the young, primarily students. He agreed with me that this was an international phenomenon not unique to Colombia.

I explained that my interest was not in this sector of the population. What I was after was information on the traditional users of marijuana. I reminded him of his earlier opinion that use here was very old. He said it was, but could not give a date. I suggested 50 years old, and he said probably less. With regard to the history of the problem he said he had personal files at home that could help me with this, as well as at least one book dealing with the situation in Colombia in the 1950s or so. He promised to trace these references down and let me see them.

I asked about the connection between traditional users and the international traffic. He stated categorically that the traffic and use seem to be separate. The international traffickers come from the upper crust of society, he said. They are intelligent, well prepared, educated, and wealthy—people with ''*cultura.*'' They are also international in origin. He gave the name of a hotel in Barranquilla where I could be put in contact with traffickers from the United States, Canada, Cuba, France—from all over the world. The hotel is one of the plushest and most exclusive in the city. It is frequented by the upper class of Colombian society.

In sum, although Alceves will not be a very good source of information on traditional users, he may be of some help on the nature of the problem in Colombia in the past.

After Alceves left something happened that I have not yet figured out. He had been gone only a minute or two when one of my best informants walked through the front door. They could not have missed passing on the street. For a moment I saw the carefully protected confidence I had built up with my informant in danger. Surely, I thought, he knows by sight the chief of the secret police. But my informant said nothing. I engaged him in the usual pleasantries about his family, his farm, etc., and we talked for some time without a hint of something wrong. He had come to tell me of a friend of his who had many friends among the users of cannabis. This particular informant is a grower. He has known his friend since 1948 and is certain that the man smokes each and every day. That is perfect, I said. I was quite eager to meet and interview him. He said he would set it up.

This event perhaps confirms the notion that the local marijuana traffic is something apart from the international traffic. It is not firm evidence, but a merchant or grower who was involved in the traffic would logically know the police in the area. Whether Alceves knew my informant by sight is another question.

[Señor Alceves had been approached by Partridge in early June in his downtown office in Fundación. Partridge paid a formal visit to him in his capacity as director of the regional office of DAS, the branch of the federal government that has the responsibility for enforcement of laws against cultivation, distribution, and consumption of cannabis. The purpose of initiating contact with the police was twofold: first, Partridge wanted them to be aware of his activities, not by rumor but by firsthand knowledge and examination of Partridge's documents; and second, Partridge wanted to gain some assurance that the police knew his activities to be of a scientific nature only. Alceves did not permit Partridge to learn anything of police operations in the region, nor did he interfere in any way with Partridge's activities. Rather, he issued a warning that he would keep Partridge under observation to see if his claim was true. He accepted for the time being Partridge's official sponsorship and his avowed scientific objectives. His exclusive interest in the international traffic in drugs made him a less valuable informant and resource, as well as only a minor threat to Partridge's data collecting activities or to informants working with Partridge. By initiating formal contact with the police Partridge hoped to avoid difficulties in the future. In order that this event be formally recognized, Partridge requested that the mayor of the town accompany him to the office of Señor Alceves and provide an introduction. This the mayor willingly did, thus eliminating the possibility of a misunderstanding later.

Kimball's letter of 13 March had stressed the importance of recognizing the danger inherent in Partridge's activities since 22 January. His suggestion was to seek the support of a person with some influence who could intercede in the event of trouble. Partridge chose the mayor of Majagua, a man of great influence locally and regionally and a personal friend of influential men in the national capital, who had known of Partridge's activities since August 1972. The support of the mayor, expressed through this introduction, constituted a kind of insurance against future difficulties.

Trouble did eventually occur near the end of the period of study and is the subject of chapter 8. The incident reported here will be seen to have been of some importance in the resolution of the problem.]

18 June 1973

I rode up to Cerro Blanco to visit Escorcia. Our arrangement was for yesterday, Sunday, but my horse needed shoes and so I had to postpone my departure.

I arrived about noon and we set out immediately to visit some friends of his with whom he claimed he had set up interviews about marijuana use.

The situation was as follows. His friends live way back in the hills on the Tucurinca side of Cerro Blanco. They are coastal peasants and sharecroppers, not *cachacos*. Escorcia is a *cachaco*, but he has friends here since they have the same *patrón* with whom they sharecrop cattle. In any case, we arrived in time for lunch and were fed. Conversation was passed back and forth for almost an hour before the subject was brought up. Escorcia did this by taking his friend aside; then when things were set he called me over to explain what I wanted and why. This I did.

The interview was taken down in writing as it progressed, and the subject seemed interested in filling me with information. At the end I requested his help in making contact with other friends who used it who lived in the area. He said certainly, there were several who had used it for years (he himself was 42 and began smoking at age 18). I emphasized the

need for mature smokers. He said he would help, sending word with
Escorcia when he had good news.

In total, this makes ten informants on marijuana. As I chart it, the
interviewing should be completed in the month of June. I can start life
histories in July if all goes well. My contacts each have been tapped to put
me in contact with others, so a final total of 20 informants seems likely. I
will be quite happy to get this many.

[Beginning in June 1973 a new note-taking system was employed. Interviews with cannabis informants were recorded separately from other notes
on Key Sort cards. Only one copy of cannabis interviews was made, and
this copy was kept in a locked trunk in Partridge's room. Partridge decided
that such precautions were necessary when he discovered, almost acci-
dently, that the progress of his study and his relations among the growers
were becoming common knowledge in the community. He became aware
of this when an informant on a host of other subjects one day volunteered
information on cannabis. Previously this informant had denied planting a
crop, although he had promised Partridge cooperation in making contacts.
He revealed he did plant a crop each year and asked whether Partridge was
interested in seeing it. Obviously, he had decided to trust Partridge on the
basis of talking with others in the highlands who trusted him. Thus,
Partridge decided to guard his notes regarding cannabis closely now that
there was general knowledge of his activities. The discussion with the chief
of the secret police in the region introduced further considerations, such as
the notes being used to harm those who had given information in trust, and
this event sealed his decision to trust neither the police nor the mails.
Interview data were recorded on cards identified only by a letter of the
alphabet. Partridge kept a copy of the key apart from the cards. Such
precautions may seem dramatic, but given the illegal nature of the activities
investigated, the precautions seemed necessary. The following are examples of these interviews recorded on Key Sort cards.]

Interview with Informant J

The man is 53 years of age and began smoking in 1942, at age 22; he has a
total of 31 years of experience with marijuana. He was born in Valledupar
in 1920, but came to Majagua as a one-year-old when his father migrated
here to work for the United Fruit Company. Later he also worked for the
company, from 1954 to 1955. His father returned to Valledupar in the
1950s and purchased a 150-hectare farm with the money he had earned as a
day laborer. For a while he joined his father, but soon returned to Majagua
to work for the company.

At the age of 15 he moved to Barranquilla and lived with his grand-
mother for three years while he attended public school. Then he took his
first job with a cement plant, Fábrica Cemento del Caribe. He made 5
pesos a day in that job. But he left Barranquilla because, as he explained it,
there were too many bad people there: thieves, attackers, etc. So he moved
to Cartagena and worked for a few months, but didn't like that city any
better. Then he moved to Santa Marta and worked for a few months, finally
returning to Majagua and his family. He got a job mixing cement for a
house builder. It was there in Majagua, not in the cities of the coast, that he
was introduced to marijuana.

He learned to smoke from his fellow workers on the construction jobs.
They used it in the morning before starting work; they smoked together
again during water or coffee breaks throughout the work day. He often
went to Valledupar in those days to visit relatives, but he did not smoke
while he was there. He had a good job and a good reputation in Majagua as
a cement worker and, as he puts it, he did not like machete work.
Sometimes he took jobs as an *obrero* or *machetero* (agricultural day
laborer), but he didn't like the work. That was what he did in the 1950s for
the company, but he did not enjoy it: he did it only until he could get a job
in construction once again. While working as a *machetero* he made 3.40
pesos a day; working cement he didn't always make much better, although
sometimes he earned as much as 5 or 10 pesos a day.

In 1969 his father got sick and so he returned to Valledupar to take
over running the farm. When he found out his father needed an
operation he contacted his brother, who lives in Medellín and has a
much better income. The brother took the father in and hospitalized him
in the city. His mother had died in 1963 and is buried in the cemetery
in Majagua. She was born here, and her family and her husband wanted
to honor her request to be buried here. A daughter and another son,
siblings of Informant J, live near here in a town called El Banco;
another son lives on the father's farm in Valledupar. My informant left
Valledupar and moved back to Majagua after his father returned from
the hospital to his farm. When his father dies he expects that the farm
will be passed on to him and his three brothers, but he intends to stay in
Majagua. He doesn't like agricultural work.

Informant J is the only marijuana smoker in his family. He taught his
brother in Valledupar to smoke, but he did not like it and discontinued
smoking shortly after experimenting with it. Informant J says this is
because his brother is *"un poco débil en la cabeza"* and this is a danger
with the plant. Those who are said to be *débil* (literally, weak) in the head
should refrain from using the drug since it *"vuelve loco"* or turns one

crazy. People with "strong" heads, on the other hand, notice no ill effects. When asked what one can do to assist someone who is *débil* and has smoked the plant, Informant J advised pouring cold water over his head, forcing him to eat green bananas, or making him drink hot black coffee. Informant J says he had never had a bad experience with marijuana. At times he feels like he is too drunk, and he simply goes to his hammock and lies down and sleeps. But this is the only negative effect of marijuana he has noticed. He says he has had long experience with the drug and does not fear it, though others who have little experience often do. But, he adds, one must have a strong head to use it.

When he learned to smoke among his work friends in Majagua all of them were roughly the same age. The only older worker on the job was a bricklayer, for whom he mixed mortar, and he also smoked with the men during work breaks. But the older man was not the one who taught him. The lesson came from an age mate who also worked with the older man. This person lives today in nearby Fundación and, like Informant J, still uses the drug. But the other young men in the group have moved on and he has lost track of them. Aside from his brother in Valledupar, no one else in his family knows he smokes marijuana. He claims his father would be very angry if he knew about it. His father believes that only criminals and vagabonds smoke marijuana.

Informant J appreciates smoking for various reasons. To help you get to sleep he prescribes a cigarette before going to bed, and calls marijuana an *aperitivo* for making love with a woman. In addition he recommends a marijuana cigarette to produce *ganas,* or desires, and for this reason it is good for work during the day. He says while working he normally smokes one cigarette in the morning and one in the afternoon. The resultant effects are described by the informant's word *temple,* meaning a mood or frame of mind. He says the *temple* produced by drinking rum is different, although he uses both rum and marijuana together some evenings. But of the two, marijuana and alcohol, he prefers marijuana because it is cheaper and the *temple* produced is pleasing.

These days Informant J always smokes alone, although he started and continued for years smoking with other laborers of his work group. His reason is that few of his old friends still live in Majagua. While moving about the coast he has lost track of some, who presumably were moving also, and others live in areas to which he does not travel. Sometimes he meets a man in Fundación who was on that early work crew when he learned to smoke; they no longer smoke while working but instead while visiting local bars, pool halls, or sitting at home on a weekend.

19 July 1973

I met my contacts for several more interviews concerning marijuana and set out in the morning to complete these. However, today I am just a bit anxious, but not out of fear that I am getting into a dangerous situation with the marijuana consumers. On the contrary. Last night I held an interview with a consumer who also markets the drug here in town, an open and quite talkative person. We got on famously (due to the fact that my friend and contact Escorcia laid some excellent groundwork in advance). In any case we talked for all of three hours about cannabis and then parted about 11:30 for home. The interview had been in the man's home on the other side of town, so we had to walk back through the center of town. At one intersection we paused to discuss the plan for the coming week (when I will be going up in the hills for more interviews) and as we talked two men walked up. They called out "mister" and came over to interrupt us. One was quite drunk; the other not quite, but on the way. Escorcia, his nephew, and I were facing them. The drunk one says to Escorcia, "Let's collaborate in something." "In what?" asked Escorcia. And then the man turned to me and said, "Lend me 15 pesos, *gringo*." I looked at him, smiling, and said "no." Then Escorcia blew up and asked, "What do you want to collaborate in?" The man was attempting to hustle me for money and was seeking the support of my Colombian companions to convince me to give it to him. The implication was that I would suffer injury if I did not come across. Escorcia told the man to pull out his arm (firearm or weapon) if he was going to because he was about to make the man "eat some shit." At this the two drunks backed off a little. My two friends and I stepped toward them. The drunker of the two made a move in my direction (he had no weapon), but the other grabbed him and dragged him off. I quickly talked Escorcia and his nephew out of attacking them, saying we would surely bring on the police. So we walked on, leaving them in the middle of the street.

I am happy (in an ironic way) that this event occurred. Now I am convinced that I am much safer with my marijuana-consuming friends than with the drunks of the town. I am rarely in the poorer barrios at night, but just the same I know (firsthand now) that robbery and assault are common here. That the *marijuaneros* are innocent of this is rather evident—they knew that in fact I had 400 pesos on me. The drunks had no idea, only a suspicion. Thus, I feel more secure with *marijuaneros* than with drunks.

During my interview, before all this took place, my host told me about payoff. He naturally has to pay the police—a custom that pertains not only to marijuana traffic but to any and all interaction with that governmental body. For example, a man who carrys a gun without a permit is fair game for a policeman. (Permits are issued by the army and are few and far between. Generally only public officials, landowners, and merchants have them.) The police can stop the man and demand his papers, and if the man doesn't have any he must bribe the cop to keep out of jail. A sum of 300 to 500 pesos is an acceptable bribe for a policeman (those who are armed, that is; the customs people get only half this much since they can not really enforce their will). Likewise, contraband runners must pay the police. But relations with the police I already knew about. What about with one's neighbors? A neighbor with whom you're on bad terms and who knows you are a seller of marijuana can simply pay a cop 20 pesos to have you arrested. What is more, he can set you up, for he can observe when you come and go with your merchandise or with customers. This interests me more than the cop-buying. My host explained to me that he maintains good relations with his neighbors, to keep them quiet, by loaning them money. He always has cash in the house, up to 20,000 pesos at a time. When one of his neighbors needs money, he said, they come to him, saying, "Lend me 20 pesos because my mother is visiting and I am broke," or "Lend me 50 pesos. My child is sick and I must buy medicine." So my host gives them money, never to see it again. The phrase "lend me" is misleading because the money is never collected—it is an investment, like insurance. He refuses large requests, but grants small ones readily, following what might be described as the "good neighbor policy."

During our discussion my host noted that many people perceive the marijuana user to be a bad person. Ever since he was a boy my informant had been told that marijuana consumers kill and rob people. It is a lie, he said emphatically. Then he told the story of an event that happened just this past Saturday. (The others present confirmed the story, since they live near the murdered man.) A neighbor of the *cachacos* Goyo and Tico was coming back from town on the truck to Cerro Blanco. The truck was stopped about half-way up the road (the road to Cerro Blanco, which is an area not settled, but simply bush). The police were blocking the road. They searched all the men on the truck for arms, and found this particular man carrying one. The man always carries a revolver when he travels, but he had no papers or permits. The police knew this: the man was like a cow that they milked at regular intervals (this comment was from Escorcia, who assisted my host with his story). The police asked him for money or they would take him back to town and put him in jail. The man refused to pay them. They sent the truck on up the mountain and detained the man. He was later brought into Majagua dead, with 18 bullet holes in his body.

Marijuaneros did not kill him, my host said, and there were nods all around the room.

[Through introductions from other informants an interview was completed with a local small-time distributor of marijuana. This distributor in turn provided introductions to a number of marijuana smokers who were also interviewed. Informant M was one of these, recorded on Key Sort cards.]

Interview with Informant M

Informant M is 42 years old. He began using cannabis when he was 18. He was brought to the banana zone of the north coast by his mother after his father died. He was 14 years old. At 17 he went to work for the United Fruit Company and, in the company of fellow *macheteros,* he learned how to smoke. He says he is the only one in his family who smokes marijuana. He explains that his male siblings do not smoke because they did not work with the same people he did when they were young. He had been working for the company a long time before his younger brothers were born. Their friends did not smoke either. Whether you smoke marijuana depends upon your friends, he concludes. Some people have the custom and some do not.

He smokes the drug "when he has the opportunity." There is no schedule to his smoking, he claims. He uses it in connection with labor on his own farm. He owns ten hectares of land planted in table crops. He also pastures about five cows on his land, only one of which belongs to him; he has only part shares in the others. With this income he can feed his wife and three young sons. He says he bought the ten hectares with savings from his days as a day laborer. He got a man with land to act as his *fiador* or cosignatory, obtained a loan, and purchased the land. He raises corn for the cash crop market here in town and is now paying off the land loan. He has had the farm for five years.

Before buying his land he lived in one of the poor neighborhoods of Majagua. Before that he had lived in Guacamayal and Sevilla. In those days he worked for the company, living in a variety of towns and hamlets all over the *Zona Bananera*. He and his mother had initially taken up residence in Rio Frío, but moved to where work could be found.

He smokes marijuana while working, about six to seven times a day. He claims that a person can smoke two or three cigarettes at one sitting if he cares to, since there is no danger of getting too much, as with alcohol. But generally he only smokes one at a time. He does not mix the marijuana with anything. Today on his farm he is the only one who smokes, as he is the only adult male in the household. He doesn't think he will teach his sons to smoke. Too many *malhechores* or criminals smoke the drug also, and they might find friends among such people, he says. But he smokes around the house, and during my visit shared marijuana cigarettes with a friend who dropped by to visit (and later turned out to be a good informant also). He compared smoking marijuana to my own habit of smoking tobacco cigarettes. Just as I offered tobacco cigarettes around to all assembled when I took out one for myself, so too he offered cannabis cigarettes to everyone assembled. If no one is around then he smokes alone.

He also drinks rum and *aguardiente* and smokes tobacco. What does he feel when in the *temple* of marijuana intoxication? It depends upon what one is doing, came his answer. If he is working he feels *incansable* or tireless. He does not have to rest as much. The herb, as he calls it, gives him strength or resistance to fatigue that he does not normally have. Do things appear different to him when in the *temple?* No, he has always felt good using marijuana. He thinks the stories about people who see snakes, condors, lions, and such are foolish. He has never experienced visual distortions. He says those who claim such experiences are lying. Can one smoke marijuana and drink at the same time? Yes, there is no harm in that, but the marijuana is much stronger and will have more effect than the rum—so it is really a waste of alcohol. It is simply not necessary to smoke and drink at the same time.

Smoking marijuana is said to be a *fortaleza* or fortifier for making love, according to Informant M. Making love is better when you are intoxicated, because it gives you force. I asked him to explain. Drinking rum or beer makes one incapable of love making, he said. One loses his force when drunk. But it is the opposite with marijuana: smoking gives one strength. Which is better, alcohol or marijuana? The marijuana is better for some things and it is cheaper, he said, easier for poor ones like him to buy. But alcohol is superior for getting drunk, for dancing, for having a party.

CONDUCTING OBSERVATIONS

Because marijuana was illegal, research into its use had to be conducted with skill and patience and not without some fear of jeopardy. But apart from the need to exercise caution, no field research can be successful without the trust and cooperation of the subjects, linked with candor on the part of the field researcher.

Partridge was granted access to the information he sought only after winning acceptance by his informants as an honorable and trustworthy individual. His avowed role of seeker of truth could be the clever front of an agent or it could be real, but his informants had no experience for evaluating him on this basis. So when Jorge told Escorcia to offer cooperation to Partridge, this was an affirmation of the trust that had been built during the previous months, as well as a manifestation of the patron-client relationship. Furthermore, we can assume that Jorge believed that Partridge knew the severity of the penalties that apply to those who violate the sanctity of a personal trust.

Once the door to acceptance had opened, the range of new data sources carried Partridge through all levels and segments of the community. He had penetrated many of them previously, but now the knowledge he gained earlier acquired new meaning. The characteristics that separated the peoples of the highlands and the coast, the *cachacos* and the *costeños,* were etched more sharply. The internal differences within each sector also began to acquire new significance. There were the constrasting life careers of workers, managers, and owners on the mechanized and commercial *fincas* of the coast alongside the cooperative settlements and remnants of the traditional cattle haciendas. The grazing and tillage pattern of the highlands represented another tradition. Finally, there was the town, the focal point for the intermeshing of these cultural diversities in the collection and distribution of goods, in the provision of professional and administrative services, and in the linkage to regional and national centers of economic, social, and political influence.

Viewed in this way, community emerges as an interlocking system of activities and institutions which orders human diversities. Through it specific individuals are linked with each other and with pan-national institutions. Thus all activities, including the clandestine practices surrounding marijuana, become diagnostically significant in revealing how the system works.

7. The Emergence of Community

In the early stages of fieldwork, anthropologists resemble pack rats in their collecting and hoarding proclivities. There is no sure guide then as to what is or is not important, so prudence suggests that everything that comes to view should be saved. But the researcher replaces the initial dragnet approach with a more selective one as he learns more about the community. Not only does he become more effective in the pursuit of his research objectives, but as his knowledge increases so also do his data become more meaningful. For example, the first fumbling attempts by Partridge in August 1972 to gather data on cannabis were failures. He had not yet matured sufficiently to handle this sub rosa aspect of community life. But by January he had formulated his first tentative model of community, a sign of increased comprehension of the organizational system of community as well as of his conceptual growth. Almost simultaneously his informants became less reluctant to discuss cannabis, an indication that Partridge had earned their trust and acceptance.

The field notes he submitted in early April cover a two-month period of intensive data collection in a rural hamlet of 25 families, a town neighborhood of 76 families, and a highland neighborhood of 11 families. Household censuses were taken, life histories and work histories were gathered, and lengthy interviews were conducted on a variety of topics. These data augment and complement much that has been presented in earlier chapters and need not be repeated here.

The detail of these materials fleshed out the broad outlines of diverse segments of the community that had been reported earlier. They also evoked Kimball's letter of 24 April in which he requested a further expansion of the model. Specifically, Kimball introduced the concepts of world view and of socialization as areas in which model testing should begin. He also called attention to the importance of ritual activities as condensed statements of social realities and as events that are rich in symbolic meaning about the nature of the social world.

During April Partridge entered his most productive and advanced stage of fieldwork in the combined roles of researcher and evaluator. He extended and deepened his knowledge of details and behavior. But the distinguishing features of this period were his model testing activities.

The material that follows includes the correspondence between Kimball and Partridge and selected portions of the field notes for the period April to August. Presented here are both the major conceptual concerns and the multiple dimensions of community. They include the description of a community encompassing ritual, the social sectors, world view, economic patterns, and an interpretation of cannabis in a community setting. The background is found in the following exchange of letters between 14 April and 27 May.

14 April 1973

Dear Dr. Kimball:

Things continue to go very well for me with my informants. The data get easier and easier to collect as people become more accustomed to what I am interested in.

My contacts with those who can assist me in event of trouble are still good. I am going to Santa Marta this weekend to make one final contact in this regard, as well as to gather information from the same person on the subject of powerful families.

I have included in these field notes an analysis of the interview data gathered so far. The picture that emerges is rather complete. It tells us that regional mobility is an important factor in any interpretation of the data.

Several conversations with informants about marijuana are also contained in these notes. My informants in this realm are becoming more confident of me and I expect this to increase as times goes on.

I will be initiating in the coming month a series of interviews in one of the barrios of the town, as a complement to and further elaboration of the interviews in the countryside. I have yet to complete the interviews in the highland *vereda,* but plan to finish them in the near future. The three should give a complete picture.

Employees of the Colombian Institute of Agriculture tell me that their records show only two days of rain in the last five months. My friends among the peasants tell me that they should have begun planting with the crescent moon of April 12. But as yet the rains have not begun. The heat is unbelievable these days.

There is little other news that is not contained in the notes. Regards to all.

Best wishes,
Bill

24 April 1973

Dear Bill:

A batch of your field notes arrived a few days back followed by a letter of 14 April. The previous letter indicated all the steps you were taking to protect yourself. You will be interested that a million dollars of marijuana was confiscated about two weeks ago by narcotics agents off the Florida coast, all neatly bagged and labeled as marijuana from Majagua, Colombia.

The plan or campaign you laid out seems time filling, but there are still two areas that I wish you would give thought and attention to. The first one is "world view." Actually there is a lot of material scattered throughout your notes on this, but you need to approach it in a specific way. What are the explanations that people use to describe how the world works; what are the criteria by which they judge events and items in the world around them; into what categories do they arrange the external world and their own behavior; what factors govern the way they respond and communicate? Usually ritual situations condense all this. I note that you have relatively little about religious behavior and thought. It might be well to interview and observe specifically around the church and evangelical sects.

Second, you need to pay specific attention to how socialization is carried on, both formally (in the schools) and informally in the household and at work and other places. What are the specifics and the processes by which individuals are turned into adults of a particular kind? If you can get some free help, or have money left and can subsidize, you might get some school teachers to help you by gathering formal data. Keep in mind the nice job that was done in *Village in the Vaucluse*.

I appreciate that these items are not part of your formal mission, but even a modicum of attention to them will be helpful in seeing the situation whole, and will permit some additional use of your notes later on.

Sincerely,
Solon T. Kimball

10 May 1973

Dear Dr. Kimball:

I received your letter and suggestions of 24 April upon my return from Bogotá recently. I am back in Majagua after having spent two weeks away in the company of my parents. They took advantage of my being here, taking their son along on a ten-day tour of the country as guide and interpreter. It was the first time in many years that we had an opportunity to talk at length. I was particularly glad my mother decided to make the trip, because her mother recently died (in March) after an extended hospitalization. The change of scene and our being together were welcome to all of us.

After they returned to Miami I took advantage of the ticket back to the coast to do some work in Bogotá. I contacted several people at the Universidad Nacional who have worked with marijuana, including an MD and a toxicologist who have worked with the secret police. They provided me with statistics regarding the incidence of marijuana violations from 1951. Further help was promised upon my next visit in August or September, at which time I will be doing some library work as well.

I hope that you saved the clipping of the marijuana haul marked as coming from Majagua, Colombia. This is further evidence of the area being a center of production. The newspapers here are full of evidence.

The interviewing in the town barrio is well off the ground with some 15 already completed. Some interesting contrasts have emerged regarding origins of the townspeople, their working lives, and work histories. I will pay closer attention to world view and socialization in the coming weeks, as you suggest in your letter. Some of this has simply not found its way onto paper yet, but is know·

Well the drought here has finally broken. The rainy season has begun and the plaza once again is green with fresh grass shoots. The burros that wander in at sundown look healthy again rather than starved. People are busy planting their gardens in table crops. The rivers are swollen to capacity and drinking water is now boiled since even from the taps in the better neighborhoods it carries a load of silt with it. It is a time when one feels that Bartok's "Duet for Two Double Bass Violins" is being performed continuously in one's bowels.

Best wishes,
Bill

27 May 1973

Dear Dr. Kimball:

Just a note to tell you some good news, and to let you know that things are going well.

The other day I received an invitaiton from Dr. Vera Rubin of the Research Institute for the Study of Man to deliver a paper at the Conference on Cross-Cultural Perspectives on Cannabis, being held 28–31 August in Chicago. I was happy to accept and submitted an abstract immediately. I plan to fly up from here to the conference and then return for a final month in the field, tying up loose ends and perhaps taking cognizance of useful criticisms of my presentation in Chicago to collect some supplementary data. I believe this to be an important opportunity to test some ideas before completely shutting down my field operation.

June and July should see the collection of details regarding the marijuana users and the collection of life histories. August will be spent polishing up documentation in Bogotá and September, tying up loose ends and researching the newspaper collection in Santa Marta. October should find me in Gainesville.

Best wishes,
Bill

RITUAL AND COMMUNITY

Following this exchange of letters Partridge had the opportunity to examine the patron saint festival in one of the satellite towns near Majagua. He describes the ebb and flow of people in and out of the town, the social groupings that compose the community, and the interdependencies among these groups.

The festival draws back to their place of origin people from all over the north coast. Among these are the wealthy professionals, landowners, and politicians, the migratory agricultural laborers, the students, and the poor. All who can, come back. The Ibrahim family provides an excellent example. Over the generations they have worked their way from shopkeepers into positions of prominence in agriculture, cattle ranching, judgeships, various professions, and national politics. Their return emphasizes their continuing attachment to the community. They are important absentee landlords and politicians, and occupy other positions of power and influence upon which the community depends for numerous services. As some of the most successful sons and daughters in the community, they are primary sponsors of the festival (this responsibility is passed among the various powerful families on a yearly basis). They hire the band, lead the procession where the statue of the saint is carried, pay for the construction of the important *corraleja,* and appoint the various officials who will be needed to carry out the activities of the ceremony. Their yearly gathering permits the reaffirmation of social and economic ties between them and the local population, ties which link them to store and estate managers, employees, minor government officials, and laborers.

As exemplified by the Ibrahim gathering there is festive drinking and eating. The adult males joke with one another, toast the town and their prosperity, and consume pork, yuca, and beef. The honorific treatment afforded the oldest brother is heartfelt and genuine: he has worked hard for his family and maintained his ties with them. He offers a ceremonial benediction on the assembly. He is a powerful man, one whose picture appears in newspapers in the cities, a man who chooses political candidates, dedicates public buildings, and crowns beauty contest winners in a burgeoning metropolis. His status brings honor to his family and to his community. In other households the same process is occurring, even if the participants are not as wealthy or powerful as the Ibrahims. The successful relatives may be the employees of urban bus companies, noncommissioned officers in the military, or clerks in the local banks. But they bring honor to the household,

The occasion is more than a renewal of the linkages that bind members to family and community. As the past is reaffirmed, the future is taking shape. The young participate only casually in the ceremonious gatherings of their elders, perhaps pouring drinks, listening to stories, or running errands. They are not yet obligated to reaffirm ties; their rights and duties are potential. Their concerns lie outside the household of their parents, lie in the households of other adults where potential spouses live. They meet in the streets, at the gambling tables, at the kitchens and beverage vendors' tables, at the *corraleja,* and at the games. The site of *la cumbia* is passed from youngster to youngster as they make plans for the evening. The *cumbia* draws them together, out of the ritual gathering of the elders and into the pool of potential adult members of the community. Here as they dance about the musicians they engage in the courtship process, a peer function and a time for experimentation and testing, a time when the young come together and forge the new families that will carry on the festival in years to come.

23 June 1973

I met with Pedro and José and started out for the fiesta. We traveled by *chiva,* as most people do, through an afternoon shower that had come up. It had ceased by the time we arrived. We were let off after the driver stopped a little way outside of the town to collect his fares—his assistant was sick and he was taking no chance that the passengers would escape in the holiday crowd without paying.

We walked through the town to the cockfights. Strung all along the main street were stands, fruit vendors, soup and fritter kitchens, gambling tables for playing a modified roulette, and of course bars set up especially for the occasion. The cock ring in El Retén is different from the one in Majagua, constructed of poles and palm thatch. The ring is surrounded by wooden benches with seats with arm rests for the "*doctores*"; the bleachers rising to the roof are of wood. The cocks here perch on poles lashed to the uprights supporting the roof rather than in cages as in Majagua and

Barranquilla. But the intense heat of the competition is the same. We arrived during a fight that threatened each minute to grow into a group brawl, with *galleros* from Fundación shouting insults to those from Majagua. The fatal words *hueputa* and *tu madre* were heard several times and the participants had to be restrained from leaping at each other's throats. I took several pictures of this interaction and of cockfights as well.

After several matches, all hotly contested, we left to see if the bullfights had started yet. At one corner near the cock ring Pedro met up with a physician, one who lives in Medellín but who had returned to El Retén for the patron's festival. He married into the Ibrahim family, who themselves are married into coastal upper-class families, being immigrants from Lebanon. The doctor escorted us to the Ibrahims' house where a private party was in progress. We entered to find about 25 adult males sitting in a circle in the living room of a concrete block house on one of the side streets. They were consuming large quantities of *aguardiente,* pork ribs, potatoes, yuca, and stewed beef. We were invited to join in and did so.

The whole clan was gathered for the event—the males for the drinking today in the home. The females will come tomorrow, they explained, for the procession and the mass in the church. Represented there were the Ibrahims of Barranquilla (one veterinarian, one doctor, and one cattle rancher), the Ibrahims of Santa Marta (one judge, numerous cattle ranchers, and several doctors), and the Ibrahims of Majagua (Alfonso, a store owner, rice farmer, and cattle rancher, and Julio, a store owner and cattle rancher). It was an important group, but all prestige settled on the head of the clan—the eldest brother of Alfonso and Julio of Majagua, a withered old man of 68 years, who had eyes like steel and the grip of a gorilla. The doctor from Medellín rose at one point and announced to the group that the old man was going to sing. Applause rang out from all. The old man rose and said he would sing a romantic song. He commenced and all conversation stopped (several men who continued their conversation were hushed by those nearby). Everyone listened as the old man sang three verses of the song. When he finished the clapping was deafening; it gave one the impression that it was sincere. The old man sat back down and smiled at everyone, accepting a shot of *aguardiente*. A moment later he rose again and said he would tell the story of a young *turco* who came to Colombia and met a Colombian girl who he then married. Applause. The man began and the interest was intense. This was an event of apparent importance to those present— a rite of intensification among the adult males of the family, a family quite conscious of the hard work and good fortune of their elders; for it was these elders who made the move from Lebanon and made their offspring judges, lawyers, and businessmen.

The *corraleja* is constructed in Majagua each year for the patron saint's festival, providing the arena for young men emboldened with alcohol to taunt the "bull" (usually a cow) and display their pride in a Spanish heritage.

We left for the bullfights several hours after we had arrived at the Ibrahim home, now in the beginning of a healthy drunk. We walked to the *corraleja,* constructed of bamboo or *caña brava* in the space between the school buildings and some public offices in the center of town. In our company now was the doctor of El Retén, one of the Ibrahims, the one who had acted the role of the drink pourer at the house, and the youngest of the clan present (the youngsters and teenagers were at the gambling tables and bullfights, and in the streets with boyfriends and girlfriends). The doctor guided us into the center of the ring or *corraleja.* The bulls (which actually turned out to be cows, complete with teats) were at the other end of the fenced-in field. A group of men were running, jumping, and waving red rags on sticks at the bull. Three horsemen, one of them *"el negro"* Acosta, a fat black man who was the owner of the cattle being beaten and badgered with sharp sticks, rode in circles around a lone cow. The cow had blood streaming from its shoulders, head, and nose. After two or three passes the cow would be provoked to rush at the men on foot with the imitation capes. One or two charges of ten feet were sufficient to scatter the crowd watching nearby. The cow settled in to await the passes of the horsemen and their pointed sticks. This went on for an hour or so, until the owner of the cattle, Acosta, signaled the end. The pen was opened and the wounded cow was herded in among other cattle, some waiting their turn, others recovering. The *corraleja* would resume tomorrow.

We walked over toward the bandstand, the porch of a school building. There a group of drunks who tooted on horns, saxophones, clarinets, and trombones were playing coastal music in time with the two drums. Several men hammered away on blocks of wood as well. In front of this band, bouncing up and down on his toes, was the Senator Ibrahim. Yet another member of this powerful family, he was introduced as the Senator. I was told that he was the patron of the band, paying them for their services and giving them drink and food during the fiesta. He was highly crocked himself, but most hospitable and happy. He danced several numbers in front of the band with the doctor and then with me. The band stayed for this special performance for the visitor at the Senator's request. Then they said they were hungry, and he waved them toward one of the kitchens on the main street, but not before they were each given swigs from the huge bottle of *aguardiente*.

When we had first arrived at the *corraleja* I had volunteered to buy a bottle for us. The doctor waved to a small black man nearby and I handed him 100 pesos and said to buy a large bottle. It was this bottle that we passed to the band, but several of them carried their own bottles of rum and *aguardiente* in back pockets. The small man who fetched the bottle (and to whom I gave the change) stayed with us late into the evening, pouring drinks. The doctor was not the one to request this service—nobody requested it that I know of. The man simply appointed himself drink pourer and stayed with us. He shared in the tugs from the bottle until it was empty, about 8:00.

From the *corraleja* we went back to the Ibrahim home in the company of the Senator and the drink pourer, our little group swollen now to seven. At the home more pork ribs and vegetables were served with hot soup. The same people continued drinking as before. Two teenagers came in and saluted their elders, sitting a moment and then leaving—the events of the drinking party were too tame for them. They mentioned *la cumbia* as they left, and I asked if a *cumbia* was to be danced. Yes, I was told, and I asked to be excused so I could go to the *cumbia*. The Senator and Alfonso Ibrahim told me to wait: the band would be on its way here when the musicians finished eating. But I wanted to see the *cumbia*. Pedro and José went with me, an excellent opportunity to leave the Ibrahim home with grace (as this was a family party).

The *cumbia* is a dance accompanied by reed flute, drums, and rasps. The flute player starts with a high lilting melody, and the drums and rasps come in together after the first phrase is ended and they augment their entrance with shouts and whoops. The dancing couple likewise say, "*Ayii,*" and they are off. The dancers are paired into male and female couples. The female holds in her right hand a bunch of five or six candles; they provide the only light for the dancing since the street is dark. The girls dance on the outside of the circle of couples, the males on the inside. The girls' movements are smooth and satin-like as they glide around the circle. The males drift about the females, holding their arms above their partner's head, or holding their arms so as to encircle her but not holding her. In this fashion the males show off their dancing partner, dancing around her, both enticing and boasting at the same moment. The girls remain erect and graceful and nonemotional, in distinct contrast to the erratic, embracing, almost worshipful gestures of their male partners. Together the couples form a circle of pairs, each pair turning on its female axis, and the whole circle turning on the axis of the band in the center.

The band pauses and then the wail of the flute introduces the next *cumbia*. Men rush to grab partners and the circle is formed. It grows and shrinks as couples come and go. The people dancing are young, finding sweethearts and lovers in the mass of people crushing in on the band. They come and go throughout the night. The landowner and cattle rancher Acosta is seen dancing with a pretty blond teenager, whom he spirits away from the crowded dance after several turns around the band. One of the Ibrahims shows up and dances with a pretty girl with black hair and light skin. An old peasant woman dances proudly with a smirk of satisfaction on her face, a cigar in her mouth, and a glitter in her eyes. Her partner is a tall young black man who dances about her as if she were a teenager, but she remains passive and dignified in the face of his adoring movements. I caught the eye of a tall, black-haired girl dancing with her boyfriend and she smiled broadly at me. I danced several rounds with her, doing my best to complement her grace with worshipful gestures.

The whole scene reminds me of the dance the Oklahoma Indian tribes call the 1949 dance, or simply "the '49er." It is said that it originated in the welcome of girl friends to the returning war veterans. These dances are always staged off from the main powwow grounds, and their main function in Oklahoma Indian society is the same as that of the *cumbia* in Colombian coastal society: it is the meeting and courting ground for youths of the two communities. They steal off from the stuffy houses full of drinking elders and somber fathers and uncles to a deserted spot. There they drink and dance among their peers, a few older people being allowed but tolerated only in exchange for their obvious approval of the event. What is really happening is the courtship process where the girls test their skills of seduction and the boys tout their prowess. The *cumbia* is a cultural element approved and loved by all ages, but in practice perpetuated by the eternal process of mating and testing among the adolescents of the town.

We left the *cumbia* about 9:00 and caught the *chiva* back to Majagua, the tiny makeshift bus crammed full of drunken fiesta-goers from our town.

SOCIAL SECTORS

Partridge's investigations during March, April, and May in the three settlements he had chosen for intensive survey, interview, and observation—the rural hamlet, the town neighborhood, and the highland neighborhood—led to a new perspective on social organization. Through tracing out the life cycles of informants in these settlements Partridge arrived at the notion of "social sectors" within the community. These he called the lower coastal sector, the upper coastal sector, and the highland sector. In his letter to Kimball on 30 June he notes that they are distinguished from "social classes" in the western sociological sense of that phrase. In a paper written at the time for the Ninth International Congress of Anthropological and Ethnological Sciences (Partridge 1975) he also utilized the notion of "social sectors."

An example will illustrate the distinction between social sector and social class. According to social class criteria, such as level of education, type of housing, level of income, etc., the managers of cattle estates and the managers of rice estates would be considered members of the same category or social class. But through his study of patterns of interaction Partridge had discovered that cattle estate managers had risen from the ranks of wage laborers and peasants in the community; maintained important bonds of reciprocal exchange with peasants, artisans, and workers; and had become skilled at handling cattle by serving a short apprenticeship under more knowledgeable cowboys, much like artisans learned leatherworking, masonry, or carpentry. In contrast, rice estate managers were descendants of the formerly wealthy families of the banana zone who had been banana producers. Following the economic crisis that engulfed these families, many of their offspring were trained by relatives in modern agricultural techniques and became active in mechanized agriculture. They maintained important ties to the most prestigious families in the community, and none with the artisans, peasants, and wage laborers. Although the rice and cattle managers were both salaried employees on large estates, their origins and connections placed them in distinctly different social spheres. As an example, the patron saint festival and the activities of the Ibrahim family illustrate another subcultural variation in this social sector. Here the Ibrahims displayed, both as public sponsors of the fiesta and in their particular familial celebration, their position and role in the life of the community.

It became evident that several distinct social fields of interaction were present in the coastal subcultural tradition. Fleshing out the details was achieved through use of several techniques. The life cycle of the highland lower sector is included here to illustrate another ordering that Partridge undertook in April and May in developing the notion of social sectors.

15 May 1973

Organization of Activity on the *Cachaco Finca*

Children up to age 3—play, no responsibilities; looked after by all members of the household at various times but usually by older sisters, aunts, and mothers.

Children 4 to 7 (males)—care of father's animals: wash them upon his return from trips, put them out to pasture, catch them in the morning; herd the cattle home in the evening and release them in the morning; receive orders from older siblings and parents to run errands such as getting firewood, cutting a stick, carrying a message, carrying water, and bringing an object.

Children 4 to 7 (females)—care of babies and youngsters; help older siblings at their tasks under their orders; bring firewood and water.

Children 8 to 14 (males)—responsibility for the cattle, such as herding them, counting them at day's end, looking for strays; chop firewood; saddle burros and mules for carrying loads; meet father at truck station with pack animals and horses on return trips; direct younger male assistants in these tasks.

Children 8 to 14 (females)—responsibility for milking the cattle in the morning and evening and carrying the milk to the kitchen; assist with the preparation of food; care of babies and youngsters; direct younger siblings in these tasks; clean house.

Children 15 and up (males)—work in the fields with father; hunt with father, siblings of same age, or friends and relatives in the *vereda;* visit potential mates from other highland households in *vereda* or between *veredas*.

Children 15 and up (females)—assist mother in kitchen in food preparation, fire building, etc.; care for babies and direct younger children in running errands; clean house; receive suitors.

Adult females—confined almost entirely to the kitchen; rarely seen in other parts of the home except in late evening when kitchen work itself is exhausted. Cooking, sewing and mending clothes, and care of infants are all centered in the kitchen so that the woman rarely leaves it. Offspring assist her greatly; daughters and daughters-in-law do a great deal of the work. All women cooperate in the care of babies, holding her own or someone else's child for periods of time but feeding and changing her own.

Adult males—range over the entire *finca,* the countryside, and the roads connecting various settlements in the area. Planting, clearing, harvesting, marketing, and household economics are in their hands. Hunt frequently with older children and with friends of the *vereda.* Father of the family is in charge of all activity on the farm and consulted each morning by even adult-age sons and sons-in-law for instructions concerning the day's activities.

[Similar information gathered in the other sectors provided part of the basis for establishing comparatively the differences among the different sectors.]

30 June 1973

Dear Dr. Kimball:

Under a separate cover I am sending you my field notes together with a copy of my paper "Cannabis and Cultural Groups in a Colombian Municipio," which I prepared over the past weeks for the Conference on Cross-Cultural Perspectives on Cannabis in August.

It is only a preliminary analysis, but it is more or less a synopsis of what I plan to do with cannabis in the dissertation. Of course, all sections will be expanded greatly and the data enlarged and discussed in detail, meaning an expansion into chapters, one of which I envision being devoted to the Use of Drugs, including tobacco and alcohol.

Recently I wrote to Dr. Carter and mentioned that I also want to include a chapter devoted to analysis of *Cien Años de Soledad* by Gabriel García Márquez. This analysis would be along the lines suggested by you several times in lunch conversations and by Dr. Wagley in his revised *Introduction to Brazil*. The reason for this is covered in my notes. Basically, I plan to draw upon the novel for several themes or statements of world view *claimed* to be typical of coastal culture, and then use my own data to explore these.

In the paper you will notice that I used the term "sector" instead of "social class." This is because I am becoming increasingly dissatisfied with the latter concept. For example, the elite and middle sectors here in town are composed of distinct groups, but my data show that they interact vis-à-vis other groups as a single group. And this is not entirely a matter of economics. Anyway, I want to devote some time to working on this concept when I return, especially now that I have read many Latin American sociologists who find themselves immersed in a tangle of ready-made social class concepts that don't fit the reality of Latin America. For this reason I used "sector" and "subculture."

The school system is still a large gap in my knowledge that I am attempting to fill. I have been hindered by a teachers' strike that has lasted now two months, but I hear it will be over soon.

Best wishes,
Bill

WORLD VIEW

A further realignment in Partridge's thinking about the model of community was stimulated by Kimball's letter of 10 July. In that letter Kimball refers again to what he meant by world view by building upon Partridge's idea of "social sectors." Kimball outlines a way of thinking about community as a number of segments, each of which has its own model of the world to which the young are exposed.

Anthropological writing about world view often defines the notion to mean the outlook upon the world that typifies an entire population (e.g., Foster's "Image of the Limited Good," which has been applied to all peasants throughout the world). This is how Partridge had been thinking about his community until he received Kimball's letter in July. Partridge's own investigation had led him to the notion of social "sectors" as discrete entities within the larger community, each having its own socialization practices, its own ritual activities, its own work patterns, and the like. Yet the notion of an overarching world view which could encompass these various sectors troubled Partridge, in fact troubled him to the point that he did not address the topic of world view in his notes until 28 July.

Kimball's letter of 10 July "set off a chain reaction" in Partridge's thinking about world view, coming as it did at a time when Partridge was developing his notion of sectors and when he was having trouble with the classical anthropological notion of world view. We can trace the results by reading Kimball's letter of 10 July and Partridge's notes of 28 July, which he wrote shortly after receiving Kimball's letter.

10 July 1973

Dear Bill:

Your letter of 30 June and recent batch of field notes and the cannabis article have arrived. I have given all these a reading and have only a few comments to make. The cannabis article is well written and organized and needs only minor polishing and a few corrections (spelling). I gather that you have worked out in great detail all the situations in which cannabis or alcohol are used separately or together, as well as by whom they are used. Have you also done this for the lesser stimulants such as tobacco, coffee, and tea? There may be some interesting sex, age, and culture group differences and combinations. Further, I think you should not ignore the recent use of marijuana by a new population. The recent use is tied to social change (in sex definitions, status, etc.), just as economic change has been tied to the middle sector picking up distribution. Is your paper clear enough on the different or separate roles of distributors and cultivators?

Now to socialization. The school system is one of the formal arrangements of the society, but there are others, such as the church for the catechism and confirmation. However, how about other segments such as the professions and government? It might be interesting to have some interviews with professionals about how they got their training and then were inducted (including your friend, the pretty prostitute). Also find out how one is inducted into the use of any of the stimulants (coffee, tea, tobacco, alcohol, etc.)—by whom, in what situation, at what age, etc. This is missing from your paper.

One should consider the community as a number of interrelated or apposite segments, each of which has its own model to which the young are exposed and which serves as the training locale for turning them into adults. Even if you cannot get the detail of this process you should get the structure of it. It will help you see differences in the table of organization of each of the subsections of the community and of the interlinkages. In this regard, make a list of the areas of tension, for the individual as well as for the group.

It is good that you now see that it is impossible to project our system of social classes to explain the nature of social divisions in Colombia. I think that if you analyze the meaning of work, the setting and consequences of socialization of the young (interaction and values), the characteristic types of social groupings, the table of organization (the personnel), the choice of a marriage partner, and the external relations of one group with another, you will have worked out the segmental structure and its dynamics.

As a start and for my information, would you summarize what you know about the organization of behavior around the preparation and consumption of food, including staple diet and its daily variation, ceremonial variation, and changes that have occurred over time with whatever explanations are available for these? Pay attention to any use of stimulants. Such a summary should alert you to any gaps in your knowledge and might give some new leads.

Summer seems to have made very little difference in the intensity of the rhythm of life here, some slight change in emphasis from teaching to other matters. Our research project is under full steam.

Best wishes,
Solon Kimball

28 July 1973

Dr. Kimball's letter of 10 July has set off a chain reaction in my thinking regarding (1) the segmentation of the community, (2) the nature of socialization, and (3) the concept of world view.

The separate segments of the community (each composed of elements we recognize as statuses or positions in the table of organization) are articulated in different ways. That is to say, there is no single organizing principle that applies to all units in the community, but rather a variety of these. The key phrase in the letter of 10 July is "segments, each of which has its own model to which the young are exposed and which serves as the training locale for turning them into adults." According to this definition, then, there are three sectors; however, they are not arranged hierarchically. This is not a social-class system, but a system of relatively closed sectors and spheres of activity. I will label them the highland sector, the lower coastal sector, and the upper coastal sector.

The distinction becomes clearer when we construct models of world view for each of these sectors (abstracted from observed interaction, values, etc.):

Highland sector—characterized by a *linear* world view in which each generation replaces the previous generation; by a sedentary, relatively unchanging existence; and by a long-term (lifelong) commitment of the individual to the (family) group.

Lower coastal sector—characterized by a *mobile-isolate* world view in which the individual exploits the world alone, with little aid from kin or nonkin; by an ego-centered world; by extenuated existence; and by a short-term commitment of individual to group.

Upper coastal sector—characterized by a *radial* world view in which some families are trunks of a network interconnecting several of these families; by an individual's taking his position where he happens to fall (trunk, branches, etc.); by a static and circular system of cooperation among families; by a world exploited by such a network of cooperating families; by control of resources; by long-term commitment, first to family and then to the network of families; and by families constantly shifting, and rising, and falling in power within the network, but seldom suffering exclusion from network.

The evidence that supports these assigned world views is extensive. The *linear* world of the highland sector is expressed in the extended three-generation family, the organization of work, the work group, the travel pattern to town, the continuing dominance of the household head long into an offspring's adulthood, and the continuity of the nature of exploitation of the land. The absence of cooperative nonkin groups is further evidence of this filial commitment. It seems to be an unchanging world, transplanted from the interior and unbending to other world views here on the coast. Customs (food preparation, cultivation techniques, celebrations) are perpetuated unchanged. The object of work and of life itself is the creation of a productive farm for the benefit of family members. A successful man can support his own parents, his spouse's parents, his offspring, his offsprings' spouses, and his grandchildren (perhaps 25 people) on the produce of his farm, his planning, his work, his intelligence. The more people a man is able to support in this fashion, the higher he is in the status hierarchy. In his path follow his lineal male descendants, who divide the land equally among themselves, perhaps colonizing other land to support the growing family. They live exactly as did their father and grandfather, seeking the same rewards.

The *mobile-isolate* world view is best expressed in the ego-centered, egotistical nature of social and economic relations among the coastal lower sector people. Life and survival itself depend upon personal contacts, friendships, and contracts obtained from patrons or employers. The family unit is the man, his wife, and his children. All others come second. And in a pinch even the children and wife must be jettisoned to permit his survival, as he takes to the city or to a distant locale to find work. He depends upon his own initiative, ingenuity, and intelligence in exploiting the options open to him. His children are taught to do likewise. They do not take over their father's position—only his world view and perhaps a few of his character traits that have made his survival possible. Each child is trained to be an individual, an ego, no more and no less; trained to cooperate when necessary, but to live on his own, keep his commitments nonbinding, short, and uncomplicated. He learns much of this between the ages of 7 and 15 in the adolescent peer groups through which he passes. He learns that others can screw you, beat you up, rob you; he learns that one can also screw others, win bets, exploit ignorance, rob others. When he gets on a bus he does not form a line and wait; he fights his way to the door. Ego is all that is important. Once on the bus he will chat peacefully and congenially with those he elbowed aside at the door. He may even help find a seat for an old lady whom he shoved out of the way. He will borrow money and then take months to pay it back, knowing the other party can often do nothing about it. He will take a job for a day, a week, a month, and then leave and go to another town. He will promise to work on Saturday and then not show up to work if he chooses not to. He is independent, mobile, resourceful, individualistic, egotistic. When drunk he will boast at the top of his lungs of his prowess, his strength, his virility. If he is farsighted and bright when young, he will see that he must either work in the fields with a machete or seek some manner of permanent employment. Of the latter, only the carefully cultivated relationship with an estate manager or landowner can ensure security in the area of agricultural labor. He will learn

deference to this man, learn to work with a group of men like himself, all
competing for the favor of the boss. He indeed views the world as
composed of rich and poor: the rich are those able to kill other men if they
care to and still remain free of legal responsibility. He consequently
recognizes that, given their all-powerful status, the rich are frequently
enemies in his world. If as a young man he looks very far ahead, he will see
that apprenticeship with an artisan is another path open to him. Like the
relation with the agricultural patron, the relationship with the artisan is a
paternalistic one. He must first seek the position of helper for dirt wages,
work very hard, and be ready to learn. The trek is a difficult one, involving
a commitment of several years. Consequently, few men from this sector
(given their world view and values) make the change to a long-term
commitment. But a few do, settling in one spot to work in the shop of a
tailor, a brickmaker, a carpenter, a saddlemaker, or a shopkeeper. There
they learn a trade after perhaps five or more years of commitment. Still
others migrate to the city and there commit themselves to mastering the art
of driving a bus or truck, also demanding several years in the status of
helper and trainee. Work in this sector carries the following meaning; one
earns money and with money one can play, have rich clothes, feed a
family, and go to the bar and whorehouse. Work is good if work pays
money, for money brings status (expressed in terms of possessions,
clothes, and bar tabs) among one's peers.

The *radial* world view of the coastal upper sector is perhaps the simplest
of all. A very few families control all available resources in Colombia, but
these families do not always maintain the same position in relation to one
another. Rather, there is a waxing and waning of prospects for families: a
family may wax in one generation and wane in the next, its power and
wealth growing or diminishing according to the abilities and training of the
offspring. But the significant fact is that it is always the same families that
radiate about the sources of power and wealth. In a particular generation
they may not be on top, but they are not far away and are helping keep the
system (the world, as they see it) on an even keel for their eventual rise to
power. The individual, then, sees the world as a series of radial networks
stemming off of the main trunks of power and wealth. His political party,
his family, and he himself may not be in direct control of this wealth and
power, but they are directly dependent upon it for their status and life, for
their survival, and for their future. For example, the son of a ruined banana
producer becomes an employee of an estate. His father knew the estate
owner in the old days, and so his position is made if he has the intelligence
to make it. The family friend may even train the boy for the position.
Likewise, the offspring of a top employee of the banana company finds

doors opening to him in the sector. His family had money once, though not now. But he can use old family ties that continue to radiate about him and win a position as estate manager. Here he can work to rebuild his fortune. Similarly, the offspring of a wealthy landowner can go into politics where his father is well known. Or he can go into a profession and then into politics. But in any of these positions or statuses his world is the same: a radial network of persons whose last names—families—he has known since birth. His task is to find out which ones are in power this year and, therefore, which are to be courted and won to his side. The players never change, merely their positions in the system. All share the same long-term commitment to the maintenance of the radius, the boundary, the limits of the upper sector, and to the control of resources that makes the radius a reality and necessity. The offspring learns this early as important people visit his home; it is reinforced as he is sent to school—and sent to complete his schooling, not to drop out—there discovering the other students who are within the radial network; and it is further reinforced when he is sent to a private school in the city along with his peers of the radial network; in some cases it may be still further reinforced by a university education, where again only his peers in the radial network will be found in attendance. The school system in Colombia is an artifact of this radial world view.

These three world views, characterized here as models called *linear, mobile-isolate,* and *radial,* are all present in the same community. And individuals are socialized and educated to see the world in one of these three ways. Depending upon individual abilities, people in each of the sectors are able to fulfill their expectations about the nature of the world. While they play a variety of roles, these can all be boiled down to three basic perceptions of the nature of the world in which they live.

(One is reminded here of the tension that sprang up several months ago when Gladys Ardila decided to marry a boy from the lower coastal sector. She comes from a family well-placed in the group that radiates about the trunk of power and wealth on the coast. Her mother was angry to the point of not speaking to her, forbidding her to see the boy. The engagement and marriage were the gossip of the town, for she was stepping outside the radial network to find a mate, a wage earner whose family was not of the radial group. The marriage took place in secret and the mother was not present, but the whole town knew. It was kept thus "secret" for about two weeks during which the mother sulked and the daughter lived at home rather than with her spouse. When he raised the money she moved in with him, but the mother continued sulking for a few more weeks, now officially let in on the "secret" by her daughter's living with the man of her choice.)

28 July 1973

Dear Dr. Kimball:

Thank you for your excellent letter of 10 July. Your suggestions were quite helpful in realigning my thinking on the nature of segments in the community, the relations among these, the nature of world view typical of each segment, and the socialization of offspring into each segment. I have worked out a first approximation of my thinking on this and have included it in my field notes, which should be on their way in a few days.

Your suggestions are really quite important in this regard and often open my eyes to ways of interpreting my data that I have simply not considered. Your sentence ''segments, each of which has its own model to which the young are exposed and which serves as the training locale for turning them into adults'' is such an eye-opener. Viewed in this way my data take on a new meaning, and the question of world view (rather, multiple world views operating together in the community) can be easily resolved. For, all along, I have been looking for a key, single principle that could explain the variety of interaction patterns, roles, beliefs, and values that I have documented. I was thinking of world view as an organizing principle present throughout the community, and now I see it as pertaining to segments. The community itself is the product of the grafting of these distinct views of the world onto each other. Thus community does not imply homogeneity of values or beliefs but merely the complementary fit among elements.

My informants on cannabis now number 15 and the number is still growing. The data continue to come in and already some of the points I made in the paper must be modified (although in general it is correct) in light of new data.

I have also worked out a treatment of the nature of food, the behavior surrounding food production and consumption, the yearly food cycle, and the ceremonial foods and drinks. This is included in the notes also.

Similarly, I am working on your suggestion regarding the data on the other stimulants such as coffee, tea, and tobacco. And I will be paying greater attention to the new population using cannabis.

On 23 August I will be flying to Miami for a few days vacation before flying to Chicago for the ICAES meetings on the twenty-seventh. I am really looking forward to the conference on cannabis, especially since Dr. Carter will be there and we can discuss some of the ideas I am working on for analyzing cannabis use.

I hope to be able to get to Bogotá and the Luis Angel Arango Library before leaving for Miami and Chicago, for only there, it appears, will I be able to get to the newspaper collections and to several rare books (all books are rare here) that are crucial to my research. I hope to spend about six days there working. If this is not possible, then I will have to spend the time in September upon returning.

As the final months of the fieldwork tick off I am more excited about the study. Each day I sit down and make lists of points that must be covered, gaps in my data, people I need to interview, etc. It is perhaps the most rewarding period in the field.

Best wishes,
William L. Partridge

15 August 1973

Dear Bill:

Your last letter and batch of notes have arrived. I always find them interesting, and begin to have the feeling that you are an old hand at the game now and know more about the area you are studying than any other person. Once, toward the end of my Irish stay, I had the feeling that I could look at a man or his clothes, listen to his speech, see his body posture, and know exactly where he fitted in the social scheme, how he thought, and how he would react to given situations. Sometimes they fooled me and I was annoyed because they deviated. (Do you have a detailed listing of clothing related to status, situation, and sex?—Now is the time to be alert to this.)

I think I suggested before that you do a typology of events. Now that you have worked out your segments and associated world views, you can bring it up to date on the basis of events occurring only within a particular segment and those that occur across segments. These are the important ones for seeing tensions. You have the one case of cross-segment crossing in marriage. Are there other instances of mobility from one segment to the other, or does each have its own internal pyramid? How then are they finally given cohesion, or rather linkage? Probably in either national or religious affairs. And you have paid no attention to the priests: what is the structuring of the Catholic church and how is it linked? Look particularly at the relation to family and rites of passage, to schooling, to politics. Does it attempt to develop a view encompassing the segmental variation?

Pay particular attention to the departure behavior of others, and what happens to yourself. How does one get separated, but not completely cut off?

Hasta luego.
Solon Kimball

ECONOMIC DIMENSIONS OF COMMUNITY

The tempo of the dialogue between senior and junior partners increased as Partridge became more deeply involved in his research. Kimball's requests became more specific and Partridge's responses more concise. On 12 September Kimball wrote from the university and asked about production-consumption units, work groups, and the like; Partridge had already recorded a great deal of information on the economic life of the community, but he had not yet organized his knowledge in a systematic way nor integrated economic aspects into the emerging model of community. Partridge responded with a descriptive outline of production units found in the community.

A summary outline permitted a comparison of the quality of data for each distinctive economic segment. Partridge discovered that he did not have sufficient data on the commercial production and distribution of cattle and cattle products. The local market was well understood, but the large-scale operations for urban markets had not been sufficiently studied. Through systematic assessment of economic information for each subcommunity, attention was directed to gaps that still remained to be examined during the final months in the field.

The six spheres of economic activity present in Majagua represent a remarkable diversity within one community form. To the untrained observer these might appear to be discrete and independent, but their articulation through the nodal functions of Majagua gives testimony to their interconnections and interdependence. Moreover, it is clear that interdependence and interconnection between the parts of community do not spell uniformity or homogeneity for the people who live there. We find the distinctiveness of the highland subcultural tradition to be compatible with the coastal subcultural tradition, the distinctiveness of the estate system to be compatible with that of the shopkeepers' small-scale cattle ranches. Economic activity is divided into separate yet interdependent spheres of activity. Thus, each subcultural tradition—with its distinct economic activities, form of work group formation, and identifiable world view—does not conflict with others but seems to mesh with other spheres through complementary relationships. Goods, services, and personnel for each sphere are not found elsewhere in the community. Because of their distinctiveness, their contribution to the life of the community is not lessened but heightened.

The economic organization that emerges further confirmed the model of community that Partridge had developed months earlier. The economic data establish clearly that distinct segments were successfully integrated into a whole. Moreover, when the organization of the production, distribution, and consumption of cannabis was finally understood, it also became clear that cannabis mirrored in all significant aspects the structure of community life discovered through the study of religious, political, familial, and economic activity.

12 September 1973

Dear Bill:

It is clear from your notes that there are several types of production-consumption systems in the locality in which you are working. Each one has its own pattern of work groups (including hierarchy), practices, technology, and ecological setting. Each also has a history, distinctive demographic characteristics, and variations of a belief system. There are differences in their orientation toward the household and toward the market.

Now I suggest that you sketch out all of these systems using the variables provided in microsystem analysis. This will show you where you have gaps that can be filled in quickly. I suspect that such a grouping will add more meaning to your social class segments, and it may also help to clarify the pattern of cannabis cultivation and use.

But there is another reason for my suggestion. It is clear that the world is in the beginning phases of a food crisis. As usual, the proffered solutions are going to be simplistic and unilinear, and at least somewhat a distortion of the facts. Here is the opportunity for anthropology to make a major contribution to the development of policy, program, and procedures. To do so we have to carry the agriculturists with us and show them that the production-technical-marketing systems are just inadequate as the basis for planning. They must see it whole, and out of science.

The preschool doldrums are with us, but some fresh student faces are about.

Best wishes,
Solon Kimball

OUTLINE OF PRODUCTION UNITS

Highland Subculture: Peasant *Finca*

Personnel
male household head, mate or wife, male offspring, female offspring, sons-in-law, daughters-in-law, grandchildren, aged parents, cousins and mates, siblings and mates

Relationships
  (1) male household head/all males in the household
  (2) mate of household head/all females
  (3) sibling/sibling
  (4) aged parents/children and grandchildren
  (5) male household head/Caja Agraria
  (6) male household head/storekeepers
  (7) male household head/other peasants

Groups
  (A) Male household head directs the work of all males present on *finca*.
  (B) Female mate directs the work of all females present on *finca*.
  (C) Siblings work in age-graded fashion and are directed by older
      siblings and adults; duties are specific to age groups.
  (D) Male household head handles all interface relations with other
      groups, arranging for the necessary services, visiting, travel, etc.
  (E) Male household head interacts with other male household heads
      from the *vereda* who cooperate in hunting wild animals, share
      slaughtered animals, exchange seeds, lend tools and weapons, lend
      animals, and sell items they have made or acquired.

Activities
  (1) clearing and burning—group A
  (2) planting—group A
  (3) weeding—group A
  (4) harvest—group A
  (5) transport to town—group A
  (6) selling—group A
  (7) hunting—groups A and E
  (8) traveling to shop—group A
  (9) slaughter of animals—group A
  (10) milking—groups B and C
  (11) cheese making—group B
  (12) cooking and food preparation—group B
  (13) tending kitchen garden—group B
  (14) child care—groups B and C
  (15) washing and cleaning—groups B and C
  (16) visiting—whole family
  (17) cattle care—group C
  (18) obtaining loans for planting—group D

Coastal Subculture: Rice *Finca*

Personnel
   Owner, *mandador,* employees, day laborers, hired services, government services, wholesaler, retailer, banks

Relationships
   (1) *mandador*/day laborer
   (2) owner/*mandador*
   (3) owner/employees
   (4) owner/government services (INCORA water supply)
   (5) owner/banks (planting loans)
   (6) owner/hired services (fertilizing by airplane, transport by truck to the city, etc.)
   (7) owner/wholesaler (purchasing and processing)
   (8) wholesaler/retailer (local general stores retail)

Groups
   (A) Nonkin male day laborers directed by *mandador;* hired by the job for a set period of time and then released; composition changes from job to job; wage labor, earning about $1.00 a day.
   (B) Nonkin male employees directed by owner and *mandador;* farm machinery operators; permanent employees; composition rarely changes; wage labor, earning about $2.00 a day; patron/client.
   (C) *Mandador* directed by owner; in charge of day-to-day operations of the *finca*; receives a plot of land to farm and a cash wage; permanent employee; patron/client; sometimes related to the owner, often friend of the family.
   (D) Production groups (above) interact with other groups not directly connected to the *finca;* these are interfaces between units. Examples are: fertilizer airplane owners, tractor salesmen, bank employees, INCORA employees, wholesalers. Such interfaces generally involve the owner and the *mandador*.

Activities
   (1) clearing and burning—group A
   (2) irrigation ditch preparation—group A
   (3) plowing and harrowing—group B
   (4) planting—group B
   (5) weeding—group D (hired)
   (6) harvesting—group B (or hired if owner lacks the necessary machinery)
   (7) shipment to city—group D (hired)

(8) administration (payment of workers, scheduling of activity, pro-
curement of resources, crossing interfaces between units to arrange
for services needed, directing daily work)—group C

Coastal Subculture: *Parcelero Finca*

Personnel
The household heads (male) of from 3 to 20 families, INCORA services,
agricultural federation services, females

Relationships
(1) worker/worker
(2) *jefe*/worker
(3) workers/INCORA services
(4) workers/agricultural federation services
(5) females of one family/workers

Groups
(A) Workers composed of nonkin male day laborers working in concert
on all tasks on the *finca*.
(B) A *jefe* or *el hombre que indica* is generally the oldest of the
cooperative members; his position is one of tacit approval by the
other workers; he has no decision-making powers (or other powers)
but functions as the leader and often spokesman of the group.
(C) INCORA provides practically all services and resources needed by
the *parcela* members: tractors to plow and harrow and plant the
land, bulldozers to clear dense brush and trees, loans for water,
loans for land (to be paid off within 15 years from the profits the
group makes), credit with the agricultural federations with whom
the *parcela* members must deal, and harvesters.
(D) Agricultural federations provide the *parcela* with seed for planting
and airplane fertilizer spraying on definite credit terms. These are
met at harvest time when the workers sell their product to the
federation to pay their bill (and make some profit to pay INCORA
and to live on).
(E) If the *parcela* is a great distance from town, one or several women
of one of the families will live on the land. They frequently cook the
main midday meal for all the *parcela* members. In some cases all of
the families live on the land; in these cases each female group cooks
only for its own males. In other cases the *parcela* families live in
town and again each female cooks for her male.

Activities
(1) clearing and burning—group A

    (2) irrigation ditch preparation—group A
    (3) plowing and harrowing—group C
    (4) planting—group C
    (5) weeding—group D
    (6) harvesting —group C
    (7) shipment to city—group C
    (8) administration (crossing interfaces between units for services needed)—group B

Coastal Subculture: Peasant *Finca*

Personnel
    male household head, mate or wife, male offspring, female offspring, siblings and mates of either head or his mate, parents of either head or his mate, sons-in-law, daughters-in-law, grandchildren (exact composition varies widely but within these limits—cousins, for example, are excluded—the basic structure being the stem family which expands and contracts over time)

Relationships
    (1) male head/male offspring, sons-in-law, siblings, and any other males living in household
    (2) mate of household head/female offspring, siblings, daughters-in-law, and any other females
    (3) sibling/sibling
    (4) aged parents/their offspring and grandchildren
    (5) male head/storekeepers
    (6) male head/petty vegetable merchants
    (7) male head/market women
    (8) male head/Caja Agraria
    (9) male head/other peasants

Groups
    (A) Male work group composed of family members; when family lives in town only work-group members travel to the *finca*.
    (B) Female work group composed of family members.
    (C) Siblings have specific duties to perform, often under direction of an older sibling or adult.
    (D) Male household head interacts with all other groups, handling all interface relationships, arranging for the necessary services, etc.
    (E) Male household head is part of a large group of peers (other peasant household heads) who cooperate in lending pack animals, sharing drinks, sharing seeds, lending farm tools, etc.

Activities
    (1) clearing and burning—group A
    (2) planting—group A
    (3) weeding—group A
    (4) harvesting—group A
    (5) transport to market—group A
    (6) obtaining loans for planting—group D
    (7) making charcoal—group A
    (8) hunting wild animals—group A
    (9) cooking and food preparation—group B
  (10) washing and cleaning—group B
  (11) child care—group B
  (12) bargaining with storekeepers, market women, petty vegetable merchants—group D

Coastal Subculture: Cattle *Finca*

Personnel
    owner (absentee), *capataz, mandador,* employees, wholesale buyer, slaughterhouse employees, retailer, hired services, government services, *selectador*

Relationships
    (1) owner/*capataz*
    (2) owner/*mandador*
    (3) *capataz/mandador*
    (4) *capataz*/employees
    (5) *mandador*/employees
    (incomplete)

Groups
    (A) Owner directs the work of his *capataz* and *mandador* in administering the operation of the *finca*.
    (B) *Capataz* directs the work of a group of employees in managing the cattle-connected operations (branding, cutting out calves, salt, vaccination, moving between pastures, etc.).
    (C) *Mandador* directs the work of other employees in clearing, burning, and planting pasture.
    (incomplete)

Activities
    (incomplete)

Coastal Subculture: Storekeeper and Peasant Cattle *Finca*

Personnel

owner (storekeeper, peasant, or *mandador* of larger *finca*), employees, government services, slaughterhouse employees, *tiendas* that sell meat, buyer

Relationships
  (1) owner/employee
  (2) owner/buyer
  (3) buyer/government services
  (4) buyer/slaughterhouse
  (5) buyer/*tiendas*
  (6) slaughterhouse/*tiendas*

Groups
  (A) Owner directs the work of one or more employees who live on the land and care for the cattle, milking them twice daily, selling the milk in town, reporting illness, etc.
  (B) Owner may sell directly to the *tiendas* that market meat to the town, but generally they sell to buyers who specialize in obtaining cattle and selling them to the *tienda* owners.
  (C) Buyer generally sees the cattle through the entire process of inspection, obtaining permission for slaughter, the slaughter, and transport to the *tienda;* owners will sell to these specialists to avoid the paperwork, taxes, etc.

Activities
   (1) purchase of calves—group A
   (2) program of vaccinations—group A
   (3) curing illnesses—group A
   (4) milking—group A
   (5) transport of milk to market—group A
   (6) changing of pasture—group A
   (7) cleaning pasture—group A
   (8) selling—group B or C
   (9) transport to market—group A
  (10) inspection—group B or C
  (11) slaughter—group B or C
  (12) transport to *tienda* in market—group B or C
  (13) marketing of meat—*tienda*

Relation of Production Unit to Consumption Units

Production Unit	Distribution Route	Consumption Units
(1) Peasant *finca* (highland)	Local petty merchant	(a) peasant family (b) worker families (c) all sectors of the town population (d) other peasant families through barter/sale
(2) Rice *finca* (coastal)	Urban market	(a) owner's family (b) employees' families (c) *mandador*'s family (d) worker families (e) urban upper class (f) urban employee class (g) urban working class (h) government employees (i) entrepreneur class
(3) *Parcelero finca* (coastal)	Urban market	(a) *parcela* member families (b) all groups included for production unit 2
(4) Peasant *finca* (coastal)	Local petty merchants	(a) peasant family (b) worker families (c) all sectors of the town population (d) other peasant families through barter/sale
(5) Cattle *finca* (coastal)	Urban market	(a) same as production unit 2
(6) Storekeeper, peasant, and employee cattle *finca* (coastal and highland)	Local petty merchants	(a) all sectors of the town population (b) other peasant families through barter/sale

CANNABIS AND COMMUNITY

Cannabis plays several roles in the life of the community of Majagua, its role varying with the social grouping with which it is associated. Said another way, cannabis means different things to different people. Almost all residents of the community are involved with some aspect of its production, distribution, or consumption. But the meaning of cannabis varies not with the production-distribution-consumption process as much as with the social groupings.

In the highland subculture, a subculture which functions as one of the three social sectors in the community, cannabis is grown but not consumed. Highlanders do not smoke it. They feel cannabis is dangerous. Yet cannabis is a valuable cash crop, like coffee or tobacco. It is as a cash crop that cannabis fits naturally into the yearly cycle of clearing, burning, planting, weeding, and harvesting. Alongside corn, yuca, beans, and coffee, cannabis is produced. Due to its illegal status, however, the system of marketing is different. The peasant sells his cannabis crop to wealthy men of the lowlands. This is his only contact with members of this social sector, and it arises from the unusual circumstances of clandestine production and the isolation of the highland farms.

Significantly, the highlanders grow tons of cannabis annually; if they cared to, they could smoke as much as they would like. But they do not. In fact, they teach their sons and daughters that only thieves and vagabonds smoke cannabis. The cannabis smoking custom, therefore, is not randomly diffused throughout a population. In the highlands it met a cultural barrier beyond which it did not spread. This directs our attention to the significant cultural differences between these highlanders and those who smoke cannabis in the lowlands.

In the coastal subculture, a subculture that encompasses the two remaining social sectors in the community, cannabis has several meanings that correspond to social sector divisions. In the upper coastal sector the traditional view of cannabis has been somewhat similar to that of the highlands. Cannabis is felt to be dangerous, smoked only by thieves and vagabonds. Upper coastal sector parents condemn childish acts by using the word *marijuanero* when they intend to describe someone who is slovenly, lazy, or untrustworthy. Yet commercial distributors of cannabis come from this social sector. The people involved in the international traffic are wealthy landowners, professionals, rice estate managers, politicians, and other descendants of important and influential families. This activity is undertaken much like other contraband activity, clandestine merchandising of illegal commodities such as alcohol, cigarettes, televisions, phonographs, and radios. Cannabis is only one of the more lucrative items in the list of contraband merchandise. Clearly the upper coastal sector holds a double set of values regarding cannabis. While consumption is negatively sanctioned, trade in cannabis is not similarly discouraged. Here again it should be noted that cannabis use has not diffused randomly throughout the population but only to certain sectors of certain subcultures.

Cannabis smoking is prevalent only in the lower coastal sector among the peasants, estate workers, and artisans of the coastal subculture. Those who own their land, such as the peasants, grow small amounts of cannabis (using techniques that vary greatly from those used by commercial cultivators of the highlands) for their own use and for trade with other members of the lower coastal sector. This distribution network contrasts greatly with highland-grown cannabis, which is funneled to the cities and foreign markets and never reaches the local consumer of Majagua. Rather, locally produced cannabis is exchanged in small amounts among friends and coworkers.

The social and cultural differences between the lower coastal sector and the highland sector can be examined here in order to discover the relationship between cannabis and social structure. To do this we shall describe the nature of the life cycle in both sectors, the composition of the work group, the processes of recruitment to work groups, and the nature of leadership in the work groups. As will become apparent, significant differences exist that are related to the presence or absence of cannabis smoking in these two social sectors.

In the lower coastal sector, cannabis smoking occurs in a specific setting called the *chagua*. Historically, the Spanish grafted onto the native cultures of the coast the cattle estate systems and the *encomienda,* a device for recruiting labor to the great estates. Alongside the estate and its tribute labor stood indigenous communities; these were taxed for the support of the Spanish cities. The device by which tributes and taxes were met, both in native communities and on estates, was the communal work party, called the *chagua*. In fact, these work groups were traditional and ordinances were passed to permit the Indians to continue "their drunken feasts upon occasion of the collective planting, on the condition that there not be excess" (Patiño 1965:393, Partridge's translation). The *chagua* persists to the present in the coastal subculture. It was modified during the period of the United Fruit Company (between 1896 and 1964), when wage labor and a migratory agricultural laboring class became typical of the coast. Today, the work gangs are composed of nonkin, whereas traditionally they were made up of kinsmen.

This form of organization traditionally involved the exchange not only of labor but also of food and drink among participants. We read the following description of the *chagua*:

> The Indians [in the jurisdiction of Santa Marta], in order to make the work
> in the fields less onerous, have introduced a change of pace, which they
> call the *chagua,* in which the Indians of a town, or part of them, gather one
> day of the week at the house of the Indian making the garden and, each
> with his axe or machete, together they clear the brush away, leaving it
> ready to plant, while the owner of the *chagua* is obligated to give food and
> drink that day, necessitating assembling much food on the part of the
> owner, and much maize beer on the part of his woman. This day for them is
> a day of rest and they treat it as a fiesta, so that it is necessary for the priest
> to say the mass early, and for the host to be careful that they pay attention.
> They return at night and if there is any drink left they form their dances
> until they tire. They retire then. When one of them must sponsor a *chagua*
> it is obligatory for the owner of the last one to participate, since he received
> this benefit (Patiño 1965:392–93, Partridge's translation).

The *chagua,* then, is a mechanism of labor organization based on the principle
of reciprocal exchange. Today as in earlier times reciprocal labor exchange is
accompanied by ritualized exchanges of food and drink. During the banana
production days the exchanges of food, alcohol, and tobacco were re-
scheduled to take place after work and on weekends, but they continued to be
important elements of the social organization of the lower coastal sector.
When the United Fruit Company departed in 1964, the region became
economically depressed and a large labor surplus resulted. As a consequence,
the exchange rituals that knit these nonkin-based work gangs together became
even more important.

Cannabis smoking became part of the exchange ritual of the work gang only
during the last 50 years (Ardila Rodríguez 1965; Patiño 1969:405). Cannabis
diffused to Colombia's north coast from the Antilles following the completion
of the Panama Canal and the vast human interchange that resulted. Laborers
from the Antilles secured jobs with United Fruit and brought with them
cannabis smoking habits. Significantly, this custom spread only to laborers of
the lower coastal sector. Life histories of smokers reveal that cannabis use
begins at the stage of the life cycle when adolescent males adopt adult work
patterns, between the ages of 12 and 22, and that initiation into cannabis
smoking takes place in the context of work in the fields and not in leisure
activity locations. Informants report between 11 and 31 years of smoking
experience, and no informant reported that his father used the drug. It is the
members of the nonkin-based work gang who initiate the neophyte.

When workers gather in the morning, and during rest breaks throughout the
day, they share cannabis, tobacco, alcohol, and food. Not all workers can
provide these items for themselves or others on any given day since wages are

very low. However, when these items are shared among work group members, there is the tacit assumption that others will reciprocate in the future. Such exchanges are viewed as traditionally appropriate among workers, having always been associated with the *chagua,* and over time such reciprocities grow into permanent relationships.

Conversely, the breach of the implicit exchange contract brings explicit condemnation from one's fellows in the form of gossip and scandal. Those who do not honor the subtle obligation to reciprocate soon find themselves ostracized by the label *vivo.* To be *vivo* in this community is to be intelligent, active of mind, but unscrupulous and untrustworthy. Such a man takes advantage of the gifts of others, a mark of intelligence, but refuses to repay, a sign of untrustworthiness. *Vivo* men are excluded from the work gang.

The meaning of cannabis use in the community, therefore, is twofold. These will be called the exegetic significance and the operational significance of cannabis, after Turner (1966). The exegetic significance, the meaning displayed by estate workers, peasants, and artisans through verbal statements among themselves and in response to questions, is that of energizer. The cannabis smokers say that cannabis reduces fatigue (*quita el cansancio*), that it gives a man energy (*fuerza*) for hard work, and that it gives a worker spirit (*ánimo*) for working well. Some men use cannabis in a daily program of health maintenance, believing it to have a prophylactic effect for a variety of illnesses (Fabrega and Manning 1972). Others use the crushed leaves to relieve pain; some say it can be brewed into a tea to calm a crying infant; but the most common and important meaning expressed is that of cannabis as an energizer (see also Rubin and Comitas 1975).

Cannabis use also has significance at an operational level, the meaning of which is reflected in the ways in which people use it in various settings. Cannabis smoking is only one part of an elaborate system of exchanges or presentations among estate workers, peasants, and artisans, the nature of which Mauss (1954) analyzed. As has been seen, cannabis use is ritualized together with alcohol and tobacco as part of the work routine of the coastal lower sector. It was also noted that failure to honor one's obligation to participate in the system of reciprocities results in exclusion from the work gang. This is an important feature of social interaction in the *chagua* and merits further elaboration.

The reciprocal exchanges seen in work rituals extend to other domains of the male's life in the lower coastal sector. Estate workers, peasants, and artisans depend heavily upon each other to achieve many of life's more important goals. To be labeled *vivo* means, in an operational sense, that a man is excluded from those activities for which he needs the cooperation of coworkers. Two of these are housebuilding and assembling alcohol for religious purposes.

Housebuilding occurs at the stage of the developmental cycle of the domestic unit that Fortes (1958) calls "dispersion," when children marry and either add members to the parental home or establish a separate residence. On the coast the latter choice is more common. Many young men and their mates spend a few years residing with parents before they build a separate house. During this time the man accumulates wood, palm leaves, bricks, and cement. Houses grow by accretion: first a mud and stick *bareque* is constructed, then a brick and concrete wall is erected around it, and finally a brick and concrete house is built to replace the *bareque*. The process may take a decade to complete, and at each stage the male of the household depends upon nonkin members of his work gang for weekend and evening labor on his new home; they provide labor, advice, and the loan of tools, in addition to contacts for obtaining materials. The young man who is building a house will spend much of his time working on the slowly developing houses of his coworkers as well.

Similarly, all men of the work gang stand at one time or another as godparents to the children of coworkers. As godfather, or on the occasion of marriage of an offspring, death of a relative, baptism, confirmation, and other events of religious life, a man is expected to sponsor a feast. Food for the feast is not lavish and the fees to the priest are minimal, but alcohol is very expensive for a worker (15 pesos for a 6-ounce bottle), and low wages do not permit a man to save any money toward purchases of large amounts. Moreover, lower coastal sector workers do not often enjoy the assistance of a wealthy patron. If saving money for such massive expenses is not a realistic goal, maintaining a wide range of nonkin reciprocal ties of obligation is. Such ties can be had by investing only a few pesos a week in alcohol, tobacco, and cannabis. When religious rituals necessitate huge expenditures on alcohol, a man turns to a number of his coworkers for assistance in meeting these obligations.

Because of a man's dependence on his work gang, to be labeled a *vivo* is a matter of important consequence. It means that assistance in achieving several of life's most valued goals is denied. All men of the lower sector seek the status of *padre de familia* (literally, father of a family), but this involves much more than paternity; it means a man must hold a full-time job, live in his own home, and meet his religious obligations to family and friends as well. For most men, achieving this status is possible only through the mechanism of winning tenure on a work gang. The ritual exchange of cannabis, therefore, is an important selective device whereby potential members of a work gang are recruited, tested, and finally accepted for membership.

The processes of achieving adult status, winning tenure on a work crew, and becoming initiated into cannabis smoking are linked in the lower coastal sector. This is not the case among males of the highland sector. Here we find that kin, rather than nonkin, dominate all choices made by individuals and provide the field of interindividual relationships that condition behavior. Unlike the lower coastal sector male, the highland male does not leave his family of orientation in order to achieve adult status or to begin adult working patterns. All significant processes of the life cycle of the highland male are structured by relationships among males of his extended family and among those of the extended families to which he is related through marriage.

As a young boy, about age eight, the highland sector male is given a machete by his father; with this he begins to assist in play fashion with tasks about the farm. As he grows older he is given increasing amounts of responsibility for the care of the farm animals, until by adolescence he has primary responsibility for this activity of the farm. At the age of fifteen the male begins work in the *roza* (mixed garden plot) of his father. He is expected to do the work of an adult, yet all tasks are carefully supervised by his father and any older siblings present.

The household head has the responsibility for marketing produce, buying provisions, obtaining loans, paying debts, and obtaining a good patron among the storekeepers in the lowland town. The young man will not be initiated into these and similar activities until his father feels it is time for him to marry and begin a household of his own. When this time arrives a portion of the farm will be transferred to the son, or he may colonize a new plot further up in the mountains. A mate will be sought, with parental assistance, among the other highland families.

Highland sector males do not achieve adulthood, however, until they obtain their own creditors, markets for their produce, and patrons in the lowland town. A young man may cultivate his own gardens, take a mate, procreate children, and be fully competent in the daily work of adult men of the highlands, but he will not be considered fully adult until he handles the interface relationships between his household and the lowlanders. When he carries the burden of travel to town, shopping, selling, obtaining credit, entering into sharecropping arrangements, and paying debts, he will be treated as an adult. This event, therefore, may come much later in life for the highland male than for his coastal counterpart.

Significantly, cannabis smoking plays no role in these processes. Important relationships are confined to kinsmen, and there is little opportunity for innovating novel behaviors. For this reason, probably, cannabis smoking never spread among the highlanders. This is not to say that the important systems of reciprocal exchanges observed in the lower coastal sector have no counterpart in the highland sector. Indeed, the exchange of butchered meat, yuca, corn and other seed, tools, alcohol, and labor is an integral part of the highlander's life. Exchanges of food and alcohol surround all important ceremonial occasions, and it is only through reciprocal exchanges of food, particularly meat, that highlanders are able to weather the long dry summers. But cannabis is not a part of these exchanges. Further, it is unlikely that cannabis ever will be a part of them, since the young are conditioned by elders for whom cannabis smoking is not customary. The abundance of cannabis in the fields makes little difference.

We see, therefore, that the social structure of the lower coastal sector provides certain incentives and constraints upon behavior that differ from those provided by the highland sector social structure. On the coast, an excess of day laborers looking for work, a depressed economic climate in which wages are minimal, and the scarcity of older filial and affinal kinsmen due to the migratory search for work mean that lower coastal sector males must depend heavily upon nonkin. In such situations cannabis smoking has become customary. Elsewhere in the same community cannabis smoking may not have become customary, because the elders who initiate the young are not cannabis smokers.

It is also clear that cannabis smokers of the lower coastal sector are productive, integral members of the community. In no sense are they marginal, parasitic, or deviant, as popular mythology in the United States often pictures the drug users. Rather, cannabis users are workers who produce the food that sustains the other residents of the community and the urban populace of the towns and cities. We have seen that the role of cannabis in this community is understood not in conditions that create deviancy, parasitism, and marginality, but rather in conditions that produce conformity, social solidarity, and productivity.

CONCLUDING COMMENTS

The dialogue during the final months of fieldwork produced an understanding of the data that had not been perceived previously. Earlier, Partridge had thought that the population could be divided into two easily demarcated groups. The dialogue directed his attention to patterns of interaction, socialization practices, and the world view. These aspects of behavior led to the discovery of three distinct "social sectors" within the subcultures. In the recurrent rituals of the yearly cycle, in the training of offspring, in the daily round of work and leisure, and in statements about the world, members of each sector revealed their identities. Partridge perceived these internal divisions only when he began to utilize behavioral analysis.

The model of community that resulted is one characterized by two broad subcultural groups: one of these forms a lower social sector, the product of recent migration from the interior; the other consists of the long-persisting division on the north coast between the elite families and their peasant-worker clients. The United Fruit Company altered this social system very little. Only briefly did a new middle sector emerge; it was subsequently absorbed by the elite of the upper coastal sector upon the withdrawal of the company.

Variations in cannabis cultivation, distribution, and consumption show surprising correspondences with internal divisions of the system. Commercial cultivation is illegal and absent on the coast, but it has intruded into the highland agricultural complex, composed of recent migrants who are willing to take greater risks for financial returns. However, marketing is relegated to the upper coastal sector, which has always controlled all human and nonhuman resources of the community. Cannabis is no different in this regard than land, hides, or rice.

Consumption of cannabis is wholly confined to the lower coastal sector, a migratory agricultural laboring population that depends upon friendships established through reciprocal obligations incurred during adolescence. The need for shifting alliances, the importance of nonkin, the central role played by ritualized exchanges of valued items, and the world view described here as mobile-isolate all fit together, not duplicated in any other social sector. Cannabis consumption makes sense only within this pattern of interaction.

It is not surprising that the habit of smoking cannabis has spread no further than the boundaries of the lower coastal sector. Nor is it surprising that cannabis smokers continue to be productive adult members of their community, since their work and ritual system sanction the use of cannabis. However, lower coastal sector people are generally looked down upon. Negative remarks about *marijuaneros* are part of a general boundary-marking behavior typical of each of the other social sectors of the community, a form of institutionalized prejudice that commonly sets social segments apart from one another. But the inferior status that this group occupies cannot be attributed solely to marijuana smoking. They were so judged long before the introduction of its use.

The community-study approach helps us to understand that although the patterns of behavior in Majagua have origins and persist quite apart from cannabis, its use does mirror some portions of the social system.

8. The Crisis of Departure

Preparation for departure from the field after an extended period of residence may be effected smoothly, or it may turn out to be a harrowing experience. There was some of both in the happenings that Partridge encountered during his last month.

Many aspects of the disengagement process recur with sufficient regularity that they deserve comment. The tempo of the fieldworker's activity increases as he hurries to harvest the last crop of data, as he attends to the detail that accompanies preparing himself and his accumulations for the trip homeward, and as he is caught up in a flurry of ritual leave-takings of greater or lesser magnitude. He is no longer beset with the pervasive anxiety that accompanied his entry into the field, since his knowledge of local groups and customs now diminishes the initial ambiguity immensely. But the process of disengagement creates new uncertainties that are embedded in the necessary alteration of behavior in the departure activity and in the anticipated exit. The new behavioral definitions extend to all those within the orbit of the fieldworker's movements. That the stresses that are implicit in change are eased through ritualization confirms an old principle of anthropology.

Every neophyte anthropologist is exposed to the cultural significance of ritual leave-taking in his study of separation, transition, and incorporation as the three phases of the rites of passage. Not only does the traditional obser- vance of departure reassert the unity of those left behind, but it also sends the defector gracefully on his way. Furthermore, the harmonious conclusion in celebration is evidence for his colleagues that he has left behind the goodwill that will ensure that other anthropologists who follow him will be cordially received.

These generalities are given specific support by the events in Majagua. During October Partridge combined his final fact-gathering with departure ceremonies. After completing his study of commercial cattle ranching, he intended to travel to Bogotá, where he could consult the newspaper accounts of the early history of the banana zone and the strike of 1928. Cattle ranching was studied through interviews with owners of large estates, veterinarians, and cowboys. Because of the limited time, several informants made special efforts to help him.

Leave-taking ceremonials were under way at the same time. It is significant that these ceremonies confirmed the division of the community into upper coastal, lower coastal, and highland sectors. There was no intermingling of these groups as they gathered to bid farewell. The elite of the town, including the mayor, several estate managers and professionals, and a school teacher, gathered at one of the estates of a wealthy rancher. There they feasted on the traditional *sancocho* (a stew made of turkey and pork and a variety of vegetables arranged on a banana leaf and eaten with gourd spoons) and consumed bottles of *aguardiente* and Scotch. The flowery words to toast the departing guest were delivered by an estate manager with whom Partridge had worked. The mayor lightened the mood by joking that Partridge would bring fame to Majagua as García Márquez had to Macondo. The revelry continued far into the night, until some departed for town while others curled up in hammocks at the estate house. Partridge interpreted this event as the ritual severing of his ties with this group.

A celebration of comparable conviviality, if of lesser elegance, was staged by members of the group Partridge had called lower coastal sector. That the *sancocho* was made of fish and vegetables and the drinks mostly paid for by Partridge made no difference in the spirit of the affair. It was held in the patio of one of his friends from the pool hall, a brickmason, and ended up back at the pool hall late at night. There men with whom Partridge had passed many hours of work and conviviality commemorated his departure by drinking beer. During the following days, people greeted Partridge on the street with an invitation to drink *el del arranque*, or bon voyage—with a friend, there is never a last drink.

Saying farewell to friends from the highland sector was a different matter. Events took place during early October that threatened the warm relationships Partridge had established with men from the highlands. The national newspaper, *El Tiempo*, carried a brief announcement on a back page of the 2 October issue of arrests of cannabis growers in the foothills of the Sierra Nevada de Santa Marta above the town of Majagua. Partridge was caught completely by surprise by this news. He knew personally all of the families that lived off of the single road leading into the foothills and he had discussed cannabis cultivation with several of them. He feared that his status as an outsider would make him an easy scapegoat, that it would be easy for these people to assume that he was a police informer. Partridge needed to take steps to protect himself against false accusations, if possible, and to reestablish good relations. He also felt that the situation was sufficiently serious that he should immediately inform his faculty advisors of this unfortunate turn of events. He dispatched letters to Carter and Kimball at once, although the possibility of a reply much before his final departure was remote.

2 October 1973

Dear Dr. Kimball:

Thank you for your letter of 12 September, which I received last week on the nineteenth, when I went to Barranquilla. All manifestations of culture shock have worn off and I am now back in reasonable field condition following the ICAES meetings. I spent a week getting the paper ready for publication.

Following your suggestion I sketched out a summary of the various production systems present in the community according to the variables developed in the applied course. This has proven satisfactory, as seen in the enclosed notes, and has revealed that information on the large cattle estates is lacking. I suspect that the haciendas will mirror the pattern of the rice estates. I will be paying close attention to filling this gap in the coming few weeks.

This appears to have been fortunate timing. The newspaper *El Tiempo* arrived this evening bringing the news of the arrest of six peasants in the foothills of the sierra, just above Majagua, the exact region in which I have been working. There is only one road and I have made it a point to know everyone living up there. Some ten hectares of cannabis were burned. The names have not been released, so I have no idea who is involved.

It will be a minor miracle if I am not blamed for this operation. I have been writing all day today and have not yet spoken to any of the highlanders. But if the rumor evolves that I am somehow responsible for the arrests, I am not certain what the consequences will be. I doubt that I will be tempted to do any investigating about the effects of this arrest. My position may not be grave, but this is not known now.

In any case, the week's end may find me altering my return schedule and closing down a little sooner than planned. I will let you know. In the event that trouble develops here I will plan to evacuate to Bogotá where I had planned some library work for later in the month anyway. Time permitting, I will have the data on the cattle estates.

Best wishes,
William Partridge

It was clear that Partridge needed to learn as quickly as possible how much jeopardy he was in and what his course of action might be. He knew the highlanders well enough to know that a violation of trust could be avenged by assassination. To journey to the highlands to declare his innocence would have been foolhardy. They might refuse to listen or he might get ambushed before he had a chance to speak; in any event, this was not the way that tense situations were traditionally handled. In contrast, the feasible course was to follow the same procedures he had used initially in establishing himself: he would search out his highland friends in bars, stores, and poolrooms where they usually assembled during the rainy season when they came into town to market produce and purchase supplies. He would also seek guidance from his friend Jorge who had been so important in establishing his first contacts with these people.

When Partridge talked with Jorge he expressed his concern for the welfare of the affected families, but Jorge dismissed the idea of assisting these families. He pointed out that the highlanders who had been arrested (and their crop burned) had behaved foolishly. They had planted ten hectares of cannabis, a huge crop even by highland standards, and had therefore invited police action. Jorge's reasoning was that too large a crop invited arrest, because the police could smell a wealthy patron or backer who would be obligated to put up a healthy bribe. Conversely, too small a crop (perhaps a single hectare) called attention to the lack of a powerful patron, permitting the police to make the less powerful grower an arrest statistic needed to satisfy superiors. Jorge felt that Partridge's concern was unwarranted, and that those arrested had behaved imprudently. To relieve Partridge's fear that he might be made a scapegoat Jorge pointed out that only one crop was burned. If Partridge had been an agent of the police the crops of many more highland growers would have been destroyed, and certainly those with whom he personally visited.

Partridge also went to the mayor of the town to discuss the implications of the arrests. It will be recalled that the mayor had accompanied Partridge to the office of the chief of the secret police and had been enlisted as a powerful protector and sponsor for Partridge's work at the local level. Partridge explained the situation to the mayor, making certain that the mayor understood that he was uninvolved in these arrests. The mayor assured him that he had never entertained such a notion.

The damage caused by the police arrests was never undone, however. Despite Jorge's opinions, the highlanders turned distinctly cool toward Partridge. Only Señor Escorcia and Guillermo remained on good terms. The others avoided him. Those who did not grow cannabis continued to greet him in the stores and streets of the town, but the growers were suspicious and maintained their distance. Leave-taking was an individual affair, sometimes almost furtive. When a friend from the highlands came to town, he and

Partridge would say their farewells at Manuel's *tienda*. A few days later another friend would be met, and so it went. By mid-October Partridge decided that further efforts to make contacts with the highlanders would be futile in the time remaining. Unwilling to travel up to the sierra *veredas* again, Partridge made ready to leave Majagua.

Even though a ritual severing of the ties that linked Partridge and the highlanders remained uncelebrated, the time to depart had come. The only remaining item on the agenda was his newspaper research in Bogotá. This finishing up included the letters to Kimball from Majagua and Bogotá. They briefly, almost cryptically, state the essentials, in striking contrast to the flowing imagery in the reports of the first days and weeks.

12 October 1973

Dear Dr. Kimball:

Please excuse my choice of stationery, but things are disorganized here and I am in the midst of packing up all of my gear and heading out.

As mentioned in my earlier letter the arrests have proven to be bad news. Most people are convinced that I am truly an agent of some kind. The townspeople with whom I have good relations are still most cooperative, but my highlander contacts have dwindled to one or two. They simply avoid me and scurry out of conversations.

In the last week I have obtained excellent data on the large cattle operations and can now confidently include these in my analysis. My guesses in the outline I sent last time were inaccurate regarding the organization of the estates, but I was right about marketing arrangements.

I have finished packing all of my gear to be shipped later this week to the States. Only a suitcase of clothes, notebooks, paper, etc., has been kept out so that I might go to Bogotá and work in the library during the remainder of October.

I received word that my paper is on the program for the New Orleans meetings, so I will be returning to Miami around November. After purchasing some kind of automobile I will drive to Gainesville, probably about the seventh.

Well, that is all for now. Any further correspondence will not be received until I pass through Barranquilla on my way out of the country. I have not typed up any further notes, but I am keeping my daily notebook up to date.

Best wishes,
William L. Partridge

20 October 1973

Dear Dr. Kimball:

Just a note to say that all is well in the wake of the local crisis, and that I am here in the capital working on documenting the social history of the municipality. I plan a final trip to Majagua before leaving for home. This will perhaps pave the way for a future follow-up of other questions.

In Bogotá I am documenting the events in the formation of the banana zone, the crisis that enveloped it in 1928, and the social changes that have occurred. This is being done through the newspaper collections in the National Library and Luis Angel Arango Library. Several highly important sources still elude me, however, so I will be sleuthing around here for another two or three days before returning to the coast for a good-bye visit. I will be in Gainesville the second week in November.

Sincerely,
William L. Partridge

The crisis that might have developed during the closing weeks of fieldwork did not materialize. All of the necessary elements were present for a true crisis: a sensitive problem involving the research objective, illegal activities on the part of some informants, a turn of events (outside Partridge's control) stimulated by the intervention of outside agencies (the police) in the community, and Partridge's status as an outside investigator. These could have combined to produce an uncomfortable situation. Partridge might logically have been suspected of gathering information for the police raid, but his long and carefully maintained relationship of trust with Jorge and the mayor, two persons of influence in the two subcultural groups of the community, protected him from suspicion and its consequences. Had Partridge not been alert to the testing of his reliability and trustworthiness several months earlier (discussed in chapter 6), he might have been vulnerable. But his informants had already satisfied themselves that Partridge kept a closed mouth on confidential information; thus, when the police raid occurred, he was not implicated.

Carter's and Kimball's replies to Partridge's 2 October letter arrived after he had left Majagua. Both recognized the unanticipated event as one of the hazards of field research. Following advice from a distance about how to extricate oneself from a sticky situation might be chancy, but it might also be comforting to know that troubles always loom about. Their letters are included here as part of the documentation.

11 October 1973

Dear Bill:

Your latest news is indeed distressing. It is, however, not totally unexpected. Please be supercautious. The last thing in the world we want is for the university to have to go to court in Colombia to get you released from prison. If you can, continue your community study work. In a situation like this you may find it hard *not* to obtain information about the arrests.

There is no doubt that the type of research in which you and I are involved creates unique field problems and stresses. We are having our share of them in Costa Rica. Frankly, our fingers are crossed there because of some developments during these past two months.

I have tried to get hold of Dr. Kimball to advise him of the latest events, but so far I have been unable to contact him. Once he learns, I am sure he will be writing to you. Let us hope that things quiet down fairly quickly and that you are able to resume your normal research. For the time being, I would suggest patience.

Regards,
William L. Carter

24 October 1973

Dear Bill:

Isn't it fortunate that the mishap about the marijuana raids came at the end of your activity rather than earlier? When Doug Oliver arrived in the Solomons the chief of the village he intended to study immediately died and the villagers were certain that he had done him in with witchcraft. He prepared to leave on the next coastal schooner, but before he could a long line of natives came with gifts and said they had been trying for 20 years to kill the old gent and asked him, Oliver, to come live with them. Unhappily, I am not certain where your refuge may be. Ask some people what you can do about it and patch it up as best you can—perhaps even ask the police, but if you are seen with police that will further convict you.

We shall be looking for you in early November. The department is going *en masse* by bus to New Orleans where we shall mount a trolley car hootenanny with a combo band for Thursday afternoon. Bring your instrument.

Other than that, much more is happening here than any of us can keep up with. All goes well.

Sincerely,
Solon Kimball

P.S. I suspect you act through intermediaries and never appear—isn't that the way to get a large number of things done without causing embarrassment or getting shot?

The advice that Kimball and Carter sent reflects their understanding of the dynamics of community life. Partridge was understandably upset by the unexpected and, in his experience, unprecedented raid on the highland growers. This was natural, since he was immersed in the situation and reacted as a participant. Kimball and Carter, on the other hand, understood that Partridge had been successful in gaining access to private information and that he had already been tested and judged trustworthy by his informants. He would not have been able to continue his work had the results been otherwise.

The highlanders' reaction to the event can be described as cautious. They understandably sought to minimize all further risk. Partridge wisely ceased his efforts to pursue information on cannabis, turning his attention to several other matters that still lay before him.

During his final weeks in the field Partridge did not type up formal notes. Shorthand notes were kept in two notebooks that he carried throughout the fieldwork period. From these records he typed the field notes that he mailed to Kimball every few months. Examples of these notes are not included here, since they are highly abbreviated. (They contain, for example, lists of births recorded at the local clinic for 1972–73 and details of the rotation cycle for beef cattle through pastures and feeder lots.) These notes and those taken in the libraries in Bogotá augmented and made more complete the model of community that Partridge had developed over a period of 15 months. They did not change his model, but they confirmed several of its aspects.

After two weeks of working in the newspaper collections in Bogotá, Partridge prepared to leave Colombia. The train that carried him from Bogotá to the coast passed through the banana zone and along the string of dusty towns that bordered the tracks. In Santa Marta he caught the bus for Majagua, arriving for a final good-bye. Yet Partridge had already said good-bye some weeks earlier. Dinner and drinking parties had been given in his honor; friends bought him beer at fortuitous last-time encounters. All the farewells had been said except for the aborted leave-taking with the highlanders. When Partridge stepped off the bus several weeks later he instantly realized that things were not the same. The town looked different. The weeks he spent in the capital made it appear this way, and his impending return to the United States and resumption of the life he had temporarily set aside also changed the way he perceived this little town.

Of course the community had not changed. The tractors continued to churn up dust in the streets as they pulled out of town for the estates. The boys still kicked the soccer ball in the plaza. The train roared by and failed to stop at 10:30. The truck full of peasants from the highlands with their sacks of produce still came up to the front of Señor Prada's store about 11:00. The proprietor of the pool hall invited Partridge to have a beer, Mayor Bernal García waved and continued with his work, and Jorge hailed Partridge from the market building to explain that he would have to mail the 50 pesos that he still owed the anthropologist. They all continued with their business of the day. The town had not changed, but Partridge had. His work here had been over for several weeks. This visit was not to be followed by others, nor did it mark the conclusion of anything that had been. This visit may have been unnecessary, except for the pleasure of a last look, or perhaps prompted by a feeling that something remained unfinished.

We find in our analysis of the departure process several steps, some of which are probably universal in anthropological fieldwork experience. First is the need to tie up loose ends, which is possible only when a clear theoretical model has been developed that can be used to delineate significance. If the objective is merely salvage ethnography or description for description's sake, then this stage probably does not occur. It is only in problem-oriented research that we can visualize the occurrence of a series of events that can be considered a tying-up of loose ends. Second, departure entails the ceremonies that always surround farewells. In the eating of the *sancocho* and the drinking of beer Partridge and his friends dramatized and made clear the significance of the event, the transition that separation universally entails. Third is the problem of departing in such a manner as to leave behind no feelings of frustration, of actions that should have been taken but were not, of acts that should not have occurred but did. For a few days Partridge was worried that this aspect of his departure would not go well. But as the events surrounding the arrests transpired it became clear to him that they were part of the life of the community into which he had won entrance. Further, he understood that the role in which he had established himself and the skill with which he had played that role precluded the unfortunate outcome that he feared. Last, we find that Partridge's final visit to the community after several weeks of library work in Bogotá demonstrates the truly decisive function of the ceremonies of farewell. These had already occurred and Partridge had bid farewell weeks before; he had already been separated from the status that he had established in the community. Community life went on as before, much as when he first saw it in July 1972. When he stepped down off the bus for his final look in late October 1973, it was as a stranger once again, a visitor who had no role to play in the ongoing life of the community. The only difference was that in late October what Partridge was seeing was familiar and warmly remembered, even when seen from the distance that the leave-taking had necessarily brought with it.

9. Research as an Operational System

THIS EXPLORATION of the dynamics of fieldwork has revealed a good deal about the workaday activities of the field researcher as well as the flavor of life and nature of community of the people of Majagua. Such a focus was an intended goal of the authors. The intellectual goal, however, was the analysis of community-study research as an operational system. The variables and objectives that needed to be examined to achieve this goal were discussed in the first chapter. A brief recapitulation of them includes the relationship between research method and data selection; the dialogue between mentor and student involving data and concepts; the successive stages in research development; and the relation between community-study method and the empirical study of community.

In this chapter we shall examine the linkages between these objectives. We begin with an analysis of relationships between concepts, methods, and model building, and the role of dialogue in joining these in a research strategy, and conclude with the conceptual aspects of community and the methods of community study. We proceed from the assumption that there is an implicit orderliness in our method that links theory, procedures, and research development and leads to the formulation of an empirical model of community.

As a first principle of scientific research it is essential to remember that the concepts and assumptions that invest the formulation of the problem influence both the procedures of investigation and the findings. For this reason any statement about the natural world must include the context of the conditions as well as other systems that constitute their surroundings. If the scientific objective is to do more than present a static description of the variety and connection of parts—the structure—then it is necessary to observe the system in operation over time. There can thus be established the chain of consequences from which statements of change are derived, those principles and processes that are analogous to the Darwinian concept of natural selection, which accounts for evolutionary modification of plants and animals in their morphology and distribution. Moreover, through comparison of differing situations, whether they be geological records in the earth's crust or living communities, further insight into variability is gained.

The perspective from which these remarks flow differs markedly from one that seeks to arrange the stars of the heavens as projected constellations of an earthly perception; that seeks to collect the range of rock specimens for a museum display; or that attempts to array kinship systems by some measure of their complexity or by some standard of moral worth. Such projections, collections, or arrays tell us little about the nature of the world other than that it contains variety. However, we might learn a great deal about ethnocentric projection, about the mentality of those who collect and classify, or about the validity of comparisons between items that have been torn from context. These procedures have all been part of the kit of science and they may still be useful for some purposes, but they are not the techniques that can illuminate the problem with which we are concerned. They do provide a contrast, however, that helps to clarify the distinctive aspects of the method of natural history.

THE EMPIRICAL MODEL

The natural history approach in community-study methodology requires a continuing dialogue between what we call a conceptual model and an empirical model. This developmental aspect can be readily grasped by examining the dialogue in relation to fieldwork stages.

A schematic diagram offers a visual device for summarizing the role of dialogue in community study. Figure 9.1 depicts on the horizontal axis the stages of fieldwork through which Partridge passed. It also shows the degree of integration that Partridge achieved over time in Majagua. The vertical axis represents Partridge's progression through the stages of academic life at the University of Florida. At one level the two processes diverge. As Partridge became more fully integrated into Majagua, he became simultaneously farther removed from the world of academe. But one of the singular features of anthropological research is that, at the point of greatest integration, the fieldworker departs abruptly to reenter the world of academe, as did Partridge.

On a more profound level, however, the divergence between the field and academe is illusory. Progressive integration into Majagua, and the resulting greater access to the lives of his informants, enabled Partridge to gather ever more effectively the data needed to accomplish his academic objectives. The dialogue with Kimball was crucial in this regard, for as Partridge progressed further into the community he also progressed deeper into the dialogue with Kimball. Near the end of the fieldwork period he had integrated fully into the

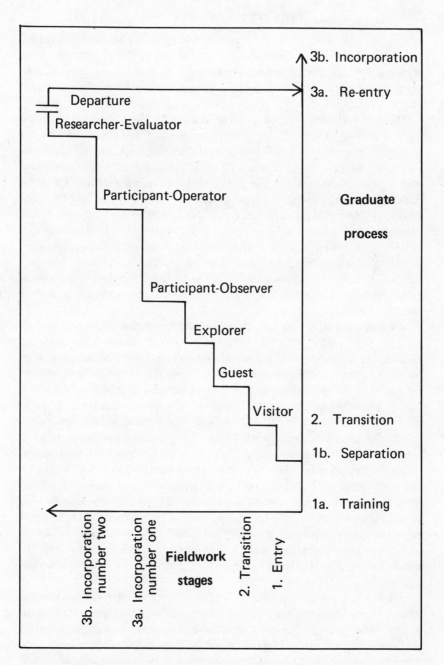

Figure 9.1.   Stages of incorporation

community, yet the data and the dialogue with Kimball about his findings are proof that Partridge was also fully integrated into the world of academe, even if physically separated. The seeming divergence, then, is actually the convergence by senior and junior partners toward a mutual goal from different perspectives.

The fieldwork period may be viewed as a double rite of passage involving both incorporation into the community under study and induction into the profession of anthropology. We have used the sequence within these rites of passage as a framework; the notations in the diagram indicate the processual stages into which each rite can be divided, providing a setting for other important points we wish to make. However, as we have argued from the beginning, the fieldwork experience should not be viewed entirely as a rite of passage. It is also a scientific enterprise that engages trained researchers and contributes knowledge to the profession. It also transmits knowledge from senior to junior partner, thus providing for continuity of the professional tradition. It is also the nexus where theory and evidence converge, the point at which dialogue as a central feature of community study is critically important and most visible.

The dialogue emerges initially out of a shared conceptual model held by both the junior and senior partners. In the first chapter we outlined our model of community; throughout this book we reiterated its major dimensions as they were substantiated in the field notes; and in intermediate chapters we developed the empirical model of community. But when Partridge stepped from the bus in Majagua that first day, his intellectual tool kit was the conceptual model. From then until his departure in October 1973 he was engaged in investigating the model that he and Kimball shared. Nothing is gained by attempting to show when Partridge began collecting data on each dimension of community. Theoretically, any point could serve as a starting place.

Empirical model-building entails two procedures: dialogue and access. Both are aspects of the natural-history approach, which demands *in vivo* observation and study. Both are instrumental to the creation of an empirical model and to the testing of the conceptual model. Most importantly, dialogue and access are so intimately linked with each other that each one fuels the other. Out of the intellectual energy thus generated the empirical model appears.

The first step toward operationalizing the conceptual model began with the arrival of Partridge in July 1972. As a visitor he played the role of guest among those who were his initial informants. There was a conscious selection of those with whom he wished to work. These included the wealthy old families, the highland peasants, the coastal cattle estate managers, and a few others.

By the end of September 1972 Partridge had entered the next phase of his field activity. His role changed to explorer as he expanded the range of his informants from whom he sought a broader knowledge of the community. During his first month in the field a goodly portion of his effort had been directed toward solving some of the problems of housing, health, food, security, transportation, and other conditions of fieldwork. Now he began to explain his research to persons whom he felt he could trust; at the same time he developed an appropriate role to play in community life. In his wide-ranging activities he attended cockfights, interviewed former workers and employees of the United Fruit Company, joined the marketing and bartering sessions in local bars and stores, and observed many other patterned behaviors that constituted life in Majagua. His treks into the countryside netted many new friendships and indebted him to those who assisted and befriended him. Out of these experiences evolved a fragmentary understanding of the groups that made up this complex social system, the distinction between *cachaco* and *costeño* emerging as a behavioral division of importance.

Like the Irish girl's father who walks the fields belonging to the prospective groom's father before giving his consent to the marriage, Partridge surveyed the social terrain of the community before committing himself. He was attempting to sort out segments of the community to know something of what lay ahead. Letters arrived from Kimball and Carter while this step was in progress, advising him to proceed cautiously but with assurance that things were going as expected. The first field report did not spark a dialogue. The responses were general, drawn from the experiences of those who had worked in similar situations. The message was clear, however, that Partridge was making progress and should not jeopardize his position by pursuing information about cannabis too quickly.

The continued exploration and expansion of activity gradually built the base for the next step. The investigation now turned to social space. Kimball's letter of 9 October 1972 responded to the second batch of field notes and called for further investigation of some situations Partridge had reported. This stimulated Partridge to begin systematic investigation of leads he had turned up during the previous three months. Utilizing the technique of event analysis, Partridge analyzed the Feast of the Immaculate Conception, a wake held for a deceased highland peasant, the New Year's celebrations, and other events in the ceremonial cycle of the community. These analyses drew Partridge's attention to the significant boundaries in social space that set some families apart from others, that separated groups from other groups and sectors from other sectors. Through perusal of published sources, study of census data, and interviews with older members of the community, Partridge also began to piece together a longitudinal understanding of the origins of the divisions he had discovered. Finally, a comparison of the *curso* in the highland *vereda* and the lowland hamlet gave the first indication of contrasting organizational structures in two distinct community sectors.

Sometime during the period from October to December 1972, Partridge achieved the role of participant-observer. Unlike the transition from guest to explorer, which had been largely a conscious effort, this transition occurred gradually as the consequence of his systematic investigation of aspects of social space. The dialogue served primarily as a stimulus. Kimball directed attention to issues that interested him in the field notes, asking questions and making suggestions. This encouraged Partridge to continue widening his scope, to record from a wide range and variety of situations while at the same time paying more attention to detail. In the process of seeking deeper knowledge of the events, groups, and organizational structures he had identified, Partridge had become transformed into a participant-observer. This was neither Kimball's nor Partridge's deliberate intention. It was the natural outcome of systematic investigation of social space.

The significance of the participant-observer role cannot be overemphasized. Through intensive and systematic investigation, Partridge was drawn into the life of the community more deeply. For example, in seeking to understand the cycle of ceremonies he was occasionally drawn in as a participant, as in the serenade for the bishop. While attempting a comparison between the *curso* in the highlands and that in the lowlands, he spent many hours in the company of informants who helped him to understand something of their lives. By returning again and again to the homes of peasants in the highlands he was able to flesh out their life cycles, the round of work and leisure, commerce and marketing, marriage and courtship, and much more. The dialogue emphasized such detail, and stimulated a more intensive penetration requiring a greater degree of access. Greater access, in turn, yielded more varied and detailed data. These data, in turn, stimulated a deepening of the dialogue.

The interplay between dialogue and greater access is evidenced in the near-simultaneous decisions on the part of Kimball and Partridge in early January 1973 that the time had arrived to construct the first model of community. In retrospect, it is now possible to recognize that this interplay between dialogue and access had begun several months earlier. For example, in the last part of chapter 4 some of the elements of the emerging model are presented: the *municipio* form of community reflecting its urban functions; the arrangements of people and groups in space; population trends over time; and the first hint of the daily round of activities of a few groups. These items necessary for the model appeared in the notes from October to December 1972. Both Kimball and Partridge recognized that enough data had been gathered to construct a working model. They arrived at this decision independently of one another in January 1973.

The model that Partridge sent to Kimball at the first of the year sparked a new stage of the dialogue and new levels of access to community. Whereas the earlier dialogue had encouraged casting a wide net to gather a great variety of information, now that the structure of community had begun to emerge it was possible to focus effectively on specific areas of interest. The substance of Kimball's letter of 24 January 1973, for example, was directed to explicit aspects of the working model. Some time would elapse before answers to the issues raised by the new model could be found, but beginning in January Partridge took the first steps by selecting three areas in which to concentrate his efforts for detailed data collection: the highland *vereda*, the coastal hamlet, and a town neighborhood. This choice derived directly from the working model, which indicated behavioral differences differentially distributed in social space. The work in these areas increased the degree of access.

A major consequence of the construction of a working model of the community was its influence in giving a direction to the research activity not previously possible. The model generated new insights and revealed areas of data deficiency. Furthermore, it provided the kind of knowledgeable guidance so essential to the critical situation that occurred on 21 January 1973, when Jorge's client offered to assist Partridge in gathering information about cannabis. This major breakthrough had been patiently awaited. It should not be construed as a fortuitous happenstance, however; Partridge had paved the way for it by establishing his behavioral maturity as a participant-observer. Now he was being advanced to the new role of participant-operator, a role that permitted him to initiate relationships with others in the interest of his research objectives.

The origins of this new operational step can be traced to the interplay between dialogue and access, which had previously stimulated the production of a tentative model of the system of community. This understanding undoubtedly assisted Partridge in interpreting Jorge's gesture correctly. Partridge was able to judge the significance of the opportunity and he took it. The spiraling expansion that flows from the interplay between dialogue and access is exemplified in this instance: it had first produced a preliminary understanding of the community; this in turn permitted Partridge to accept deeper commitments and obligations, to achieve greater access, and to contribute new data to the continuing dialogue.

From January through the remainder of the fieldwork period Partridge moved freely in probing for cannabis and had little difficulty collecting the data he sought. Through February, March, and April he gathered information on cannabis cultivation and other activities. In May his contacts with the cultivators led to both distributors and consumers of cannabis. It was during these months that the interplay between dialogue and access achieved a new intensity. Yet the productivity of this relationship became even greater in the months ahead.

Beginning in April 1973 Kimball gave new momentum to the dialogue by expanding and testing the developing empirical model. He called attention to the principle of reciprocity and raised the issues of world view and socialization of the young. He was not questioning the presence of reciprocity nor the adequacy of the collected information. Rather he was asking if the details that explained the cultural forms and functions of reciprocity in this community could be described using the model Partridge had developed. Kimball, aware of the significance of Partridge's newly achieved role of participant-operator, suggested that he employ the empirical model to trace out reciprocal relationships within the system of which he was now part. In this manner the dialogue stimulated a new level of access, one in which the model could be validated through testing in the field.

Partridge now began to explore further that aspect of the model that included relationships of reciprocity. As an actor in the organizational structure—the role we called participant-operator—Partridge had access to situations in which he could manipulate the system and observe the response; he could also find himself manipulated by others, and judge the appropriateness of his responses by the reactions of others. As he pursued this course he advanced to a new role that we shall call researcher-evaluator. Within this role Partridge was able to test the validity of the model he had constructed by employing it as a guide to evaluating the behavior of others and of himself.

As a patron of some individuals and a client of others, Partridge was in a position to examine the validity of his perception of fictive kinship, cash loans, sharecropping arrangements, credit at stores, visiting during life crises, distribution of food, marketing of produce and products, and numerous other connections among people. By assuming the behaviors he observed and judging others' reactions, and by tracing out the actions of others and asking his informants about their significance, Partridge constructed a series of tests of the validity and reliability of his model. By June 1973 Partridge had arrived at his notion of "social sectors" through the use of this technique. He was confident that he could demonstrate the existence of three such sectors on the basis of situational context, social space boundaries, ritual behavior, and reciprocal exchange relationships. The dialogue had stimulated a new level of access, the researcher-evaluator role, and the field reports that went back to Kimball in turn stimulated a new level of dialogue.

The productivity of the interplay between dialogue and access reached its peak just before Partridge's departure from the field. Chapter 7 describes the dramatic series of events that document this fact. Utilizing Partridge's concept of social sectors, Kimball in a letter of 10 July 1973 called for summary statements of congruencies in the nature of world view and socialization. It was then that Partridge took the operational step involving specification of interdependencies among variables. In his reply, Partridge extended the model to include a concise explanation of world view and socialization. A further example of the high level of productivity of the dialogue was the subsequent request by Kimball for a summary outline of production-distribution-consumption units. Access was so complete at this point that the outline (with only a few gaps that were filled in the next few weeks) was worked up immediately.

We have shown that dialogue between senior and junior partners moves the investigator into ever greater access into the community. Greater access provides ever more detailed and complete data, which in turn stimulate the dialogue and permit ordering into an abstract, preliminary model. The preliminary model sparks a new level of access and becomes the object of a higher level of dialogue. Maximum access and the highest level of dialogue are achieved when model testing and verification in the field take place. The conceptual model shared by the investigators is now brought into comparison with the empirical model. Operations are carried out that constitute important tests of the conceptual model and the empirical model. Where discontinuities are noted or gaps in the evidence are discovered, further investigation is conducted. In this manner the conceptual model is modified against the evidence of the field data. Such a reordering took place on several occasions, but the example included here referred to Partridge's concept of world view. Clearly the empirical model forced a reformulation of this concept, providing a feedback mechanism, which is an essential part of community-study process.

Herein lies the importance of the flexibility of the community-study methodology. Research formulations, the preliminary models developed in the field, can be tested and modified as they are created. Theories, conceptual models carried from the university, can be similarly tested and modified in the field as they are compared to empirical models. Model testing of both kinds is an integral procedure of the community-study methodology, and provides a mechanism of verification that few other methods can duplicate.

THE CONCEPTUAL MODEL

What was the conceptual model that Partridge carried with him into his field research in Majagua? Community stands for the encompassing social grouping in which *Homo sapiens* combines the transmission of both genetic and cultural heritages. Although many different types of communities have evolved and continue to persist, ranging from the once pervasive hunting band to simple agrarian villages to more recent urban variations, each type exhibits certain characteristics that are common to all. For example, we have already mentioned the conservator-transmitter function of the genetic-cultural characteristics of a population. This function is a consequence of the interdependence between biological, ecological, and cultural aspects of the human condition. Specifically, these may be observed in the universal and basic division of human groups on the basis of sex, age, and status. But from one perspective these characteristics are also derivatives of the rules or customs that humans follow as they conjointly meet their multiple needs—physical, psychic, or social—as cooperating members of social groups. Such groups may be the domestic groups of hearth and home, work groups of field or factory, political groups of council or bureaucracy, religious groups of sacred grove or temple, or any of the myriad other types of organization through which humans solve their problems of survival or enjoyment.

Human communities differ from one another in the types and number of groups they comprise and in the relationships between them; in the activities in which each group engages; in the customs governing these; and in the perspective or world view held by a group's members. Although we know that these dimensions and others are intimately interwoven into what we metaphorically label the web of life, we are still far from making explicit their connections and understanding them.

The main features of a conceptual model of community are implicit in the explanation offered above. It would seem useful, however, to expand the explanation of the significant variables before we consider some of the principles and processes operating in a community in action. Four major dimensions of the community model can be distinguished. These include: (1) the variety of cooperating groups and the situations in which they function— the *social structure;* (2) the rules of behavior that govern the activities in which these groups take part—the *customs;* (3) the cognitive system of identities, explanations, and valuing of all aspects of the experienced and perceived universe—the *world view;* and (4) the setting, natural or modified by man and his technology—the *conditions.*

These abstract dimensions of community—social structure, customs, world views, and conditions—and the systematic relationships among them are articulated with two other dimensions. These are the *temporal-spatial context* and the *table of organization.* These two additional dimensions complete the conceptual model of community.

Communities possess life histories. They have beginnings, develop, propagate by dispatching members to establish comparable new communities, may be transformed, may perish. The constituent parts of a community, individuals and groups, also move through life cycles from birth to death or dissolution. Depending upon the richness or poverty of the conditions surrounding their existence, individuals, groupings, or communities may prosper or decline. The course of their life histories operates within the context of location so that territory and activity become identified with individuals or groups. The daily round of eating, working, playing, or sleeping of hunter, farmer, or merchant occurs within well-habituated confines of place and transit. The inhabitants commemorate seasonal changes or great events of the past as festive gatherings in plaza or temple. Individuals experience rites of passage as they move from one status to another in the life cycle. These ritual observances of individual, group, or community are rhythmically orchestrated in temporal sequences and by number of participants and degree of elaborateness. Recall the privately celebrated service for the dead of the *cachaco* family or the community-wide celebration of the saint's festival in El Retén.

Communities have inhabitants. These are flesh and blood individuals who selectively join others to form cooperating groups. They differ from each other on the basis of age, sex, and other criteria. According to these characteristics they occupy positions in the table of organization of a community. Individuals achieve their distinctive identities and distribution in time and space from participation in community; to fix attention on only a portion of community ignores the systematic relationships through which individuals gain their significance.

Attention to the table of organization and the temporal-spatial context leads naturally to the problem of boundaries. The geographical bounding of communities has posed nagging problems for researchers (such as rural sociologists) and for administrators. In Europe and Asia, unrest and even war have arisen from the tension produced by violation of the community-rooted loyalties of such peoples as the French, Germans, Greeks, Arabs, and Basques, where political boundaries have split these people apart. Where tribal groups have been administratively separated by colonial powers, as in Africa, administrative problems have been exacerbated. If we use observed behavior as the basis for resolving problems of boundaries, we follow a basic principle of the natural history method. We learn that boundaries should be thought of not necessarily as enclosures but as the spatial extension of interaction systems. Boundary in this sense becomes a variable. The nucleated village of New England is situated within the defined geographic limits of township. Such clear-cut lines cannot be drawn for rural Ireland, where kin-connected families live in dispersed homesteads in the environs of a crossroads hamlet combining church, school, and public house. Among the Navajo, community is expressed through ritually recurring gatherings of linked lineages that are territorially identified but not necessarily contiguous. Undoubtedly the tidy-minded will be distressed by the absence of neatly delineated territorial units among the Irish and Navajo, but the examples cited here illustrate the value of a model derived from reality.

This then was the conceptual framework in which Partridge tested his fieldwork experience. This base provided the intellectual scheme in which the three divisions of coastal, highland, and urban sectors were ordered and their interconnections established. From this approach came the understanding of the relations between social structure and change, and the functional place of marijuana in the whole.

Such understanding, however, is also a function of the fieldwork dialogues. In this instance, Partridge first became involved in the field and accumulated the empirical data in conjunction with cooperative informants. Only after such specifics of setting and behavior had become available could Partridge and Kimball then exchange ideas and advice, fleshing out the earliest models of the community and pointing the direction for further research. Finally, the dialogue became a dialogue of one, the cerebral processing within Partridge by which he adjusted prior conceptual formulations with observed reality. Through such a sequence of fieldwork dialogues the community-study method orders the structure and activities of groups and their associated values, symbols, and settings into the interconnected regularities we identify as community.

Epilogue: Ethical Dilemmas

by William Partridge

T HE OPERATIONAL system described in earlier chapters can be generalized to
other situations, and the ethical dilemmas that attended this particular research
have parallels in many other situations. Ethical choices are inherent in all
scientific research involving human beings as subjects. Our central concern as
scientists is that our procedures and the uses to which the results are put will
add constructively to knowledge but will not be harmful for the subjects of our
study, the agency or foundation sponsoring the research, or our professional
colleagues. Our central concern as humanists is that the scientific aims,
procedures, and results of our work not harm our subjects, but enhance their
human potential.

A "code" of ethics for anthropologists does not exist, nor is there a
professional society that judges conformity with such a code in the fashion of
review boards in the medical profession. Instead, anthropologists have recognized through many years of thoughtful debate that a fixed code would be
counterproductive. We subscribe to a set of guidelines established by the
American Anthropological Association (AAA 1970). Such a guide is of more
value than a code-review process, for ethical dilemmas are culturally specific:
what is responsible behavior in one place or at one time is perhaps irresponsi-
ble elsewhere. A viable ethical guideline must be precise enough to be
understood, yet general enough not to preclude flexible and continuing adaptation to changing cultural conditions.

The present case, research on an illegal activity, introduces special difficulties that deserve separate treatment here. Ethical choices centered on three
dilemmas that occurred in the following sequence: (1) problem choice and
definition, (2) the behavior of the investigator in the field, and (3) the uses of
the research results. Every anthropologist who enters another culture (as well
as those who focus their analytical skills on the culture into which they were
born) confronts these dilemmas. Each in turn must stand behind the choices
made, ready to be personally and individually responsible for the conse-

quences of his or her choices. A flexible and continually adaptive professional ethic rests ultimately in individual commitment. Thus the choices made in the course of the cannabis research are presented here as an addendum to the foregoing chapters, providing a personal statement that complements, but is distinct from, the operational system analyzed above.

The first dilemma is problem choice, for what one person sees as a "problem" worthy of extended study may be seen by another as a trivial matter undeserving of special attention. Yet most observers would agree that drug use and abuse are problems in contemporary cultures of the world. Drug use has been studied by scientists since before the turn of the century, and in the decades immediately preceding my research scientific work in this area had dramatically increased. In the 1970s, however, drug abuse was declared more prevalent than ever (Mitchell 1970), and policies and programs designed to control it were reported to be unsuccessful in the majority of cases (Artinian 1974). The paradox of vastly increased scientific work coupled with a rise in the severity of the problem and the failure of public policy to control abuse is evidence of the contemporary significance of the problem. In the United States, society has not traditionally valued the use of drugs other than alcohol in its religious heritage and has purged drugs other than tobacco and alcohol from the secular realm; the response of lawmaking and enforcement agencies to the rising incidence of drug use and abuse reflects the perceived significance of the problem. Penalties for drug possession, cultivation, or sale have increased in severity through time. In the case of cannabis, by 1970 this trend had culminated in sentences of life imprisonment for first-possession offense in Missouri and the death sentence for sale to a minor under twenty-one in Missouri and Louisiana (Brecher et al. 1972:419–20).

Once a research problem is identified, it is then defined precisely in terms that will permit data collection and analysis. In the present case, as discussed earlier, I thought that much of the previous research on cannabis use was not useful for the purposes of understanding the drug user or for evaluation and design of public policy dealing with drug abuse. From 1937, when the Marijuana Tax Act was passed in the United States, to the present, the Federal Bureau of Narcotics has insisted that cannabis users are criminals who support themselves by preying on society (Brecher et al. 1972:38). While a great deal of scientific research has been devoted to this question since 1937, very little of this research is useful either for evaluating the claim made by the Bureau or for understanding the drug abuse problem. A major reason is that questions of social policy cannot be answered by laboratory and clinical experiments (Hollister 1971). Paradoxically, there has been almost no research on the use of cannabis in natural social settings (U.S. Dept. HEW 1971). Data collected in such facilities as laboratories, clinics, and prisons are not useful because of the placebo effect, where perceptions of drug effects and the social and psychological behavior of subjects are more the product of the institutional setting of the study rather than of the drug itself. In order to examine the link between criminality and cannabis use the problem was defined in terms of the community context of cannabis use: it was hypothesized that, in the absence of enforcement of laws restricting cannabis use or where enforcement has traditionally been lax to the point of nonobservance, the use of cannabis would not be associated with criminality, deviance, or marginality. Cannabis users were predicted to be mature adults, integral members of the community who had achieved over their lifetimes economic, religious, political, and social parity compared to nonusers.

The ethical implications of this problem definition may not be immediately obvious. First, to have accepted the Federal Bureau of Narcotics definition of the drug user as criminal, deviant, and marginal in the absence of any evidence (for there never has been any evidence supporting this assertion outside of societies restricting cannabis use) would have been fundamentally unethical. The bureau and numerous other law enforcement agencies depend upon arrests of cannabis and other drug users not only to generate their operating budgets, but also to legitimize their existence in the eyes of the public. Such agencies benefit from the widespread belief in the causal link between cannabis use and criminality; therefore their assertions regarding this linkage must be viewed cautiously.

Second, to have accepted the bureau's assertion would have violated the anthropological commitment to holistic problem definition; this in turn would have been unscientific and unethical. In anthropology we recognize that any behavior finds its significance at the community level within the context of the full round of local life. If we are to understand that behavior, we must understand its nexus in community processes. If my only consideration had been to obtain a grant and earn a doctorate, undoubtedly I could have located several funding sources that were not scientifically rigorous and would not recognize the contradiction inherent in demonstrating the correlation between criminality and cannabis use by studying incarcerated populations. But ethical considerations dictated that the link between crime and cannabis be empirically tested in the community context.

The second dilemma involves the behavior of the investigator in the field, a situation fraught with numerous choices with ethical implications. This dilemma is in fact an arena of ethical choices, for there is not one choice to be made (as is implied when one speaks of "the role" of the fieldworker), but several, sequential choices that through time become a complex of commitments on the part of both the investigator and the people with whom he or she works. These choices begin the moment the investigator arrives in the field, and cease only when his or her ties are finally severed with the companions and collaborators in the work undertaken. In the present case, my major choices were with regard to three questions: Which people in the community will be good informants? When and to whom should the details of this sensitive research project be explained? To what extent should I participate in the illegal activity I was studying?

The first question could not be answered without a certain amount of patient testing of the waters and calculated risk taking. An example will clarify my meaning. Jorge Duran is a Colombian peasant who, while serving in the Colombian army during the military government of General Rojas Pinilla, was interim mayor of Majagua. His wife is from one of the old coastal elite families of the region, and today teaches in one of the primary schools. They have seven children in school and others under school age or for other reasons not attending. From the first week that I took up residence in the town I was warned against Jorge by the townspeople. The message was clear and came from all sides: Do not trust this man! There was every reason to heed this warning, which came from important people, including government officials, because to ignore their advice might alienate them from my small group of friends. My research topic was sensitive, and any enemies I might make could use it as a pretense to try to drive me out of the community. Still, I did not act immediately to put any distance between myself and Jorge, for I realized that I did not yet understand the conflicts and tensions (which are a part of any community's life) characteristic of this situation. I decided to be patient.

My first contact with Jorge had been shortly after my arrival. The mayor's nephew had helped me to get settled in the town and, when I pointed out that I would need to buy a horse, he introduced me to Jorge. I knew nothing of horses, having been raised in Miami, Florida. But after riding the animal about the cleared area near the market building I was satisfied that it was fast and spirited. I had in the back of my mind the need for such a horse in the event my probing in the countryside met with violent response. We agreed upon a price and the sale was made.

Jorge assisted me in finding pasture for my horse, in locating and buying a saddle, bridle, and the rest of the gear I would need, and with several elementary riding lessons. He invited me to drink beer with him at local stores when we met and always asked after my horse and joked about my riding abilities. I found him to be intelligent, good-humored, entertaining, and a hard-working man. But still the townspeople persisted in warning me about him, each time with greater emphasis. I learned that Jorge was a consummate horse trader, drinker, and farmer. Although he lived in town, his farm was located in the highlands of the foothills of the Sierra Nevada overlooking the town, and his neighbors there were highland peasants. Among these highlanders, who had migrated into the area only recently, Jorge was universally respected. They called him *"Sargento"* or Sergeant in recognition of his having risen to that rank in the Colombian army. But the townspeople considered Jorge unscrupulous; he was a highlander who had married into one of the old families by virtue of the accident of a military government in Colombia. After his stint as mayor, Jorge had returned to being a highland peasant and horse trader.

Although I did not know the depth or importance of the division I had discovered in the community, it was apparent that Jorge was unpopular with townspeople and popular with highland peasants. I made the decision that I would work to retain a good working relationship with him, despite the warnings. Here I was clearly taking a chance. It was possible that Jorge was a police informer, and that the townspeople were cannabis users and distributors attempting to keep me away from danger. Or Jorge might have been a middleman himself, and the townspeople could have been trying to keep me from getting any information from him. At the time I did not have any of the facts necessary to make an intelligent decision, but it was clear that something of significance was occurring. It was also clear that, had I terminated my relationship with Jorge, I would come to depend upon only his enemies for information. This was something I could not risk. In order to investigate the community context of cannabis, I needed to maintain access to all of the groups that composed full round of local life in the community. At this stage I could not afford to make judgments based on gossip or other insufficient information that might alienate anyone.

As time passed I learned that Jorge was indeed a significant figure in the life of the community. The right choice had been made. The division between the *cachacos* of the highlands and the *costeños* of the lowlands, as seen in earlier chapters, is a basic organizing principle of this community. Jorge was a *cachaco,* yet he lived in town and had married a coastal woman. Initially he stood as a champion of the *cachacos;* later he was a bridge between the two subcultures. Through Jorge I gained access into the world of the highland subculture. He proved to be a willing and intelligent informant who grew to appreciate my work, to learn why I asked the questions I did, and to volunteer information that extended my understanding of his community.

The second question, when and to whom should the nature of my sensitive research be disclosed, is intimately related to the first question. It was seen earlier that I had initially explained my objective in detail to anthropological colleagues in Bogotá, and upon arrival in Majagua had given a more general explanation (the study of medicinal plants, one of which is cannabis) to my initial contacts. This explanation was given in order to protect myself and the people that had assisted me up until that point, and to preserve my capacity to test informant reliability, honesty, and trustworthiness. First, I had to protect myself from possible danger. The secret police in the area are trained professionals (schooled in the United States for drug control activities) who are automatically suspicious of foreigners, many of whom come to the coast hoping to make contact for drug trafficking; they are more than willing to arrest foreigners perceived as vulnerable and wealthy. I did not think a letter of sponsorship from the National Anthropology Institute would be much protection from harassment or from having to bribe my way out of difficulty, although it might eventually get me out of jail. For this reason I could see no reason to immediately identify my interest in cannabis. Second, since cannabis is illegal I was aware of the potential harm that might come to the people in the community who assisted someone interested in illegal activity (whether they did so knowingly or unknowingly would not matter when the information entered the gossip network of the community). Therefore, in the early stages I thought it best to be cautious until I had a better idea of the potential risks for those who worked with me. Third, every anthropologist knows that a central part of his work involves training local people to be good informants. Not every individual has the time, interest, or intelligence needed to attempt to explain his or her culture to an outsider; those that do have these qualities make excellent informants. In the process of trying to explain what is (to them) obvious, to translate into terms the anthropologist understands, they eventually achieve a perspective of their world quite different from the one they had previously. Investigator-informant relationships are built slowly to the point where the informant begins to understand the intellectual concerns that lie behind flat requests for information, and begins to anticipate areas of interest and to direct the researcher's attention to important facts. Such relationships are built through mutual testing and probing of another's personal qualities and values. By defining my objectives broadly, though not misleading or falsifying my special focus, I was able to stimulate the interest of those with whom I became acquainted in the first few months in the community. With those who lacked such interest, little could be done. But with individuals who wanted to know more, I was in a position to exchange information, to take them into a deeper relationship and satisfy their curiosity about me, my purposes, and the precise questions that concerned me. To have immediately broadcast my interest in sensitive subjects would have removed the opportunity to build relationships founded in mutual trust and confidentiality.

The last question I had to resolve as an anthropologist in the field is the extent to which an investigator should participate in illegal activity in order to achieve the objectives of scientific research. It will be recalled that I participated in cannabis cultivation with a highland man, in this way learning not only about cultivation but about distribution as well. From there I was able to expand my contacts to include cannabis users on the rice and cattle estates. This may prompt some readers to wonder, ''Whose side are you on, that of the cannabis grower-distributor-consumer or the police?'' It is a misleading question. The anthropologist's participation in the lives of people does not imply approval or consent to aspects of their lives that might in other contexts be unworkable. Examples such as female infanticide, warfare, and witchcraft come to mind. Further, an anthropologist engaged in value-critical, empirically grounded research knows too little at the outset to align himself or herself with a particular side in a conflict. If evidence were sufficient to permit such a decision, then the research would become value-committed. The objective would no longer be hypothesis testing or holistic problem definition and data collection; the objective instead would be to collect data that support certain values in such a way as to permit action in defense or assertion of these values. Such a priori value commitments are inappropriate in community studies where we lack the evidence upon which to base a decision. Since this was the first study in Colombia of cannabis use in a naturally occurring human community, there could be no such decision.

A major concern, however, was the impact of the research upon the well-being of informants. Because my research entailed engaging with others in illegal activity, I was joined with others in a relationship that involved risks that we each had to calculate and evaluate. The real question is not whether I was in fact at risk, but whether the relationship between me and my informants was an honest one, founded upon equal perception of the risks involved and equal vulnerability to the consequences. The only possible ethical posture in such circumstances is the willingness to suffer the consequences of possible misfortune. I had to be prepared to be arrested along with those who collaborated with me and to accept the brutality, psychological abuse, unhealthy jail conditions, and the like for which the coast of Colombia is famous. In the back of my mind I knew that my Colombian and United States colleagues, my university, and my family would come to my aid in the event of misfortune (although friends had advised me that the United States government would do very little in such cases); yet it would be months before such help would result in freedom, and the monetary cost was unknown. My informants likewise would be able to count on their networks for assistance, which I expected to be more effective than mine. In any case, acceptance of risk in this case was real and mutual. I never promised to be able to get anyone out of jail or deliver immunity from police action, for this was impossible. All I could promise was mutual responsibility for the consequences of our actions. No doubt this commitment, which I continually made clear to my companions, in no small way accounts for some of the trust I was able to build with informants. This is not to say that in the end I had in fact chosen a side with which to ally myself. Through participation I was merely exposing myself to the consequences of illegal activity, just as I exposed myself to the risks and consequences associated with legal activities such as helping to move a herd of cattle to winter pasture (with the attendant risk of being thrown from a horse or bitten by a poisonous snake).

Finally, we come to the third ethical dilemma, revolving around the uses to which the data are to be put. The information gathered in Majagua is potentially sensitive within Colombia. The outsider with little experience among drug using populations and law enforcement officers often guesses that the identities of the participants in drug-related activities are unknown, and that disclosure of identities would be the major sensitive issue. However, law enforcement officials rarely lack such information. Identities are always known. What precipitates law enforcement action is the opportunity for large profits, either in terms of the legal rewards resulting from the capture of a shipment destined for clandestine markets or in terms of bribes or profits stemming from the threat of such action. The vital information needed for either action is when and where a substantial amount of money is changing hands, an amount substantial enough to warrant the risk of confrontation with the armed and usually powerful individuals involved. This was information I did not have. The secret police in Majagua concentrated upon evicting squatters from the large estates, not upon intervention in the drug traffic. The reason was quite simple: the wealthy families of the community were engaged in drug traffic and owned the large estates. There was little profit either in terms of career advancement or in terms of monetary advancement from threatening the drug trade, whereas there was profit of both kinds in protecting the lands of the wealthy from squatters.

Protecting the identities of my informants, therefore, was not the major issue in this ethical dilemma (although I have consistently used fictitious names in writing about them, since conditions might change). After six months of probing, when I finally began to identify those involved in the drug networks, it became clear that everyone at every level of the local authority structure (from the mayor to the secret police) knew which individuals were the growers, distributors, and smokers. People in the drug traffic had nothing to fear from my research in this regard.

But the results were nonetheless sensitive for others who had helped me in my research. These included those informants from the community who, though not connected with the cannabis trade, might conceivably be hurt by the identification of their community as the site of illegal activity, particularly if published in the national press or in a Spanish-language scholarly journal in Colombia. Similarly, the Colombian anthropologists who assisted me were vulnerable to political pressures from their colleagues, who could conceivably criticize the controversial nature of the work and the unfavorable image of Colombian law enforcement or Colombian drug suppliers conveyed in several ways by my research. In light of the negative publicity Colombia had already received in the early 1970s for its prominent role in the international drug trade, my colleagues could conceivably suffer a good deal from association with a foreigner who added further evidence. For these reasons, in my writings on the subject of cannabis in Colombia, I have never acknowledged by name those anthropologists who were truly instrumental in my work in 1972 and 1973, instrumental to the extent that it could not have been accomplished without their assistance.

Almost exactly a year after leaving Colombia I had completed my doctoral dissertation, and I returned to Colombia with copies of that document, an article published in English that same year, and the draft of an article I intended to submit to another English-language publication. These I gave to several of my Colombian colleagues, telling them that they would have to be the judges as to whether and when my work might be made available to their countrymen. In my opinion only they can adequately judge the political climate that would make possible an open scientific debate on the topic of cannabis in Colombia. At present the immense profitability of drug enterprises and the pressures from the industrial countries, particularly the United States, to control drug traffickers make the political climate much too hot for any serious scholarly discussions on these issues. (The Foreign Assistance Act of 1971 requires vigorous enforcement of drug control laws on the part of the recipients of U.S. foreign aid.) Applying the guideline I used during fieldwork I decided that since I would not be in Colombia to share the consequences of publication within the country with my Colombian colleagues, I could not ethically create such risks. Nor would it be sufficient to do so and disguise the place where I worked, for the diligent political enemies of my colleagues or informants could undoubtedly identify the community from descriptions contained in the field notes (e.g., size of municipality, population, number of buildings, and major features and landmarks). The common convention of using false names in order to protect informants and colleagues is thus ineffectual when used in the society that encompasses the people studied, for members of that society can easily find out the true names and places and from there identify the actors.

On the other hand, I have written about the results of my work in English-language publications. And I would like to think that to some extent this has influenced the gradual processes of change in perceptions of the nature of drug use and abuse in the United States and other English-speaking countries. Yet it is reasonable to ask to what extent these English-language publications may be damaging to my informants and colleagues in Colombia. Many Colombian scientists are perfectly bilingual in English and Spanish and have access to the results of the research. The protection I have sought for my informants and colleagues, by letting the scientific professionals in Colombia determine the uses to which the results might be put in their country, makes sense only when it is recognized that Colombian bureaucrats and politicians are generally monolingual in Spanish. Colombian scientists subscribe to the scientific criteria for data identification and collection, analysis and theory building, and professional debate and criticism; they are therefore the primary source of protection for the people who assisted me in the research. These scientific criteria and the men and women who value them are, ultimately, the only guarantee that the research results will not be used to harm those who made the work possible. The petty bureaucrat or ambitious politician looking to build a public career on a controversial issue is as common in Colombia as in the United States. As scientists with ethical commitments to those who make our work possible, we can only keep controversial information out of the hands of the political piranha and do what we can to make scientific information available to those honest and diligent politicians (who are also as numerous in Colombia as they are in the United States).

Although honesty, decency, and integrity may be universal virtues, no such applicability can be claimed for ethical considerations. Different groups carry obligations that vary one from the other and exacerbate cross-purposes. The field researcher may be caught between the obligations to make his research findings available to his colleagues and the need to protect his informants. There is no single resolution of these ethical dilemmas.

Glossary

abono, manure

abrazo, embrace

administrador, manager

agua con panela, drink of water, raw sugar, and lime

aguardiente, cane alcohol distilled and sold by departmental governments

alcalde, alcaldía, mayor, mayor's office building

aldea, hamlet

almacén, store

Arawako, name given the Ijka of the Sierra Nevada de Santa Marta by local Colombians

arepa, bread made from pounded corn and milk and cooked on a griddle in the highlands

arriba, up, above

arroba, weight of 25 pounds

arrocera, rice farm in irrigated lowlands; rice grower; rice dealer

bareque, traditional coastal house of wattle and daub, plastered with white clay, having a peaked thatch roof

bautismo, baptism

bollo, lit. "bun," "loaf of bread"; coastal dish made of ground corn boiled, then cooked to the consistency of cold grits, and wrapped in a corn husk

cabecera, county seat of a municipality

cachaco, term used by coastal people to designate highland people from the interior

campamento, encampment

campesino, technically, a peasant who owns his own land and is engaged in subsistence and cash-crop farming; locally used to refer to any agricultural laborer

caña brava, bamboo

capataz, overseer, foreman, on an estate

caserio, series of houses

casero, housekeeper

chagua, collective work party of agricultural laborers

chicha, maize beer brewed for ceremonial and festive events

chiva, lit. a female goat; locally an old car or truck converted into a vehicle for transporting passengers

chorro, gush of water

civilizado, mixed blood, compared to full Indian

claro, clear

cliente, one who is indebted to another socially, politically, economically, and/or ritually and is expected to repay in kind or in loyalty and respect, or both

cocina, kitchen

cofradia, religious society, brotherhood

colono, squatter on private or public land; also called *invasor*

comisariato, commissary owned and operated by the United Fruit Company

compadre, friend

compartimiento, in highlands, a dividing line between Indian and mestizo territories; in lowlands, a collection of worker row houses on United Fruit Company estates

consejo, elected municipal council

corraleja, bamboo and wood structure built for bullfights during patron saint festival

corregimiento, satellite town over which the county government has jurisdiction

cosecha, harvest; product of one planting, as a *cosecha* of corn

costeño, one born on the north coast

crema, cream (of society)

cumbia, a dance of coastal adolescents to reed flutes and drums *curso,* course of lectures given to promote a program or policy

desarrollo, development

doctor, lit. physician; locally used to address powerful landowners, professionals, or politicians regardless of education or training

empleado, public employee

espíritu, spirit

espuela, control station

feliz, lucky

finca, farm

fique, fiber of century plant or agave cactus

fogon, hearth

frijoles, beans

gallero, one who raises, trains, and fights cocks; *gallera,* cockfighting ring

ganadería, cattle ranch

gripe, flu

guarapo, fermented sugarcane juice

hacienda, property, farm; *hacendado,* farmer, landholder

hato, cattle estate specializing in beef production; also called *estancia*

hectare, 2.47 acres of land

hombre que indica, labor broker responsible for recruiting work crews on United Fruit Company plantations; today refers to recruiters for private estates as well

huepa, exclamation indicating surprise or enthusiasm

huerta, see *roza*

indio, derogatory term for Indian, *indígena* being more respectful

invasión, invasion; *invasor,* see *colono*

jefe, anyone in charge of anything

latifundia, large expanse of land controlled by one person, family, or corporation

libertad, freedom

líder, leader

machetero, agricultural wage laborer usually with only enough land to build a house; also called *obrero, jornalero, trabajador*

mandador, administrator of large estate

marijuana, plant and product of cannabis; types harvested; also called *mona, mota, hoja, ella*

marijuanero, one who smokes marijuana; general term for agricultural laborers used by higher status persons

matadero, slaughterhouse

medio, surroundings, medium

mestizo, person of mixed Spanish, Indian, and Negro ancestry

minifundia, landholding of less than five hectares

mochila, woven shoulder bag made of century plant fiber, cotton, or wool

monte, bush, scrub, or weeds

moreno, mestizo with negroid features

municipio, administrative unit of urban state corresponding to a county

padre de familia, literally, the father of the family, but meaning a respected adult male of the community

panela, raw brown sugar

parcela, peasant cooperative sponsored by the Colombian Agrarian Reform Institute

patrón, powerful benefactor who provides social, economic, political, or ritual services in exchange for other services

personero, municipal officer in charge of street maintenance, gardening in plaza, etc.

placita, small plaza, square

quinta, villa or large estate-house complex

quintal, 100 kilograms

racimo, stalk of bananas

roza, mixed garden of peasant farmer planted in corn, beans, manioc, plantain; also called *huerta, labranza*

sancocho, traditional festive meal on the coast; a stew of many vegetables, chicken, pork, and/or fish

sapo, lit. toad; gossip or talebearer

selectador, a fruit selector at the rail spur loading docks

sirviente, servant

tamal, tamale

tanquepe, fruit cleaner

técnico, technician

temple, disposition; in this context the mood produced by smoking marijuana

tienda, shop, stall

tiple, small guitar

trapiche, sugar mill

turco, term given Lebanese merchants on the coast

vereda, lit. path; neighborhood of dispersed, individual peasant family farms in the highlands; rural census unit in the lowlands

verdad, truth

voluntad, will, determination

Zona Bananera, an area 40 by 100 kilometers stretching from Santa Marta south to Fundación and from Sierra Nevada de Santa Marta to the Ciénaga Grande

Bibliography

Aguirre Beltrán, Gonzalo.
  1967. *Regiones de refúgio*. México: Instituto Nacional Indigenista.
American Anthropological Association.
  1970. Principles of professional responsibility. *Newsletter of the American Anthropological Association* 11 (9).
Ardila Rodríguez, Francisco.
  1965. *Aspectos médico legales y médico sociales de la marihuana*. Tesis doctoral, Universidad de Madrid, Facultad de Medicina.
Arensberg, Conrad M.
  1955. American communities. *American Anthropologist* 57:1143–60
  1959. Summation and comments. *Plantation systems of the new world,* edited by Vera Rubin, pp.184–87. Social Science Monograph no. 7. Washington: Pan American Union.
  1968. The urban in crosscultural perspective. In *Urban anthropology,* edited by Elizabeth M. Eddy. Southern Anthropological Society Proceedings 2:3–15. Athens: University of Georgia Press.
Arensberg, Conrad M., and Kimball, Solon T.
  1965. *Culture and community*. New York: Harcourt, Brace, Jovanovich.
  1968. *Family and community in Ireland*. Cambridge: Harvard University Press.
  1969. Community study: retrospect and prospect. *American Journal of Sociology* 73:691–705.
Artinian, Barbara.
  1974. Identity and change in a therapeutic community. Ph.D. dissertation, University of Southern California.
Bailey, Fred G.
  1969. *Stratagems and spoils: a social anthropology of politics*. New York: Schocken Books.
Berreman, Gerald.
  1962. *Behind many masks*. Society for Applied Anthropology Monograph no. 4.
Brecher, Edward M., and the editors of *Consumer Reports*.
  1972. *Licit and illicit drugs*. Boston: Little, Brown.
Cancian, Frank.
  1965. *Economics and prestige in a Maya community*. Stanford: Stanford University Press.
  1972. *Change and uncertainty in a peasant economy: the Maya corn farmers of Zinacantan*. Stanford: Stanford University Press.
Carter, William E.
  1965. *Aymara communities and the Bolivian agrarian reform*. Gainesville: University of Florida Press.
Casagrande, Joseph B., ed.
  1960. *In the company of man: twenty portraits of anthropological informants*. New York: Harper Torchbooks.

Chapple, Eliot D., and Arensberg, Conrad M.
  1940.   Measuring human relations: an introduction to the study of the interaction of individu-
           als. *Genetic Psychology Monographs* 23:3–147.
Departamento Administrativo Nacional de Estadística.
  1959.   *Censo de población de 1951, Departamento de Magdalena.* Bogotá: Imprenta Na-
           cional.
  1971.   *XIII censo de población y II de edificios y viviendadas, Julio 15 de 1964, Magdalena.*
           Bogotá: Imprenta Nacional.
Dix, Robert.
  1967.   *Colombia: the political dimensions of change.* New Haven: Yale University Press.
Doughty, Paul L.
  1970.   Behind the back of the city. In *Peasants in cities,* edited by William Mangin, pp
           30–46. Boston: Little, Brown.
Fabrega, Horacio, Jr., and Manning, Peter K.
  1972.   Health maintenance among Peruvian peasants. *Human Organization* 31:243–56.
Fals Borda, Orlando.
  1955.   Peasant society in the Colombian Andes. Gainesville: University of Florida Press.
Fortes, Meyer.
  1958.   Introduction. In *The developmental cycle in domestic groups,* edited by Jack Goody.
           Cambridge Papers in Social Anthropology no. 1. Cambridge: Cambridge University
           Press.
Foster, George M.
  1942.   *A primitive Mexican economy.* American Ethnological Society Monograph no. 5.
  1948.   *Empire's children: the people of Tzintzuntzan.* Institute of Social Anthropology Publi-
           cation no. 6. Washington: Smithsonian Institution.
Gaitán, Jorge Eliécier.
  1972.   *1928: la massacre en las Bananeras.* Bogotá: Ediciones los Comuneros.
García Márquez, Gabriel.
  1970.   *One hundred years of solitude.* New York: Doubleday.
Gillin, John.
  1947.   *Moche: A Peruvian coastal community.* Institute of Social Anthropology Publication
           no. 3. Washington: Smithsonian Institution.
Goffman, Erving.
  1967.   *Interaction ritual.* New York: Doubleday.
Hammel, Eugene.
  1969.   *Power in Ica.* Boston: Little, Brown.
Hollister, Leo E.
  1971.   Marihuana in man: three years later. *Science* 172:21–29.
Kamalaprija, V.
  1965.   *Estudio descriptivo de la estructura del mercado del banano Colombiano para la
           exportación.* Bogotá: Instituto Latinoamericano de Mercadeo Agrícola.
Kimball, Solon T., and Pearsall, Marion.
  1955.   Event analysis as an approach to community study. *Social Forces* 34:58–63.
Kimball, Solon T., and Burnett, Jaquetta H., eds.
  1973.   *Learning and culture.* Proceedings of the 1972 Annual Spring Meeting of the Ameri-
           can Ethnological Society.
Latin American Center, University of California, Los Angeles.
  1968.   *Statistical abstracts of Latin America.*
Mangin, William.
  1970.   *Peasants in cities.* Boston: Little, Brown.
Mauss, Marcel.
  1954.   *The gift: forms and functions of exchange in archaic societies.* Glencoe, Ill.: The Free
           Press. First printing, 1925.
Mitchell, John.
  1970.   John Mitchell on marihuana. *Newsweek,* September 7, p. 22.

Modiano, Nancy.
1973. *Indian education in the Chiapas Highlands*. New York: Holt, Rinehart and Winston.
Moore, G. Alexander.
1973. *Life cycles in Atchlán: the diverse careers of certain Guatemalans*. New York: Teachers College Press.
Nader, Laura.
1970. From anguish to exultation. In *Women in the field: anthropological experiences*, edited by Peggy Golde. Chicago: Aldine Publishing Co.
Parsons, Elsie Clews.
1945. *Peguche: a study of Andean Indians*. Chicago: University of Chicago Press.
Partridge, William L.
1973. *The hippie ghetto: the natural history of a subculture*. New York: Holt, Rinehart and Winston.
1974. Exchange relationships in a community on the north coast of Colombia with special reference to cannabis. Ph.D. dissertation, University of Florida.
1975. *Cannabis* and cultural groups in a Colombian municipio. In *Culture and cannabis*, edited by Vera Rubin. The Hague: Mouton.
1977. Transformation and redundancy in ritual: a case from Colombia. In *Drugs, ritual and altered states of consciousness*, edited by Brian M. du Toit. Rotterdam: A. N. Balkeina.
Patiño, Victor Manuel.
1965. *Historia de la actividad agropecuaria en América equinoccial*. Cali: Imprenta Departamental.
1967. *Plantas cultivadas y animales domésticos en América equinoccial: plantas misceláneas*. Tomo III. Cali: Imprenta Departamental.
1969. *Plantas cultivadas y animales domésticos en América equinoccial: plantas introducidas*. Toma IV. Cali: Imprenta Departamental.
1970. *Plantas cultivadas y animales domésticos en América equinoccial: animales domésticos introducidos*. Tomo V. Cali: Imprenta Departamental.
1971. *Factores inhibitorios*. Cali: Imprenta Departamental.
Peacock, James L.
1968. *The rites of modernization*. Chicago: University of Chicago Press.
Peattie, Lisa Redfield.
1968. *View from the barrio*. Ann Arbor: University of Michigan Press.
Perez, Juan B.
1952. Intoxicación por la marihuana. *Antioquía Médica* (June).
Redfield, Robert.
1930. *Tepoztlán, a Mexican village: a study of folk life*. Chicago: University of Chicago Press.
1934. Culture changes in Yucatán. *American Anthropologist* 36:57–59.
1941. *The folk culture of Yucatán*. Chicago: University of Chicago Press.
Reichel-Dolmatoff, Gerardo.
1951. *Datos histórico-culturales sobre las tribus de la antigua Gobernación de Santa Marta*. Bogotá: Banco de la República.
Reichel-Dolmatoff, Gerardo, and Reichel-Dolmatoff, Alicia.
1966. *The people of Aritama*. Chicago: University of Chicago Press.
Rubin, Vera, and Comitas, Lambros.
1975. *Ganja in Jamaica*. The Hague: Mouton.
Stein, William.
1961. *Hualcán: life in the highlands of Peru*. Ithaca: Cornell University Press.
Steward, Julian H., ed.
1946. *Handbook of South American Indians*. Vols. 1–6. Bureau of American Ethnology Bulletin 143. Washington: Smithsonian Institution.
1956. *The peoples of Puerto Rico*. Urbana: University of Illinois Press.

Turner, Victor W.
  1957.   *Schism and continuity in an African society*. Manchester: Manchester University Press.
  1966.   The syntax of symbolism in an African religion. In *Philosophical transactions of the Royal Society of London*, edited by Sir Julian Huxley, ser. B, 251:295–303.
  1969.   *The ritual process: structures and anti-structure*. Chicago: Aldine.
United Nations Educational, Scientific, and Cultural Organization.
  1965.   *The question of cannabis: cannabis bibliography*. New York.
U.S. Department of Health, Education, and Welfare.
  1971.   Marihuana and health: a report to the Congress from the Secretary. Washington: Government Printing Office.
Valdeblanquez, José María.
  1964.   *Historia del Departamento del Magdalena y del Territorio de la Guajira, desde el año de 1895 hasta el año de 1963*. Bogotá: Editorial El Voto Nacional.
Val-Spinosa, Allen Steele.
  1969.   Colombia's semana trágica: the banana strike of 1928. Master's thesis, University of Florida.
Vergara y Velasca, F. J.
  1901.   *Nueva geografía de Colombia*. Tomo I. Bogotá: República de Colombia.
Wagley, Charles.
  1941.   *The economics of a Guatemalan village*. American Anthropological Association Memoir 58.
  1949.   *Social and religious life of a Guatemalan community*. American Anthropological Association Memoir 71.
  1952.   *Race and class in rural Brazil*. Paris: UNESCO.
  1953.   *Amazon town: a study of man in the tropics*. New York: Macmillan.
  1971.   *An introduction to Brazil*. Rev. ed. New York: Columbia University Press.
Wagley, Charles, and Harris, Marvin.
  1955.   A typology of Latin American subcultures. *American Anthropologist* 57:428–51.
Warner, W. Lloyd.
  1959.   *Living and the dead: a symbolic life of Americans*. New Haven: Yale University Press.
  1964.   *A black civilization: a social study of an Australian tribe*. New York: Harper and Row.
Wauchope, Robert, ed.
  1969.   *Handbook of Middle American Indians*. Vols. 1–6. Austin: University of Texas Press.
Wheatly, Paul.
  1972.   The concept of urbanism. In *Man, settlement and urbanism*, edited by P. J. Ucko, R. Tringham, and G. W. Dimbleby, pp.601–37. London: Gerald Duckworth.

Author Index

Subject Index

Acción Cultural Popular. *See* Radio Sutatenza

Agriculture: in highlands, 71, 73, 95–96, 120; estates in lowlands, 117–19; organization of, 131–35; variations in, 144–45; of cannabis, 165–67; types of production units, 201–9

Almacenes: description of, 124–25. *See also* Shopkeepers

American Anthropological Association: ethical guidelines, 239

Anthropology: as a natural science, 16

Antioquia, 30, 69, 87, 89, 109

Arabs (Turks), 69: as shopkeepers, 141, 186. *See also* Shopkeepers

Arawak Indians, 87, 136

Artisans, 119

Assembly patterns: list of, 143–44

Banana zone, 20, 56, 86, 88–89, 90–91, 134–35, 137, 177; *fincas*, 92–93. *See also* United Fruit Company

Barranquilla, 23–24, 25, 33, 34, 37, 38, 39, 53, 57, 62, 84, 86, 114, 135, 141, 170, 173, 186

Biological base: of community, 1–2

Bogotá, Colombia, 25, 28, 44, 57, 58, 84, 86, 182, 183, 222–23

Boundaries: ritual control of, 22

Cachacos: as residents of highlands, 73; hotel catering to, 87; barrio in Majagua, 89; bar and pool hall of, 103; drinking places for, 117; *vereda,* 132–33; influx of, 134, 137, 138; habitat of, 139; as peasants, 141; farm pattern of, 145. *See also* Highlands

Cannabis: research problem, 9–10, 21; published data, 27; area of cultivation, 29; cultivation in sierra, 38; absent from highland visit, 44; first contact with cultivator,

45–47; minimize research on, 53; sighting of first plant, 57; sale of, 59; limitations in research, 60; and Jorge , 62; users of, 63; concern of research in, 128; *cachaco* growers, 134–35; as social artifact, 148; probing for, 153; and migration, 155–56; and crime, 156; discussion with informants, 160–78; cultivation of, 165–67; and visit from police, 169–70; life history account of, 172–74; reputation of users, 176; users' account of, 177–78; and community, 210, 213; in highlands, 210, 215, 217; on coast, 210–11, 213, 216–17; in work ritual, 211–13; exchange of, 214; arrest of growers, 219; end of data quest, 225; caution about, 231; ethics of research in, 239–48

Carter, William E., 9, 18, 24, 155, 192, 225, 231

Catholic Church: location of cemetery, 89; visit of bishop, 94–95; ringing church bells, 102–3; baptismal records, 105–6; function of priest, 114; bell tolling as signal, 149

Cattle. *See* Livestock

Cattle estate: definition of, 7; in *municipio,* 114; *finca,* 145

Cemetery, 82, 89

Ciénaga, 34, 37, 43, 56, 58, 64, 69, 96, 120, 137, 141

Client. *See* Patron-client relationship

Coastal subculture: contrast of, 92; observation of, 146–47; hamlet organization, 152; production units of, 204–8; cannabis in, 210–13, 216, 217

Cockfights. *See* Rituals

Colombia: research in, v; research locale in, 18

Colombian anthropologists: anonymity of, v; initial contact with, 24; further assistance from, 28; visit to, 86; protection of identity, 247

UNIVERSITY OF FLORIDA MONOGRAPHS

Social Sciences